The End of Empire in French West Africa

The End of Empire in French West Africa

France's Successful Decolonization?

Tony Chafer

Oxford • New York

First published in 2002 by
Berg
Editorial offices:
150 Cowley Road, Oxford, OX4 1JJ, UK
838 Broadway, Third Floor, New York, NY 10003-4812, USA

Berg is an imprint of Oxford International Publishers Ltd.

Library of Congress Cataloging-in-Publication Data
Chafer, Tony
    The end of empire in French West Africa : France's successful
decolonization? / Tony Chafer.
        p. cm.
Includes bibliographical references (p.) and index.
        ISBN 1-85973-552-5 -- ISBN 1-85973-557-6 (pbk.)
    1. Africa, French-speaking West--History--1884-1960.
2. decolonization--Africa, French-speaking West. 3. Africa, French-
speaking West--Colonial influence. I. Title.
        DT352.5 .C48 2002
        960'.917541--dc21

                                                        2002001531

British Library Cataloguing-in-Publication Data
A catalogue record for this book is available from the British Library.

ISBN 1 85973 552 5 (Cloth)
        1 85973 557 6 (Paper)

Typeset by JS Typesetting, Wellingborough, Northants.
Printed in the United Kingdom by MPG Books Ltd, Bodmin, Cornwall.

To the memory of my father, Doug Chafer, who died in May 2001 just as I was completing this book.

Contents

List of Figures

Preface

The original idea for this book was born in the early 1990s, while I was in Dakar doing research for my PhD thesis on the politics of education in French West Africa. As I sat working in the dusty surroundings of 'le Building', home of the Senegalese National Archives, it became increasingly clear to me that, buried in the documents I was consulting, there was a story, and a history, of decolonization in French West Africa that had not been told in the existing literature on the subject. This book is the product of that original idea.

In doing the research for it, I have visited archives and libraries in Senegal, Côte d'Ivoire, Mali, France and Britain. I have interviewed over thirty people, many of whom were key actors in the decolonization process and are now quite elderly. Indeed, some of those interviewed have since died and, as this has happened, a living library of the period has also disappeared. Their testimony has been an invaluable complement to the written sources used in the preparation of this book.

Tracking down these people has sometimes been a challenge: on one memorable occasion, I was unable to leave Dakar because of an air traffic controllers' strike and as a result missed a series of interviews in Côte d'Ivoire that had taken months to organize. On another, I took a bus journey from Abidjan to Yamoussoukro to interview someone, only to find on arrival that the person in question had just left for Abidjan. In the end, however, the frustrations have been more than compensated for by the joys and discoveries.

During the book's long gestation period, many people have helped me. Some have given generously of their time to answer my questions: Thierno Bâ, Abdoulaye Fofana, Abdoulaye Gueye, Boubacar Ly, Souleymane Ndiaye, Assane Seck, Iba Der Thiam, Pierre Kipré, who found time in his busy schedule as Minister for Education to see me, Mme Dagri Diabaté, Thierno Ibrahima Barry, Monsieur Konaré, Assouan Usher and Joachim Bonny. I am most grateful to Joseph-Roger de Benoist, Paul Désalmand, the late Joseph Eyraud, Amadou Ndene Ndaw and Jean Suret-Canale for not only giving generously of their time but also for giving me access to their own personal archives. Chance encounters have

Preface

also played their part; for instance, I spent many long, hot hours talking to a Monsieur Sangaré on the train from Dakar to Bamako, as a result of which I now appreciate much better some aspects of political realities on the ground in Soudan during the decolonization period and also understand far more than I did before about the pitfalls of trying to analyse African election results through Eurocentric eyes.

Archivists and librarians in Europe and Africa have helped me to track down elusive information and references. In this respect, I should like to give particular thanks to the staff at the Institut Fondamental d'Afrique Noire (IFAN) and in the National Archives in Dakar, who work in often difficult circumstances and whose knowledge, help and patience have been indispensable in the preparation of this book. At the National Archives, the Director, Saliou Mbaye is invariably *disponible* to researchers and willing to share his personal experience and knowledge of the archives, and I should like to make special mention of Mamadou Ndiaye, who must have worn out several pairs of shoes in his treks into the basement of 'le Building' in search of documents I have requested. I cannot thank him enough for his professional help, but also for his warmth, good humour and friendship.

Others have helped me in different ways. Emmanuel Godin and Michel Brot have consulted documents in the Aix archives on my behalf. Rod Kedward gave invaluable advice in helping me to prepare the research proposal and application for research leave, from which this book has emerged. Martin Evans, Janet Bryant, Alice Conklin, Paul McVeigh, John Hargreaves and Berg's anonymous external reader have all read and made helpful comments on earlier drafts of the book. Thanks to them, this is a better book than it would have been and I should like to thank them most warmly for giving up their valuable time to help me in this way. If problems remain, needless to say, they are down to me. I wish to thank Paul Wright for preparing the map of French West Africa and colleagues in the French and European section of the School of Languages and Area Studies for their support throughout these last few years - and also for covering for me when I was away! I also wish to thank the Arts and Humanities Research Board of the British Academy and the Centre for European Studies Research at the University of Portsmouth for their financial support, which made possible the research trips and the research leave in 1998–9 without which this book could not have been completed. Finally, I should like to thank Anne who, when she married me, probably wondered if she had also married this book. She has helped me constantly by chasing up references and information, has given me invaluable advice and has shared patiently in the frustrations and rewards of the book's gestation. She has also read various drafts and her attention to detail has helped me to produce a better, clearer text.

A Note on Names and Translations

The French colonial territory of Soudan (present-day Mali) is spelt in the French way throughout, in order to distinguish it from the Sudan in East Africa. All translations from the French are my own.

Tony Chafer
Southsea
August 2001

Glossary

AEF	The federation of French Equatorial Africa, comprising Congo, Oubangui-Chari, Chad and Gabon, the Government-General of which was based in Brazzaville. Following the Treaty of Versailles in 1919, the former German colony of Cameroun was entrusted to France and Britain under a League of Nations mandate. The French-administered part came under the authority of Brazzaville.
AOF	The federation of French West Africa, comprising the territories of Mauritania, Senegal, Soudan, Niger, Côte d'Ivoire, Haute-Volta (created in 1919, abolished in 1932 and re-created in 1947: called Upper Volta in English), Guinea and Dahomey, the Government-General of which was based in Dakar. Following the Treaty of Versailles in 1919, the former German colony of Togo was entrusted to France and Britain under a League of Nations mandate. The French-administered part came under the authority of Dakar.
Assemblée de l'Union Française	Consultative elected assembly, based at Versailles, which discussed Union affairs.
assimilé	A person who is the product of assimilation, having assimilated French culture and lifestyle.
capitation	In AOF (q.v.), the tax was a flat rate for all native taxpayers and was payable per head, hence the name 'capitation' (poll tax).
centrale	French metropolitan trade union federation.
chef de canton	A French-appointed chief who worked for the colonial administration (see also *indirect rule*).

Glossary

colon	A European settler.
colonie	Dependent territory of an imperial state (for example France). In theory French colonies were usually ruled directly, unlike protectorates (q.v.) and often settled by metropolitan settlers.
CGT	Confédération Générale du Travail, one of the main French trade unions established in 1895. Representative of mainstream social-democracy until after the Second World War when it became predominantly communist.
commandant de cercle	Local French colonial officer, roughly equivalent to the British District Officer.
Conseil de la République	France's indirectly elected second chamber, also known as the Senate.
député	Elected member of the French National Assembly.
direct rule	The system of colonial rule under which colonies were governed directly by the colonial administration, excluding traditional local rulers or institutions.
évolué	In the vocabulary of the period ('educated native' is the equivalent term in British colonies), an African who had received an education of a European type and who was therefore, in part at least, acculturated. *Evolués* often worked as clerks, skilled workers or minor officials.
FIDES	Fonds d'Investissement pour le Développement Economique et Social: Investment Fund for Economic and Social Development, established in 1946.
forced labour	Forced labour took a number of forms. Every man liable was supposed to provide eight days' work a year, in theory under the supervision of the *commandant de cercle* (q.v.). However, Africans were forcibly recruited by the Administration, notably in

Côte d'Ivoire, to work on European-owned plantations. Forced labour was also used as a punishment. Injustice and abuse were widespread, thus feeding discontent.

Grand Conseil The Grand Conseil was the indirectly elected federal body that met in Dakar. The first elections to it were held in 1947 and each territorial assembly elected five representatives to sit on it.

indigénat A legislative code that allowed colonial officials to punish any native with a prison sentence or a fine as a matter of discipline and without trial.

indirect rule The system of colonial rule under which colonies were administered indirectly by the colonial administration, using traditional local rulers (or their replacements) as intermediaries who retained some measure of competence and authority, for example tax-raising powers.

interlocuteurs valables Means literally 'valid representatives'. The term was used by France to describe African political leaders who were friendly towards France and with whom it was prepared to negotiate.

Loi-Cadre Framework Law or Enabling Law, defining the framework and principles to a subsequent set of more detailed legislation. The Loi-cadre of 1956 (also known as the loi Defferre, after the minister responsible for guiding it through the National Assembly, Gaston Defferre) set the framework for legislation implementing a measure of self-government in the French colonies of sub-Saharan Africa. It was superseded by the provisions for the French 'Community' in the constitution of 1958.

négritude A cultural movement for the promotion of black culture and values, started in Paris in the 1930s by Aimé Césaire and Léopold Sédar Senghor.

Glossary

protectorat Legal-administrative entity established to enable rule of one polity by another without the full transfer of sovereignty as in colonies (q.v.). Often used to impose 'law and order' and ensure the economic viability of bankrupt regimes. In theory, the existing ruler continued to rule subordinate to the 'Protecting Power'.

RDA Rassemblement Démocratique Africain. A grouping together of a number of territory-based political parties, the most important of which were the PDCI-RDA (Côte d'Ivoire), the PDG-RDA (Guinea) and the US-RDA (Soudan).

SFIO Section Française de l'Internationale Ouvrière. Formed in 1905 as a unitary organization of working-class parties. Main socialist organization in France until the split at the Congress of Tours in 1920 which led to the creation of separate and antagonistic Socialist and Communist parties.

tirailleurs sénégalais African infantrymen. Contrary to what their name suggests, they were in fact recruited from throughout French Black Africa.

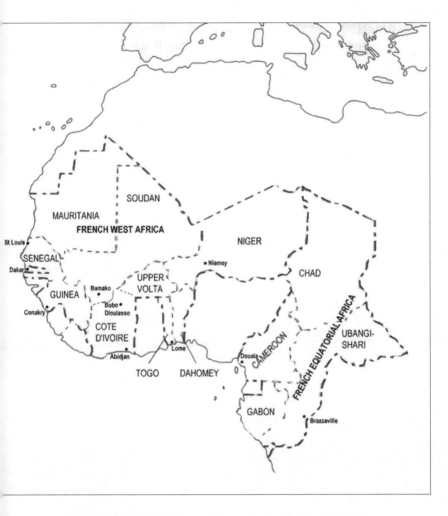

Figure 0.1 French West Africa and French Equatorial Africa (1947–60)

Introduction

In June 1995, the Senegalese National Archives organized a major inter national conference in Dakar to commemorate the centenary of the creation of the federation of French West Africa (Afrique Occidentale Française: AOF). The conference's opening session was chaired by the President of Senegal, Abdou Diouf, and attended by the Prime Minister, Habib Thiam, together with other members of the government. Also present was the French Minister of Cooperation, Jacques Godfrain. The closing address was given by the last French High Commissioner in Dakar, Pierre Messmer. A month later, and just six weeks after his election, Jacques Chirac's first official visit abroad as President of the Republic was to Francophone Africa. His visit took in Morocco, Côte d'Ivoire, Gabon and Senegal. The visit was clearly intended to mark the continuing importance of French links with, and the French presence in, its traditional sphere of influence in Africa, because it took in France's strongest ally in north Africa and its closest allies in, respectively, former French West Africa and French Equatorial Africa (Afrique Equatoriale Française: AEF). These two events are symbolic of the continuing close links between France and its former African colonies and of the perceived importance of these links for French *grandeur* and the maintenance of France's world power status. Apparently taken for granted as normal in both France and Francophone Africa, such events would have been unimaginable in the former colonies of Anglophone Africa, such as Ghana and Nigeria. One could not conceive, for example, of a conference being organized in Accra thirty-five years after independence to mark the beginning of British colonial rule. Nor could one imagine a newly elected British prime minister making his first official visit abroad a tour round Britain's former colonial possessions in Africa. Such events would, incidentally, have been equally unimaginable in Algeria or former Indochina, where French decolonization was so much more traumatic than in Black Africa.

In his closing address at the Dakar conference, Messmer used the opportunity to praise France for the climate of peace it created in French West Africa, to underline the way in which France had brought about the economic integration of West Africa and to draw attention to the 'stability' of French sovereignty. As evidence of this, he cited the CFA Franc, which, he claimed, still had the same value then as it had had a century earlier – a claim that was greeted with some hilarity in the audience, since it apparently overlooked the fact that France had successfully obtained a 50 per cent devaluation of the CFA franc against the French franc just eighteen months earlier, in January 1994. He suggested that this integration had also been promoted by the schools, communications and military service that France had brought to Africa. Returning to the stability of French sovereignty in that part of the world, this was, according to Messmer, combined after 1945 with a French ability to adapt to 'the course of events and to African ways of thinking'. This evolution had, he asserted, been peaceful and democratic, largely thanks to the French training of Africans between 1945 and 1960 which had brought about a 'peaceful and democratic transition to independence'.

His speech has been covered in some detail here, because it contains within it several of the myths concerning the French colonial presence and the decolonization process in French West Africa.[1] These myths operate at a number of different levels, in both France and Black Africa. The first relates to the nature of the French presence in Black Africa, which is implicitly seen as enduring and therefore somehow natural, hence the reference to the 'stability' of French sovereignty. The fact that French control over its colonial territories in Black Africa was not fully established until after the turn of the century and that French sovereignty over these territories had formally ended in 1960, meaning that French rule lasted for barely sixty years, was conveniently forgotten. The second relates to the benefits that French colonial rule brought to Black Africa, which have traditionally been linked to France's self-appointed 'civilizing mission' in Africa. In this speech Messmer expressed these benefits more specifically in economic and political terms: at the economic level, it was regional integration, notably through the establishment of a common currency within the Franc zone,[2] modern communications and a common public school system; and at the political level, it was the smooth transition to independence, thanks to France's 'colonial peace' and its training of the qualified personnel Africa needed in order to prepare for a successful decolonization. The fact that the rival colonial presences of, notably, France and Britain in West Africa, have in practice been a significant obstacle to regional integration was conveniently overlooked: in this respect, one need only think of the absurd borders of Senegal, which is literally divided in two by the former British colony of the

Gambia, a country some three hundred miles long but never more than thirty miles wide. As for the smooth transition to independence being attributable in some way to French training of the qualified personnel that Africa needed in order to make a success of independence, most historians have suggested, rather, that one of the reasons for the reluctance of French West African leaders to call for immediate independence in the 1950s was the economic, political and administrative dependence of their territories on France, a product – in part at least – of the dearth of qualified Africans![3]

These myths, which were –and still are – widely shared by members of the generation of France's governing élites with direct knowledge or experience of the French colonial presence in Black Africa, have helped to create another myth: that of independence intentionally granted as a 'gift' to Black Africa in order to ensure a continuing close relationship with France.

This raises the question why these myths have been so enduring. Part of the answer to this lies in the way in which they tapped into deeply rooted elements of French national culture, both underpinning and justifying the notion of France's *vocation coloniale*. This notion was linked, in turn, to ideas of French universalism and the superiority of French culture, a notion widely held on both the right and left. At the same time, they served, on the right, to sustain myths of French *grandeur*, particularly in the military and diplomatic fields, while on the left, they served to legitimize the notion that French colonialism was modernizing and progressive through the export of the republican values of liberty and equality and the promotion of economic development. Now detached from the *vocation coloniale*, they have continued to underpin French attitudes and policy towards Black Africa in the post-colonial period. Taken together, these myths have served to legitimize, implicitly if not explicitly, the maintenance of France's presence in Black Africa in the post-colonial period. Linked to this, and just as importantly, they have acquired an explanatory function by suggesting that the largely peaceful transition was the product of a deliberate government strategy.

The narrative of a France in control of the decolonization agenda in Black Africa is an appealing one, but it does not reflect how things looked to those in charge at the time. As government records of the period show, France's governing élites were far from taking any such peaceful outcome for granted in the 1950s. On the contrary, they were worried by the rising tide of African nationalism and, haunted by the spectre of Algeria, they feared a descent into violence and the consequent loss of political control.

So, if the peaceful outcome was not the product of government strategy, how did it come about? How can we explain it? Why did French West Africa, and more generally French Black Africa, go the way it did, whereas in Indochina and Algeria the end of colonial rule was marked by war and, ultimately, the eviction of the French? Tony Smith's typology of nationalist élites can help us here. In his comparative study of French and British decolonization, he suggests that there are three situations in which nationalist élites can be expected to enter into violent conflict with an imperial regime: 'where a native élite dependent on foreign power has never been created; where such an élite, once created, is destroyed; and where such an élite has been displaced by the rise of a rival political formation'.[4] None of these cases applied to French West Africa, where the native élite was, as we shall see, very much dependent on France. Moreover, this native élite was in a weak position because it was obliged to fight on two fronts, against the imperial power on the one hand, and against more radical local groups striving to replace it on the other. As Tony Smith again points out, dominant élites in this situation are prudent to avoid open confrontation with the colonial power: 'This is not only because it is sensible to recognize that, given the great disproportion of military resources, it is mostly their fellow citizens who will be killed. The élites understand as well that the first military setbacks they can expect to suffer may well release the centrifugal forces of class and ethnic division which so profoundly mark most colonial societies'.[5] In the predictable chaos that ensues, the dominant élite may well find it loses out to rival leaders.[6]

The foregoing describes well the situation in which African political leaders such as Senghor (Senegal), Apithy (Dahomey) and Houphouët-Boigny (Côte d'Ivoire) found themselves after the Second World War. They were constantly forced to look over their shoulders, fearing initially Communist influence and, later in the 1950s, the spread of radical nationalist ideas, because both of these represented a threat to their strategy of cooperation and negotiation with the colonial power, which depended for its success on the maintenance of both a stable situation within the colony and stable relations with France. This was the main reason for Houphouët-Boigny's decison to break with the Communist Party in 1950 and was also one of the reasons for his subsequent decision, in 1956, to support the 'balkanization' of Africa through the granting of internal autonomy to the separate territories of French West and Equatorial Africa, rather than to the federations as a whole as the more radical elements within the nationalist movement wanted. To achieve their aims, they needed French political support. This was not the whole story, however, because much of the French-educated élite in Black Africa bought into aspects of the myths about the French presence in Black Africa, albeit in different and complex ways. This was as true of the radical nationalists who demanded immediate independence as it was of more moderate nationalists who wanted to maintain close links with France. They were impressed, for instance, by French superiority in the military, technical, scientific, economic and cultural fields, and sought to share in the benefits of this superiority through the acquisition of French education and though closer contact with France. Even after this superiority began to be questioned as a result of France's military defeat in 1940, French republican ideals of democracy and equal rights continued to exercise a powerful force of attraction. They also encouraged significant sections of the French-educated African élite to see French colonialism as modernizing and progressive and to believe that African emancipation would take place through integration within a Greater France, rather than through secession from it. This belief endured in significant sections of this élite right up to, and beyond, political independence. Even those more radical members of the French-educated élite who advocated secession from France found themselves inextricably caught up in the logic of the French colonial presence. Like the nationalist leaders whose moderate stance they rejected, they were French educated; and it was by reference to French models and norms that they demanded the expansion of education for Africans, equal rights, equal status and equal pay for equal work. Such contradictions and ambiguities were to be actively exploited by African political leaders who sought to challenge the legitimacy of the radical nationalists' position. We shall return to this theme below.

A number of issues emerge as a consequence of the above that are significant with regard to the approach to decolonization that is adopted here. Firstly, the nature and outcome of any decolonization process cannot be taken for granted. Decolonization brings into play a range of actors, on both the colonial and nationalist side, whose goals are diverse and often in conflict. In this respect, it is important not to view decolonization as a straightforward 'us' and 'them' situation that pitched the colonizer against the colonized. Even if the ultimate goals on each side were broadly shared, there were multiple opportunities for tension and conflict within each side over policy priorities, which in turn fed into divisions over strategy and tactics. However, it is arguable that even this attributes too great a commonality of purpose to the various actors involved on each side. The decolonization process was in practice a good deal less 'tidy' than this suggests. It drew in various European and African participants whose aims and loyalties were multiple and shifting. During the process of negotiation significant commonalities of interest could emerge between actors from either side of the colonizer/colonized divide, which might be greater than, and in some situations might even override, the commonality of purpose that is supposed to unite the metropolitan and colonial governing élites on the one hand, and the different elements of the nationalist movement on the other. The proposition here is that it is only through an analysis of the complex interaction between the different actors involved that a fuller understanding of the specific nature and outcome of a particular decolonization process can be attained.

Secondly, decolonization does not take place in a vacuum. There are clearly alternative paths to decolonization and for this reason methods do differ. But they are not the product of a free choice owing to the play of a range of factors over which the actors concerned do not have control, such as geopolitical considerations, the wider international context, economic power, logistical strength, the degree of ideological control, and the strength and depth of opposition. Each of these will be a significant variable for each side. For example, if we take the question of the strength and depth of opposition, this is a factor that affects the relative strength, and thus also the stance and strategy, of both the colonial power and the nationalists. On the government side, domestic legitimation is inevitably a major concern. The likely scale and effectiveness of metropolitan opposition – and the fear of widespread problems if a particular stance is adopted can be just as significant a consideration as the actual expression of opposition – will certainly affect the government's position. Similarly, on the side of the colonized, the scale and nature of opposition to nationalist leaders from within the nationalist movement will have an impact on the negotiating stance they adopt and on the relative strength of their position vis-à-vis the government. This will not necessarily happen in straightforward and predictable ways. For example, a moderate nationalist leader, such as Houphouët-Boigny, may actually have his hand strengthened in negotiations with the colonial government by the perceived threat that he could be replaced by a more radical leader who would be less amenable to compromise and thus less acceptable to the colonial power. Or conversely, a radical leader fully in control of his movement may induce the government to adopt a more intransigent position, if it is perceived that making concessions to the nationalist position would not be likely to further its aims. This happened in the case of Guinea in 1958. Moreover, personalities, and the personal chemistry between different actors, can influence outcomes in ways that are not easy to predict.

Thirdly, decolonization can be smooth or otherwise for either party. There are alternative perspectives on the overall question of decolonization and one's view on this will depend crucially on the goals of the respective participants and on one's perspective in relation to these goals. For example, if we posit that for France a central foreign policy consideration throughout the twentieth century was the assertion and maintenance of French great power status, and that colonial empire enabled such a goal to be pursued successfully, then we can assume that, from the French perspective, a smooth decolonization will be one that allows it to maintain its great power status.

A related point can be made from a nationalist standpoint: whether or not decolonization is seen as successful will depend on one's perspective on the process and its perceived outcomes. For the political leaders of the newly independent states, one can assume that decolonization will be seen as a smooth and well-managed transition if it enables them to secure the transfer of power without bloodshed and then successfully to assert their authority over the country they now govern. If, however, the country were to descend into civil unrest, or political instability were to lead, for example, to a military takeover, then their view of the decolonization process would be rather different. On the other hand, if one were to shift one's perspective from the nationalist leaders who inherited power at independence to that of groups within the nationalist movement who took part in the struggle for independence but then found themselves sidelined or, worse, banned or imprisoned by the new regime, then one's perception of the success or otherwise of the decolonization process would again be different. It will be shown here that this was what happened in much of French West Africa: nationalist leaders who were active in the trade union, student and youth movements often found themselves marginalized at independence, and their movements repressed, banned or politically neutered through forced absorption into the dominant political party as the new governments sought to assert their authority. Thus, while they might indeed be prepared to concede that the decolonization process had indeed been smooth, insofar as large-scale bloodshed or civil war had been avoided, they would certainly question whether it had been 'successful'. Moreover, as a result of this sidelining, the questions they posed about the nature of the newly won independence could not be addressed in public. How genuine was it? Were the African post-colonial governing élites in hock to the former colonial power to such a degree that the country still was not genuinely independent? And how viable, in economic and political terms, were these eight small, and in most cases very poor, countries that emerged from the former federation of French West Africa?

Much of the existing literature on French decolonization, which has traditionally concentrated on the conflicts in Indochina and Algeria and paid scant attention to events in Black Africa, has tended to 'iron out' these complexities and treat decolonization in French West and Equatorial Africa as, implicitly if not explicitly, straightforward and largely unproblematic.[7] This relative neglect of Black Africa is understandable, insofar as decolonization in Indochina and Algeria was so much more traumatic for France than it was in Black Africa. The focus has naturally tended to be on what went wrong in those parts of the Empire, rather than on Black Africa, where France apparently got it right. Moreover, no monograph on the politics of decolonization in French West Africa has appeared in English since the 1960s: Ruth Schachter Morgenthau's *Political Parties in French-speaking West Africa*, published in 1964, remains a seminal work in the field, while William Foltz's *From French West Africa to the Mali Federation*, published in 1965, and Edward Mortimer's *France and the Africans*, published in 1969, are still useful sources of information. Thus, just as Black Africa was for many years the Cinderella of the French Empire, so decolonization in French Black Africa has remained the Cinderella of research and scholarship on French colonialism.

In revisiting the politics of decolonization in French West Africa, the present study aims, at one level, to retell the story of the end of empire in this region of the world. The justification for this is that it is a story – or rather a plurality of stories – the details and complexities of which remain relatively little known, at least in the English-speaking world.[8] Knowledge about the politics of this period remains at best fragmentary. A small number of 'landmark' events, such as the Brazzaville Conference, the Loi-Cadre, De Gaulle's 1958 referendum and political independence in 1960, have been well covered, as has the role of certain key actors, such as De Gaulle, Senghor, Houphouët-Boigny and Sékou Touré.[9] The broader political picture remains little known, however. What kinds of goals were being pursued by the different actors in the process? What were the constraints and variables which helped to determine their actions? The present study seeks to establish and explore these.

The political story is not only worth retelling for this reason however. Unlike earlier studies of the politics of decolonization, which were written at the time, or in the immediate aftermath, of the events being described, the present study has benefited from the insights afforded by the recently opened archives from the period, particularly in Africa but also in France and Britain. Complemented by interviews with key political actors of the period, which were conducted in the light of this newly available material, it is clear that the widespread impression of French decolonization in West Africa as a successfully managed transition needs to be substantially qualified. It is misleading to suggest, as John Chipman has done, that in Black Africa 'independence was intentionally granted as a "gift" whose acceptance by the newly created states was implicitly meant to ensure a close relationship with France'.[10] On the contrary, policy making was far from monolithic. While there was broad agreement between policy makers over the ultimate goal being pursued – the maintenance of French influence – there were deep-seated tensions within and between both the government and colonial officials over priorities and strategy. As a result, the policy-making process was far from monolithic and decolonization in French West Africa, rather than a successfully managed process, actually consisted of periods of policy inertia, during which pressure from the nationalist movement on the government increased, leading to gathering political crises, which were followed by timely concessions and political compromises at key moments. Moreover, the neglect of the role of the nationalist movement in the existing literature on decolonization in French West Africa has lent support to the predominant view, carefully orchestrated by both the French political establishment and those African political leaders who inherited power at independence, of decolonization in Black Africa as a smooth transition successfully managed by well-intentioned French politicians and civil servants and a small group of enlightened African political leaders. In contrast to this traditional view, it will be argued here that there was no overarching French strategy. Rather, French tactics were subsequently dressed up as strategy, which in turn has served to underpin the conventional view of French decolonization in Black Africa as a successfully managed transition.

However, it is not only the dominant narrative of decolonization in French West Africa as a successfully managed transition that the retelling of this story will lead us to question. The nationalist narrative of an anti-colonial movement, broadly unified after the Second World War under the leadership of a French-educated élite which successfully led Africa to decolonization and political independence, emerges here as equally problematic. The roots of African nationalism were many and diverse. One consequence of this was that the immediate political priorities and goals of the different elements of the nationalist movement were frequently in tension. Moreover, the reasons for, and acuity of, these tensions did not remain static, as the aims of the different groups within the nationalist movement were themselves constantly shifting to take account of new demands and new situations as they arose. Fred Cooper, in his study of the labour question in French and British Africa in the period of decolonization, showed how the objectives of trade unionists were often at variance with those of African political leaders. Although both claimed to be representing the nationalist cause, the imperatives of the class struggle were not always easily reconciled with the principle of African unity and the task of nation building.[11] Other groups that played a key role in the nationalist movement, such as the student and youth movements, also had their own agendas. This study seeks to establish the goals of the various actors involved, and to explore the constraints and variables that helped to determine the choices they made and which contributed to shaping the nature and outcomes of the decolonization process.

* * *

In addressing the issues outlined above, this book aims to fill a number of gaps in the existing literature on decolonization in French West Africa. In so doing, it seeks to advance our historical understanding of the contemporary period in three ways. Firstly, it can contribute to the study of French history by adding to our understanding of the changing role and status of France in the wider world during the twentieth century. Secondly, it can make a contribution to our understanding of African history by examining the complex roots and nature of African nationalism. Thirdly, through its aligning of Eurocentric and Afrocentric perspectives, it can help us to arrive at a fuller appreciation of the nature of the decolonization process and of France's colonial legacy in Black Africa. By focusing on the end of empire in a specific spatial and temporal context, we can draw out common threads with decolonization processes elsewhere in the world while identifying features that were specific to the decolonization experience in French West Africa. The comparative dimension makes it possible to illustrate more sharply the key differentiating characteristics between this and, for example, the British experience of decolonization, as well as with other French experiences of decolonization. As we look back from the vantage point of the twenty-first century, the end of empire and its many legacies appear as one of the defining themes of twentieth century history. The hope of the author of the present study is that this book might inspire other historians to undertake further comparative studies in this field.

If we now turn to the first of our themes, the changing role of France in the wider world during the twentieth century, we can see that the building of French great power status was a constant preoccupation of French policy makers.[12] Colonization allowed this goal to be pursued successfully and, by the end of the First World War, empire had become the benchmark of great power status. However, since that time French power has been in decline. But how has this power declined? The weakening of France's position as a result of the destruction caused by two world wars in Europe and its economic and political decline in the context of the rise of the US and the Soviet Union account for the more marginal position of the French empire by the end of the Second World War. What did France hope to achieve in this situation? How has it tried to maximize its position with respect to its goal of maintaining great power status?

A comparison with Britain, which also emerged weakened from the Second World War, is instructive here. Faced with the emergence of the US and the Soviet Union, both France and Britain were forced to recognize that they were no longer world powers in the way that they had been and that they needed to adjust to this situation. Gradual withdrawal with appropriate compromise and the positioning of friendly élites would make sense if it could be engineered. Britain sought to do this and maintain global influence by, in effect, substituting an imperial role for colonial rule. In order to achieve this, a three-pronged strategy was pursued: to shed colonial 'liabilities' so as to be better able to exploit remaining assets; to cultivate 'friendly' nationalists in these remaining colonial territories; and to share the costs of this new imperial role with the US through the 'special relationship'. French policy makers were prevented by the legacy of the past, in terms of both ideas and procedures on imperial matters, from pursuing the first of these strategies; it was for this reason that France found itself implicated in two highly destructive colonial wars, first in Indochina and then in Algeria. Indeed, even as late as 1957–8, the prime focus of policy makers in Paris was how to restructure the colonial link with Black Africa so as better to maintain it, rather than on preparing the colonies for self-government. Nor was it in a position to pursue the third of these strategies, although the foundation of the Common Market under French impulsion in 1957 can be seen at one level as a strategy for achieving this sharing of costs, but with European partners rather than an American one. On the other hand, it did have some success in West Africa in its pursuit of the second strategy. Yet France was apparently in an even weaker position than Britain to undertake such a policy of adjustment at the end of the war. Not only had it been occupied by Germany for much of the war, but the capacity of its domestic political institutions to deal with a problem of the magnitude of decolonization was diminished, compared to that of Britain, both by its lack of regime stability, thanks to the constitutional wrangling of 1945–6 and the fall of the Fourth Republic in 1958, and by the power of France's 'colonial myth' in determining the mindset of France's post-war governing élites. Given these constraints it seems that, compared to Britain, France was remarkably successful in achieving its key policy objectives in Black Africa. The decolonization process was largely peaceful and it was this smooth transition that enabled France to maintain a high profile French presence in the region after independence. At a political level this is exemplified by French presidential visits and the annual Franco-African summits. This has been accompanied by a significant economic effort: since 1960, between half and two-thirds of bilateral French economic development aid has consistently gone to its former colonies in sub-Saharan Africa.[13] The political and economic effort has in turn been underpinned by the Franc zone, by the maintenance of permanent French military bases and the promotion of French language and culture through cultural cooperation and the organization of La Francophonie.[14] None of this would have been possible if the decolonization process had been marked by violence and bloodshed, as happened elsewhere in the French Empire.

Yet if, as is suggested here, the comparatively smooth decolonization process was not the product of French strategy, then this 'accidental' success story needs to be explained. If France actually achieved its objectives incrementally and without any grand plan, how come it has done so well at shoring up its long-term position in Africa? Part of the answer lies in the French capacity to create a discourse on decolonization and ultimately to achieve the triumph of relatively friendly élites, which bought them time to re-establish a discourse with its own momentum to maintain French influence in the area. In order to understand this, we have to go back to the origins of what Jean-François Médard has called French 'messianism' and its association with French imperialism.[15] This messianism dates back to the French Revolution and its 'universal' message of liberty, equality and fraternity, as expressed through the Declaration of the Rights of Man and the Citizen, which proclaimed a duty to export French republican ideals beyond the frontiers of metropolitan France and bring the message of liberty to peoples living under regimes less modern and progressive. In this way France's revolutionary message led to, and became associated with, imperialism. It enabled France to create a discourse of French imperialism as emancipatory, progressive and modernizing, which served to legitimate it in the eyes of many across the political spectrum from right to left. This was significant when it came to decolonization, as it enabled France's post-war governing élites to generate a discourse which suggested that decolonization could take place through closer integration with the *métropole* rather than through secession from it. Nationalist élites in Indochina and Algeria did not buy into this discourse, in the former case because, as Tony Smith has pointed out, 'a nationalist élite that might have had an interest in cooperating with the French after 1945 was destroyed', and in the latter case because 'a strong Muslim élite which depended for its position on the good favour of the French was simply never created'.[16] In Black Africa, on the other hand, nationalist leaders did buy into the idea that French imperialism was modernizing and progressive, at least to the extent that they could exploit this discourse in order to sell to their electorates the idea that maintaining close links with France would bring developmental benefits to Africans. This is not to suggest that they believed in assimilation, in the sense of wanting full integration with France or wishing to become 'Black Frenchmen', but it does mean that they could point to the material and other social benefits to much of the population of maintaining close links with France. Implicit, and sometimes explicit, in their stance was the notion that these benefits might be lost if there was a sudden rupture with France.[17] Instead, the idea that France and Africa should become partners for development was promoted, which enabled France to maintain a sphere of influence in the region after independence.

It is doubtful, however, if a purely socio-economic discourse would have been sufficient for African political leaders to carry their peoples with them in this project. Something else was needed: an ideal. As Houphouët-Boigny put it in 1957, if Côte d'Ivoire had been colonized by the Anglo-Saxons, 'there is no doubt that we would have chosen independence even at the cost of economic disadvantages. But in France we think we catch a note of human fraternity'.[18] And this is where the cultural aspect of French imperialism, and its association with French messianism – that is, with a certain idea of France and of the French nation – have been so important in helping to produce a real sense of a common, shared identity between French and African post-colonial governing élites. The notion of the modern French nation as progressive and modernizing and its association with the republican ideals of liberty, equality and fraternity, were of crucial importance, as they enabled De Gaulle during the Second World War and French governing élites after the War to develop a discourse of French imperialism as emancipatory and egalitarian. In this way, decolonization did not have to mean secession from France, but could mean instead closer association with it.

There is an intriguing comparison to be made here between French and British discourse on decolonization. In the quotation from Houphouët-Boigny just cited, he hints at a fundamental contrast between the French and British approach by suggesting that one of the distinguishing features of French colonial imperialism was the cultural dimension and that this marked it out as clearly different from British colonial imperialism, the ostensible motive for which was much more explicitly commercial and economic. However, this is to overlook the Commonwealth ideal of a partnership between sovereign nations. The history of the Commonwealth idea is a complex one and it is true that it was not originally intended to apply to Africa, yet it was not without effect even here and, importantly, it did provide a 'discourse' within which to envisage continuing relationships with Africans.[19] The difference between the French and British approach is not, therefore, the lack of such a discourse. It is, rather, the salience of the cultural dimension in French discourse: not only is the messianism more prominent, it is also expressed more consistently and with more formal rhetoric than in the British case.

The image of De Gaulle as the Liberator of France was also important in this context, because it facilitated the promotion of the notion that it was through association with France, with 'true', republican France, the France of liberty, equality and fraternity represented by De Gaulle, rather than the reactionary, racist and authoritarian France of Vichy, that African emancipation could be achieved. Testimony to just how powerful and enduring such ideas were in laying the basis for maintaining close links with France is provided by a speech made by President Félix Houphouët-Boigny to the Ivoirian National Assembly seventeen months after Côte d'Ivoire gained its political independence from France:

> We gained independence in friendship with France . . .
> Indeed how could it be otherwise, since there is no longer any political problem between us.
> France does not seek to impose a doctrine upon us.
> The love of freedom and democracy, that we share with France, brings us together.
> What we do know . . . is that, if some French people are Communists, or Socialists, or Radicals, or Christian Democrats, or people of the centre left or right, or conservatives, France itself is neither Communist, nor Socialist, nor Radical, nor conservative.
> It is France, the country of democracy, liberty and friendship with all the peoples of the world.[20]

To be sure, the development of a specific discourse on decolonization does not, on its own, explain the relatively smooth political transition in French West Africa. Education, and especially the insistence on using French as the language of instruction, was an important factor in the acculturation of the new élites throughout French Black Africa.[21] The election, under the Fourth Republic, of twenty Black African *députés* to the National Assembly in Paris (and of a number of Black African senators to France's second chamber, the Conseil de la République) was a powerful symbol, albeit in reality little more than that, of African political assimilation. The very fact that it was possible for Black Africans to be elected to France's national parliament was certainly a distinguishing feature of French colonial practice in Africa: no Black African was ever allowed to represent Britain's colonies in the House of Commons, for example. Importantly, it enabled African politicians, who were in many cases to become the political leaders of the newly independent nations, to forge close links with France's post-war political leaders and develop a taste for *la vie parisienne*, where they enjoyed the pleasures of a relatively affluent upper middle class lifestyle. The fact that French colonial officials appear to have had closer relations with Africans than their British counterparts, who generally maintained a greater distance in such relations, was undoubtedly also a factor.[22] Finally, transcending their political differences on other major issues, France's post-war political élites of both left and right shared a certain mindset, which linked empire to French Great Power status and which Bruce Marshall has characterized as the 'French colonial myth'.[23] This did not of course put an end to disagreements about strategy, which fed on occasion into conflicts over African policy, but the point is that these conflicts were acted out within the context of an overall objective which was broadly shared. As a result, and in contrast to the situation in British West Africa where decolonization was accompanied by substantial British withdrawal and the British government was much less willing to intervene in African affairs after independence, there was a clear and consistently pursued government policy, during the last years of French colonial rule and after, to maintain the French presence in the region.[24] In this respect, France has behaved very much as those commentators who adopt a 'realist' perspective on international relations would expect it to behave: it has acted to defend and promote what it sees as its key strategic national interest. One of the central themes of this study will be to show how French policy makers sought to pursue this policy during a painful and difficult period of transition while attempting to come to terms with the loss of empire.

Secondly, the book aims to contribute to our understanding of African history through a study of the nationalist movement in French West Africa. Nationalism in a colonial context is, first and foremost, anti-colonial. It is rooted in people's divergent experiences of colonial rule: the grievances felt by different groups against the colonial regime, which fed nationalist feeling, took many different forms. Thus, recognizing that the roots of nationalism were complex and diverse and that African nationalism, as elsewhere in Black Africa, operated at different levels in French West Africa, this book does not adopt a single definition of African nationalism. Rather, it seeks to capture some of this diversity, which resulted in the 'segmentation' of the nationalist struggle and was one of the reasons why it proved so difficult to forge a united nationalist movement in the colony.

Benedict Anderson has rightly pointed to the ways in which the *métropoles* shaped what he called the 'last wave' of anti-colonial nationalisms during and after the Second World War. These new nationalisms, he suggests, have to be seen in the context of existing European models, since modern nationalist leaders can, and do, draw on these models.[25] Two examples will suffice to indicate the relevance of this to French West Africa. As already indicated, cultural universalism has traditionally been an important aspect of French imperialism; it is not therefore surprising that the earliest expressions of modern French West African nationalism in the inter-war years reflected this and took a cultural form. *Négritude*, as Senghor envisaged it, was about the valorization of black culture, it was 'the manner of self-expression of the black character, the black world, black civilization', the origins of which were to be found in Africa.[26] The title of the work in which this definition appeared, *Négritude et civilisation de l'universel*, can be seen as a deliberate attempt to counter the claimed universalism of French culture with its own claim to universalism for black culture. Secondly, the way in which French West African politicians after the Second World War appealed to republican France was significant: 'Children of Senegal, totally devoted to the destiny of these ancient French lands, our only ambition is to serve, as effectively as possible, within the framework of a Republic which gives a little reality to the fine slogan "Liberty, Equality, Fraternity". Long live France! Long live Socialist Africa! Long live the Republic!'[27] In this text, which is taken from Lamine Guèye's and Léopold Sédar Senghor's manifesto for the 1945 Constituent Assembly elections, republican France represents both an ideal and a tribune, to which they appealed for change over the heads of reactionary Vichyite colonialists in French West Africa. Both of these aspects, the cultural dimension and the appeal to republican values, were to feature regularly in the discourse of African nationalist leaders after the War. Moreover, as the last part of this quotation suggests, it is clear that they saw themselves as simultaneously African nationalists *and* part of a wider French community. The two were not perceived as contradictory.

This was only part of the story, however. As Anderson recognized in the second edition of his *Imagined Communities*, it was not only the *métropole* that played a key role in fashioning these new nationalisms, but also, just as importantly, the local colonial state.[28] This is of crucial importance to an understanding of nationalism in French West Africa for two reasons. It is significant firstly because of the way in which the colonial state arrogated to itself the right to intervene in every aspect of African economic, social and political life: in this respect, colonial rule became a vast experiment in social engineering, in which the colonial state undertook a project to 're-make' indigenous society, not so much in the image of metropolitan society, as most colonialists were ultimately ambivalent about Black Africans becoming too much like them, but sought to refashion African society according to some idealized image that was the product of the imaginings of colonial policy makers and officials.[29] It was these imaginings, which helped to shape the political ideas and ambitions of the nationalist leaders of Black Africa, that were to be the seed-bed of the authoritarian tendencies of official nationalism in the post-colonial states.[30] In this respect, French West Africa was no different from much of the rest of Black Africa.

However, there were two other respects in which the specific nature of the local colonial state was to have a profound impact on French West African nationalism. This was linked at one level to the way in which French West Africa had been administered, until the Second World War, under two completely distinct regimes: the Four, subsequently Three, Communes of Senegal,[31] the residents of which were French citizens and enjoyed certain political and electoral rights, and the rest of French West Africa, which was administered as a protectorate. In the latter, Africans were subject to the *indigénat* and forced labour and had no political rights.[32] The key position of the Four Communes in French West Africa, with their long tradition of assimilationist politics, had a formative influence in shaping nationalist demands and the nature of early nationalist politics in French West Africa in the immediate aftermath of the Second World War.

At another level, French West Africans were subject to a bifurcated colonial state within Africa, with a federal Government-General in Dakar and local territorial governments, answerable to Dakar, at the level of each of the constituent territories of the federation.[33] Its key significance for the nature of French West African nationalism was the way in which it served to create overlapping, and sometimes conflicting, African identities. For example, members of the French-educated African élite who had travelled outside their home territory, perhaps to train as teachers or medical assistants at the Ecole William-Ponty in Senegal, could feel culturally Guinean, Ivoirian or Soudanese while at the same time seeing themselves as part of a larger federation. More seriously for African nationalists seeking to build a united nationalist movement in French West Africa, one consequence of this colonial administrative structure was that nationalism, particularly in the territories furthest from Dakar, such as Dahomey and Côte d'Ivoire, was also bifurcated. At one level it was anti-colonial, insofar as it represented a reaction against the French colonial regime in Africa, while at another level it emerged as a reaction against the domination of the federation by Senegal: the 'enemy' could be Paris, or Dakar, or both.

Another result of this was that the nature of the colonial state experienced by the Senegalese who lived in the Four Communes was very different from that of the rural populations in the protectorate, where the leaders of the Muslim Mouride brotherhoods worked closely with the French authorities, and this in turn was profoundly different from the colonial experience of Ivoirians, where there was a significant *colon* (European settler) presence and Africans were recruited in large numbers for forced labour on the European-run plantations. As a consequence of their different experiences of colonialism, the roots of anti-colonial nationalism in the different territories and for different groups within the territories were very different. This posed problems when attempts were made after the Second World War to build a united nationalist movement. A central theme of this study will therefore be the 'segmentation' of the nationalist struggle. Different groups had divergent objectives which were often difficult to reconcile, so that it is in this sense perhaps more appropriate to talk of national*isms* in French West Africa, rather than a single united nationalist movement. Combined with the difficulties of communication and the problems of coordinating actions across the vast distances of French West Africa, these factors represented major obstacles to the creation of a united nationalist movement.

Despite these problems, it is argued here that an effective nationalist movement was nevertheless on the verge of emerging in French West Africa in the mid-1950s and that the threat which it represented to the maintenance of the French presence in West Africa was only defused at the eleventh hour, through the combined actions of the French government, top colonial officials and certain African political leaders. In focusing on the specificity of the nationalist movement in French West Africa, on its diverse origins and manifestations and the difficulties it faced, this study aims to throw into sharper relief the key differentiating characteristics between this and, on the one hand, anti-colonial nationalist movements elsewhere in the French Empire and on the other, nationalist movements which emerged under the other colonial powers, notably Great Britain, in other parts of Black Africa.

The third level at which the book aims to contribute to our understanding of the contemporary period is through its aligning of Eurocentric and Afrocentric perspectives in order to arrive at a fuller appreciation of the nature of the decolonization process in French West Africa. Although the end of empire appears as one of the defining themes of twentieth-century history, the term 'decolonization' encompasses a vast range of different experiences: the old colonial empires came to an end for an array of different reasons, and the nature and length of the process varied greatly from one colonial power to another and from one region of the world to another. France adopted a very different approach to decolonization in West Africa from that adopted by Britain and from that which France itself adopted in Indochina and Algeria. Also, as indicated above, the nature of the nationalist movements in these regions differed greatly. In order to appreciate the reasons for these differences, we need to understand the specific nature of the interactions between the *métropole*, the local colonial state, and the nationalist movements which challenged them. Both structures and discourse played a role in fashioning these interactions.

One example will be used to illustrate this point here. In both British and French West Africa, the colonial power was forced onto the defensive by African nationalist movements and obliged to make concessions to them; in each case it adopted a strategy of limited interventions in an effort to defuse nationalist pressure. However, this strategy was generally more effective in French West Africa than it was in British West Africa. It is argued here that this was to a considerable degree thanks to the idea of Greater France and the universalist ideals of French republicanism. Against this background, each demand by Africans – for improved pay and conditions, for the right to family allowances, for access to full metropolitan education, for instance – could be justified by reference to the French Union's constitutional commitment to a 'one and indivisible republic'. In the British case, on the other hand, there was no comparable discourse to suggest that the colonies of British West Africa might one day become an integral part of a Greater Britain. Thus, French concessions to African nationalism took place within a wider framework which appeared to hold out the promise of emancipation through integration with Greater France. Membership of this community in turn offered access to the world of progress, modernity and liberty. British concessions to African nationalism, in contrast, could only be seen as preparation for self-government, because no other political option was on offer.

The point was made earlier that decolonization should not be viewed as a straightforward 'us' and 'them' situation which pitched the colonizer against the colonized. Colonial power did not simply operate through force, coercion and repression, but also used manipulation, influence, co-option and persuasion. Indeed, colonial authority operated most effectively when the colonized, or their representatives, could be encouraged or induced to do what the colonial power wanted them to do without the use of coercion or force.[34] For this to happen, both the colonizer and those speaking on behalf of the colonized need to operate within a shared system of references and values. In French West Africa, republican ideas transmitted through colonial education played a key role in creating such a shared framework and laid the basis for the relatively smooth political transition in French West Africa.

The recognition that decolonization is not a simple 'us' and 'them' situation is also of central importance to an understanding of the nature of the French colonial legacy and its ongoing impact in West Africa after political independence. When we talk of decolonization and the end of empire, we naturally think in terms of closure, the end of an era. At one level this is of course true, because the former colonial territories gain their political independence and become sovereign nations, but the use of such terminology can obscure the many continuities that exist between the colonial and post-colonial periods. In this respect, decolonization represents not so much the end of an era but a period of transition from colonialism to neo-colonialism, in which the links between the former *métropoles* and the newly independent states were maintained 'in the form of economic dependency, development assistance, foreign invest-ment, and the political, social and economic compatibility of objectives among the involved élites'.[35]

These continuities have been widely documented in social, cultural, economic and anthropological studies, but it is important to stress that they also existed at the political level. This is especially significant in the case of French decolonization in West Africa, where France invested much effort in maintaining its presence in the region after African independence through a range of economic, military, technical and cultural accords and thanks to the close personal relations forged between French and African political leaders in the post-war period. Against the background of the recent cultural turn in post-colonial studies, this story – the political story – risks getting lost. However, it should be clear from the foregoing that, in placing the political history of decolonization centre stage, the intention is not to downplay the cultural dimension. On the contrary, the contention here is that an understanding of the interplay between the cultural and the political is essential to an appreciation of the decolonization process and the nature of the French colonial legacy in West Africa.[36]

Finally, an aligning of Eurocentric and African perspectives is essential because decolonization does not take place in a vacuum, insulated in some way from developments on the wider international stage. Some historians have suggested that 'the history of the expansion and contraction of European empire is best understood by giving primary emphasis to the study of the "periphery", or colonial areas'.[37] However, as John Darwin has remarked, 'we will make little progress in unravelling its causes unless we take seriously the complicated interplay between domestic, colonial and international politics, and view cautiously the claims of any of them to primacy'.[38] It needs to be recognized that developments in the colonies took place against a background of world events that were in large measure determined by the actions and interactions of the world's major industrial powers. Any study of decolonization needs to take account of this by attaching due weight to the impact of the Second World War, the Cold War, the relations of the colonial powers with the US, and the profound formative influence of the colonial powers, economically, culturally and politically, on the colonies they administered. Thus we need a balance: we need to recognize the central importance of the European powers in the forging of modern Africa, while acknowledging that African agency played an important role in shaping the decolonization process. We also need to recognize that, in this whole process, neither the European nor the African participants were entirely free agents. The former were subject to international constraints, notably from the US and to a lesser extent the United Nations, and to the constraints of their own recent history, as well as domestic economic and political constraints. The latter were subject not only to these international constraints but also to the deeper constraints imposed by their recent history of European colonial domination, which combined with the longer term social, cultural and ethnic heritage of pre-colonial societies to have a determining influence on the nationalist movements they led.

Thus, decolonization was not the product of free choices, but an often chaotic process in which the variables of international, national, regional and local politics, as well as accidents of luck and timing, all played a role. The present study seeks to unravel these for French West Africa and, in so doing, to provide material for comparison with other experiences of decolonization elsewhere in the world.

Notes

1. 'Myth' is here used in the sense in which Roland Barthes uses the term, that is, of a discursive strategy that aims to 'évacuer le réel' by representing it in a depoliticized and ahistorical manner, *Mythologies* (Seuil, 1957), p. 230.
2. The Franc zone groups together thirteen countries in sub-Saharan Africa (all except one, Equatorial Guinea, former French colonies) and the Comoros Islands in the Indian Ocean. Their currency, the CFA Franc, is tied to the French Franc at a fixed rate which was, until January 1994, 50 CFA to the French Franc and has, since then, been 100 CFA to the Franc. Countries that are members of the zone are required, under the terms of membership, to hold the majority of their foreign currency reserves on deposit at the Banque de France in Paris.
3. See for example, Crowder, M. and Cruise O'Brien, D., 'Politics of decolonisation in French West Africa, 1945–60', in Ajayi, J. F. A. and Crowder, M., *History of West Africa*, vol. 2, 2nd ed. (Longman, 1987), pp. 759–61.
4. T. Smith, 'Patterns in the transfer of power: a comparative study of French and British decolonization', in P. Gifford and W. R. Louis, eds, *The Transfer of Power in Africa. Decolonization 1940–60* (Yale University Press, 1982), pp 109–10.
5. Ibid, pp. 107–8.
6. For a discussion of the key role of indigenous collaborative élites in determining the nature of the decolonization process, see J. Springhall, *Decolonization since 1945* (Palgrave, 2001), pp. 213–17.
7. To take just two examples, both Raymond Betts' and Charles-Robert Ageron's studies of French decolonization devote a mere ten pages to French Black Africa 1944–60, of which a mere three in the latter cover political developments: C.-R. Ageron, *La Décolonisation française* (Armand Colin, 1991); R. F. Betts, *France and Decolonization, 1900–1960* (Macmillan, 1991). G. Pervillé's *De l'Empire français à la décolonisation* (Hachette, 1991) dedicates a little more space (fourteen pages) to decolonization in French Black Africa, whereas A. Clayton's *The Wars of French Decolonization* (Longman, 1994), apart from a few pages on Madagascar, Tunisia and Morocco, focuses exclusively, as its title suggests, on Indochina and Algeria.
8. The two most detailed narratives of French decolonization in West Africa have never been translated into English. They are J.-R. de Benoist, *L'Afrique Occidentale Française de 1944 à 1960* (No

velles Editions Africaines, 1982) and *La Balkanisation de l'Afrique Occidentale Française* (Nouvelles Editions Africaines, 1979).

9. See for example J. L. Hymans, *Léopold Sédar Senghor. An Intellectual Biography* (Edinburgh University Press, 1971); J. G. Vaillant, *Black, French and African. A Life of Léopold Sédar Senghor* (Harvard University Press, 1990); S. Kobelé-Keita, *Ahmed Sekou Touré, l'homme du 28 septembre* (INRDG, 1977); I. B. Kake, *Sekou Touré: le héros et le tyran* (Jeune Afrique, 1987); D. Guèye, *Sur les sentiers du temple. Ma rencontre avec Félix Houphouët-Boigny* (Les Rouyat, 1975); P.-H. Siriex, *Félix Houphouët-Boigny: l'homme de la paix* (Seghers, 1975).

10. J. Chipman, *French Power in Africa* (Blackwell, 1989), p. 86.

11. F. Cooper, *Decolonization and African Society. The Labour Question in French and British Africa* (Cambridge University Press, 1996).

12. See P. Cerny, *The Politics of Grandeur* (Cambridge University Press, 1980).

13. J. Adda and M.-C. Smouts, *La France face au Sud* (Karthala, 1989), pp. 32–3; T. Chafer, 'French Public Development Aid', *Modern and Contemporary France*, NS4, 4, 1996, p. 556.

14. On the French military presence in Black Africa, see T. Chafer, 'Military agreements between France and African states', in ibid, pp. 557–64; on the linguistic and cultural dimension of French policy, see G. Parker, 'French language policy in sub-Saharan Africa', in ibid, pp. 471–81.

15. J.-F. Médard, 'Les avatars du messianisme français en Afrique', *L'Afrique Politique 1999: Entre transition et conflits* (Karthala, 1999), p.17.

16. T. Smith, 'Patterns in the transfer of power', p. 110.

17. See E. J. Berg, 'The Economic Basis of Political Choice in French West Africa', *American Political Science Review*, 54, 2, June 1960, pp. 391–405.

18. *West Africa*, 12 October 1957.

19. J. D. Hargreaves, 'Approaches to Decolonization', in D. Rimmer and A. Kirk-Greene, *The British Intellectual Engagement with Africa* (Macmillan, 2000), pp. 90–111.

20. Quoted in *Modern and Contemporary France*, NS4, 4, 1996, p. 554.

21. Commentators have often pointed to the more rigorous application of the policy of assimilation in the educational field as a key factor in explaining why the governing élites of post-colonial French Black Africa were more 'Frenchified' than their British counterparts, cf. A. A. Mazrui and M. Tidy, *Nationalism and New States in Africa*

(East Africa Educational Publishers, 1984), p. 377. This is, however, difficult to prove: while it appears to be true if we compare Senegal or Côte d'Ivoire with Nigeria, one would probably not draw the same conclusion if one were to compare, for example, Mali with Kenya.

22. O. White, *Children of the French Empire. Miscegenation and Colonial Society in French West Africa, 1895–1960* (Clarendon Press, 1999), pp. 16, 24, 36.

23. D. B. Marshall, *The French Colonial Myth and Constitution-Making in the Fourth Republic* (Yale University Press, 1973).

24. A. A. Mazrui and M. Tidy, *Nationalism*, pp. 378–81.

25. B. Anderson, *Imagined Communities* (Verso/New Left Books, 1983), p. 104. Cf. also E. W. Said, *Culture and Imperialism* (Vintage, 1994), p. xxvii: 'Western imperialism and Third World nationalism feed off each other, but even at their worst they are neither monolithic nor deterministic'.

26. L. S. Senghor, *Liberté 3: Négritude et civilisation de l'universel* (Seuil, 1977), pp. 269–70.

27. *L'AOF*, 5 October 1945, p. 1. Also in AAOF 17G419/126.

28. B. Anderson, *Imagined Communities* (Verso/New Left Books, second ed., 1991), p. xiii.

29. This is one of the themes of A. Conklin's *A Mission to Civilize* (Stanford University Press, 1997); see also, for example, G. Wilder, 'The Politics of Failure: Historicising Popular Front Colonial Policy in French West Africa', in T. Chafer and A. Sackur, eds, *French Colonial Empire and the Popular Front* (Macmillan, 1999), pp. 33–55.

30. For a recent discussion of what he calls the colonial *imaginaire autoritaire* and the ways in which it has influenced social movements and shaped post-colonial systems of domination in Africa, see A. Mbembe, *De la postcolonie* (Karthala, 2000), pp. 69–70.

31. Gorée was attached to Dakar in 1927, thus reducing the Four Communes of Senegal to three.

32. The *indigénat* was a legislative code that allowed colonial officials to punish any African subject with a prison sentence or a fine, as a matter of discipline and without trial.

33. The boundaries of the territories that comprised AOF were periodically changed: for example, Haute-Volta was abolished in 1932 and re-constituted in 1947. But this did not prevent distinct territorial identities emerging.

34. Steven Lukes' discussion of the ways in which power operates is apposite here: see his *Power* (Macmillan, 1974), esp. pp. 24–32.

35. G. Wasserman, *Politics of Decolonization: Kenya Europeans and the Land Issue, 1960–1965* (Cambridge University Press, 1976), p. 174.
36. Yves Person has used the term 'symbolic violence' to describe the cultural domination to which the colonized were subject, notably through the imposition of French education, and which resulted in the negation of Africans' identity and civilization. The cultural alienation to which this gave rise among those who were to become French West Africa's new governing élites after 1960, and its political consequences for Côte d'Ivoire, are analysed in Y. Person, 'Colonisation et décolonisation en Côte d'Ivoire', *Le Mois en Afrique*, August–September 1981, pp. 15–30.
37. Cf. T. Smith, 'Patterns in the transfer of power', p. 115. One historian who has adopted such an approach in relation to French West Africa is H. Brunschwig, 'The Decolonization of French Black Africa', in P. Gifford and W. R. Louis, eds, *The Transfer of Power in Africa*, pp. 211–24.
38. J. Darwin, 'Diplomacy and Decolonization', *Journal of Imperial and Commonwealth History*, XXVIII, 3, 2000, p. 5.

–1–

Prelude to Decolonization: The Popular Front and the Second World War

French West Africa before 1936

Between 1895 and 1904, France's largest colony in Black Africa, the federation of French West Africa (AOF: Afrique Occidentale Française), was formally established by a series of six decrees. Covering a surface area of over 4.6 million square kilometres, the colony was placed under the responsibility of a governor-general, who represented the French government and was answerable to the Minister of Colonies in Paris. His powers were wide ranging as he had overall responsibility for finance, defence and security, public works, economic, political and social affairs, justice, administration and staffing, public health, education, information and communications in the colony. From 1902 onwards he was based in Dakar, which became the federation's capital in that year. The federation itself grouped together eight territories, whose number and boundaries changed from time to time and to which was added a part of the former German colony of Togo in 1919.[1] Each of the territories was administered by a governor who answered directly to the governor-general, the one exception to this being Dakar and Dependencies (covering Dakar, Gorée and Rufisque), which had been separated from the territory of Senegal in 1924 because of fears after the First World War about the growing political influence of Africans who were citizens of the Four Communes.[2] Dakar and Dependencies was therefore administered directly by the governor-general himself. Despite this change, the Four Communes maintained their distinctive position within AOF. They had a political tradition and a history of competitive elections dating back to 1848, when they first won the right to elect a deputy to the French National Assembly in Paris, and they were the only towns in the federation to elect their own mayors, until these rights were suspended in 1939. Residents of the Four Communes – *originaires* as they were called – had also been French citizens since 1916.[3]

In 1936 the population of French West Africa numbered some fifteen-and-a-half million Africans, of whom approximately 100,000 were citizens in the Four Communes, whilst just 2,400 were citizens in the whole of the rest of AOF. The rest of the population were classified as subjects; they had no political rights and were subject to the *indigénat*, a legislative code that allowed colonial officials to punish any African with a prison sentence or a fine as a matter of discipline and without trial. Dakar was the only major urban centre in AOF at this time, with a population of 92,500; no towns outside Senegal had a population of over 25,000, so that society in the great majority of AOF was essentially rural and 'traditional'. There were some 20,000 Europeans, of whom approximately 4,000 were civil servants working for the colonial administration and another 3,900 were French military personnel. This meant that there was only one colonial official or military person for every 2,000 Africans. However, Europeans were even thinner on the ground in the rural areas than these figures suggest, because most of them lived in the towns and remained largely isolated from this peasant-based, rural society. It is not therefore surprising that, while the French presence was everywhere visible, notably in the person of the *commandant de cercle* who represented the colonial administration at local level throughout AOF, French culture had by this time rarely penetrated in all but the most superficial ways into African 'traditional' society. Where such penetration had taken place, it was usually thanks to French education. Although no more than 5 per cent of the population of AOF had attended a French school at the outbreak of the Second World War, this was sufficient to create a new class of African *évolués*, as they were called in the colonial language of the time. Composed mostly of civil servants working for the Administration, for example as interpreters, policemen, teaching assistants and clerks, and employees of European trading companies, they were at least partly acculturated. Within this new class, a more thoroughly acculturated French-speaking élite had emerged, composed of medical assistants (*médecins africains*), pharmacists, primary school teachers (*instituteurs*) and administrative officers (*commis de l'administration*), many of whom had graduated from the Ecole William-Ponty.[4] Thanks to their education, this French-educated élite gained access to French ideas and values. Moreover, French schools opened a new route to social promotion for young people within African society, because those who had obtained a French education enjoyed both material privileges and, in the eyes of an increasing number of Africans, enhanced status within African society.

Approaches to Colonial Rule: Assimilation and Association

The question of the approach France should adopt to governing its African Empire gave rise to much debate among French politicians, colonial administrators and academics. In this debate, the concept of assimilation has traditionally been opposed to that of association. The basic idea underpinning assimilation was to recreate France overseas. There were a number of different dimensions to this. Firstly, it could mean the representation of the colonies in the parliament of the mother country. Such political assimilation might also extend to the idea that all new laws in the mother country should automatically apply in the Empire unless specific exceptions were made, and that the administrative structures and procedures of the mother country should also be trans-ferred to the colonies. A second aspect of assimilation, which might or might not accompany the first, was the assimilation of the colonized population into the culture and way of life of the mother country, the creation, in effect, of 'black Frenchmen'. Thirdly, the term might be used to refer to the economic assimilation of the colonies through the application of the same tax and tariff regime in the colonies as in the mother country. Finally, it might be used to refer to the personal assimilation that occurs, for example, through mixed marriages and regardless of the political or administrative regime put in place by the colonial power. In the early years of the twentieth century, as the practical impossibility of implementing a policy of assimilation was increasingly recognized, association was developed to provide an alternative approach to administering the colonies. It was supposed to be less disruptive of African political and social structures than assimilation since, in principle at least, it accorded greater value to traditional African cultures, as it did not imply an aspiration to eliminate them and replace them with French culture.[5] Instead, Africans would be retained in their traditional culture, which was in the past, and African societies would be allowed to evolve at their own pace and along their own lines, with the important proviso, of course, that their chosen path of evolution did not threaten French dominance or offend French sensibilities. They therefore needed to be insulated from modern ideas so that they could be more easily controlled, although the underlying assumption remained that they would gradually become more *francisé* ('Frenchified'). In these respects, its underlying principles, if not its practice, were similar to those underpinning the British approach of indirect rule.

Recent historiography, however, has suggested that the debate over whether France was assimilationist or associationist 'is to some extent a useless one, since most students of the subject agree that from the end of the nineteenth century on, France was both'.[6] In any case, the debate between assimilationists and associationists was of little interest to colonial administrators out in the bush confronted with the practical need to rule over an area about which they had little or no direct knowledge. In French West Africa, political and administrative assimilation was applied only in the Four Communes; in the rest of AOF, an essentially paternalistic administrative regime was adopted, in which the colonial power ruled through African intermediaries who agreed to collaborate with it in the administration of the colony. Thus, the colonial administration appointed approximately 2,200 *chefs de canton*, who were its African intermediaries and in some places became close allies of the *commandant de cercle*, while the 48,000 African *chefs de village* largely continued to exercise authority in the area of civil and communal disputes. Chiefs carried out many unpopular tasks on behalf of the colonial administration: they undertook the census, on which tax demands were based, collected taxes, recruited forced labour, and assisted with conscription and with the maintenance of law and order. Conseils des Notables Indigènes, chaired by the *commandant de cercle* and comprising native leaders nominated by the governor, existed in each *cercle* (administrative district), at least in theory, since 1919. However, they were not an effective vehicle for the political expression of the indigenous population as they were unelected and their role was purely consultative.[7]

As for assimilation in the sense of creating black Frenchmen, this was never pursued systematically as an aim of official policy in AOF. It would have required the immigration into the colony of far greater numbers of French people and the investment of far more resources, notably in education, than actually occurred. This did not however mean that the idea of assimilation disappeared from French colonial discourse. Indeed, one commentator has suggested that 'assimilation was the doctrine preferred by those who felt a public need to justify colonialism; association was preferred by those who had actually to administer the colonies, for whom the high ideals of assimilation were both abstract and dangerous'.[8] The rhetoric of assimilation thus continued to occupy a prominent place in the discourse of metropolitan French politicians, colonial apologists and others. Moreover, assimilation continued to be seen by many republicans associated with the imperial project as a long-term aim of French colonialism. To them French imperialism, closely linked as it was with the ideal of assimilation and the universalist ambitions of France's 'civilizing mission', was modernizing and progressive. The long-term goal of assimilation thus became a key justification in their own eyes for the colonial project in which they were involved and also served to legitimize this project to domestic public opinion and the outside world.

Signs of Change in the 1930s

At the beginning of the 1930s, the situation in French West Africa was apparently one of general calm and tranquillity. However, important forces were at work, laying the foundations for a new African political consciousness. Partly, this was a product of the economic dislocation caused by the worldwide economic depression, which began in 1929 and greatly reduced demand for the primary products on which the economy of AOF depended. The principle had been established in 1900 that the colonies should pay for themselves, so that the cost of administration and development would not be borne by the metropolitan government.[9] The decline in exports therefore left the colonial administration with no choice but to raise taxes on their African subjects while reducing expenditure, notably on education and health. A new approach to colonial rule was clearly needed and in this respect the Depression represented something of a watershed in French West African history as it led France to try to exploit its colonies in a more systematic way, for example through the rounding up of peasant farmers to work on development projects such as the Office du Niger cotton-growing scheme.[10] However, this growing administrative pressure, which coincided with an increase in taxes and a fall in the prices paid to Africans farmers for their produce, fuelled the discontent many Africans felt with colonial rule, thereby helping to undermine whatever legitimacy the colonial regime might have achieved in the previous thirty to forty years.[11] Among the French-educated élite, a growing African political consciousness emerged, which was further sharpened by Italy's invasion of Ethiopia in 1935. It was at this point that the Popular Front came to power in France with promises, albeit vague, of colonial reform.

The Popular Front: A New Start for French West Africa?

The Popular Front's arrival in power on 4 May 1936 was greeted with enthusiasm in French West Africa. Marius Moutet became the first Socialist Colonial Minister and chose as his collaborators Louis Mérat, an economist, and two well known reformers, Robert Delavignette, a liberal Catholic, and René Barthes, whom he appointed his *directeur du cabinet*.

Change was, apparently, in the air, but the new government's priority was its domestic reform agenda. For the colonies, it did not have a detailed reform programme, but instead set up a commission of enquiry into the political, economic and cultural situation in France's overseas territories. There were no specific policy proposals for French Black Africa. However, in August, the Socialist Marcel de Coppet was appointed Governor-General of AOF. Married to the daughter of the writer Roger Martin du Gard, he joined the colonial service in 1905 and received his first posting to AOF in 1910. De Coppet served in Casamance (southern Senegal) from 1912–17, where he first acquired his reputation as a liberal and a *négrophile*, and was appointed Governor of Chad in 1929, then Dahomey in 1933, Somalia in 1934 and Mauritania in 1935, before becoming Governor-General of AOF in 1936. He was a friend of the writer André Gide, who had published his *Voyage au Congo* in 1927 and whose reformist, humanitarian ideas he shared.[12] Gide was highly critical of French mistreatment of Africans in the Congo. His work represented a call for justice and an appeal for France to remain faithful to its true civilizing mission in Africa, but it was not anti-colonial in the sense of advocating the liberation of the colonies from French rule. Rather, Gide belonged to that strand of opinion that saw French colonial rule, properly applied, as essentially progressive and modernizing.[13] It was not only for his humanitarian views that de Coppet was appointed Governor-General, however; his role in splitting the nationalist movement, as Governor of Dahomey from 1933–4, by seeking out moderate, French-speaking nationalists with whom he felt he could do business, was significant in setting government strategy for dealing with African political activity throughout AOF.[14]

The view of French colonialism as modernizing and progressive was shared by both de Coppet and his superior, Moutet. It was also, in essence, the stance of the political parties – the Radicals, the Socialists and the Communists – that made up the Popular Front. None was unconditionally anti-colonial; even the Communist Party had, by 1936, softened its outright opposition to empire, subordinating its traditional anti-imperialism to the need to combat the fascist threat in Europe.[15] It is important to underline this point: the colonial humanists responsible for making colonial policy under the Popular Front were reformers, but they were not anti-colonialists in the sense of being opposed to colonial rule *per se*. Rather, they conceived of colonialism as a work of collective solidarity, a partnership from which both the colonizer and the colonized could benefit, not only in material but also in moral terms. Renewed emphasis was put on the 'civilizing mission'. Unlike the traditional colonialism of the right, left colonialism was presented as modernizing, progressive and generous. The new policy was summed up as *colonisation altruiste* ('altruistic colonization'), in which colonization represented the moral responsibility of superior races towards inferior ones to improve the material and moral conditions in which the latter lived.[16] Accordingly, a number of reforms were introduced to mitigate some of the more repressive aspects of French colonial rule: freedom of the press and freedom of movement were introduced in French West Africa, as was the right to belong to a trade union although this was restricted to those who had received a French education; and exemptions to the *indigénat* were brought in so as to lessen its impact. There was, however, to be no major change in economic policy, and the industrial road to development was to remain closed to Africans.[17]

Although it was short-lived, the Popular Front left two important legacies in policy terms. Firstly, it consolidated the implication of the French left in France's imperial project. Secondly, in seeking to provide a new start for France's African empire, the Popular Front's reform programme exposed a contradiction, which was latent within the republican imperial project but was thrown into sharper relief by the Popular Front's reformism, between the idea that French colonialism could be generous, humane and civilizing and its in-built tendency to authoritarianism. In the end, however, this issue did not have to be directly confronted at this juncture. Within little more than a year of its accession to power the Blum government fell, and it was less than another year before the Popular Front disintegrated completely.

The Popular Front's Impact in French West Africa

Throughout AOF, the arrival of the Popular Front in power raised hopes of reform, especially among the French-educated African élite. This enthusiasm was particularly noticeable in the coastal areas and the main towns, where contact with French rule was greatest. In Dakar, for example, on 14 July 1936 there was a colourful 5,000-strong procession through the streets, led by some 40 Europeans, with red flags, clenched fists and 'Popular Front' logos stuck onto colonial helmets![18] A similar demonstration also took place in Saint-Louis. The impact of the Popular Front was not, however, confined to these areas. African teachers, often encouraged by their French colleagues, carried the Popular Front message into the interior of AOF and Popular Front committees sprang up in towns throughout the colony.

Later in the year, Marius Moutet became the first Colonial Minister to visit AOF. His decision personally to install the newly appointed Governor-General and the speech he gave on arrival in Dakar, which ended with a commitment to improved human rights and greater freedoms for colonial peoples living under French republican rule, raised African hopes for substantive change: 'The Republic is the country of the liberation of men, whoever they are'.[19] His 'universalist' language is significant for the way in which it reflected the socialist view of the French republican imperial project as leading to the liberation of all men 'whoever they are'. The use of such language by French politicians was one of the factors which set the terms within which the decolonization debate took place in AOF after the War, by suggesting that decolonization could take place *within* the colonial relationship while retaining close links with France. This was to be a defining feature of the decolonization process in French West Africa, which distinguished it from that in British West Africa, for example.

The Popular Front's declared intention to legalize trade unions led to an upsurge in union activity. By December a wave of strikes was beginning to unfurl in Dakar and Kaolack (the peanut capital of Senegal). There were also strikes in Guinea and Côte d'Ivoire, where Moutet's visit in April 1937 was greeted by a strike among forestry workers, and trade union activity spread inland along the railway lines of French West Africa. Strikes were not previously unknown in French West Africa. Railwaymen and seamen in Dakar had struck in the 1920s, for example. But the 1936–7 strike wave was different, partly because of the scale of the strike action and partly because of the backcloth against which it took place. Unlike in the case of previous strikes, the Governor-General, de Coppet, was essentially sympathetic to trade unions, and the Popular Front wanted to encourage responsible, organized trade unionism as part of its modernizing project for French West Africa.[20] Nevertheless, the Administration became worried at the scale of the strike wave. The authorization of trade unions and recognition that African workers had rights and legitimate grievances led it into uncharted territory. The problems involved in pursuing such a strategy were dramatically illustrated by the tragic events at Thiès in September 1938. Following two brief strikes by some railway workers in the town, which had, since 1937, been the headquarters of the Dakar-Niger railway, the government became worried by the threat to public order. It sent in troops, who apparently panicked when confronted by the strikers; they opened fire, leaving six workers dead and 60 injured.[21] By this time, the Popular Front government had fallen and de Coppet was recalled to Paris by the new Colonial Minister, Mandel, on 15 October.

The Popular Front was short lived and its concrete realizations were, in practice, limited. Its historical importance for French West Africa lies elsewhere and can be discerned at three different levels. The first of these is at the level of language. Responding to the new, or rather renewed, discourse of French colonialism as generous and civilizing, French-educated Africans demanded the same political rights as French citizens, such as freedom of association, freedom of movement and the right to belong to a trade union, and 'equal pay for equal work'. This campaign was launched by Lamine Guèye's Socialist Party under the Popular Front and became a rallying cry of the French-educated African élite. Born in 1891 in Soudan, Lamine Guèye went to school in Saint-Louis, then went on to take a law degree in Paris. After graduating, he taught for a few years before entering the colonial service, serving in La Réunion and Martinique before returning to Senegal in the 1930s to embark on a political career. In 1934, he stood unsuccessfully against Galandou Diouf in the election for a *député* to represent the Four Communes in the French National Assembly. Despite his defeat, which was attributed by many Africans at the time to administrative interference, he rapidly established a reputation as a brilliant lawyer and an effective advocate of African interests. He created the Parti Socialiste Sénégalais in 1935 and by 1936, when his party joined forces with the French Socialist Party (SFIO: Section Française de l'Internationale Ouvrière), Guèye was already one of the Four Communes' best-known *assimilés* and the leader of what was by then the dominant African political force in the colony. His political programme was to ensure that France applied the same laws in its overseas territories as it did at home and to extend French citizenship to all Senegalese.

This was not the first time the 'assimilationist' demand that republican values and practices be extended to Africa had been used as a campaign theme in French West Africa.[22] It had been a central theme, for example, in the citizenship campaigns of Blaise Diagne's Jeunesses Socialistes in the Four Communes during and after the First World War and it was a recurring theme of Four Communes politics.[23] What was different in 1936–7 was that French-educated Africans throughout AOF began to exploit the theme. The key significance of the Popular Front was thus that it marked the point at which the discourse and values of French republicanism were first used beyond the confines of the Four Communes to mobilize a campaign against the colonial regime in French West Africa.

This was to emerge as a defining characteristic of nationalist discourse in French West Africa after the Second World War.

The second level at which the Popular Front had an impact was the way in which it raised African hopes and aspirations. William Cohen has suggested that the raised hopes and the upsurge in political activity 'portended the development of nationalism in all the overseas territories and the subsequent dissolution of the French Empire'.[24] While this may have been less immediately the case in French Black Africa than elsewhere, it is nonetheless true that the dashed hopes and disillusionment that followed did have a significant long-term impact on African attitudes. The return to a harsher form of colonial rule after the fall of the Popular Front and under Vichy forced the new social movements to suspend their activities, at least overtly, until the end of the war. However, nothing could change the fact that new horizons had opened up for many Africans. Political and trade union activity had entered into people's minds and experience and could not now be erased.[25]

Thirdly, the Popular Front is significant in the context of a pattern that had its roots in the very acquisition of empire in the previous century. Once France was in possession of this empire, the question confronting all subsequent governments was what to do with it. The reason why the Popular Front marks a defining moment in the French process of coming to terms with empire lies precisely in the ambivalence of its responses to these questions. Faced with the reality of empire, yet at the same time keenly aware of its exploitative nature and the abuses to which it gave rise, reform was seen as imperative. But the government, at least those within it who were interested in colonial matters, was equally well aware of the economic and political obstacles to implementing a colonial reform programme. The financial resources necessary for such a programme simply were not available to the Colonial Ministry, given the priority attached to the government's ambitious, and expensive, domestic agenda. On the political front, quite apart from the opposition to reform from colonial business interests, some colonial officials and *colons* in the settler colonies such as Algeria, there was another reason why the government decided to proceed cautiously, which was the need to maintain stability. The government wanted to improve conditions in the Empire, both to meet the expectations of its metropolitan supporters and to do something to meet the aspirations and demands of the French-educated élites in the colonies, but it also knew that, if it tried to go too far too fast, even more unrealistic expectations of change would be unleashed in the colonies. The result would be increased demands, political unrest, more strikes, and more accusations from their political opponents in the *métropole* that they were undermining the empire. The government could not take this risk and chose instead a compromise solution: 'Caught between the Radical and right-wing parties on the one side, which expressed a strong imperialist ethos, and the Communists on the other side, who declared themselves resolutely anti-colonial, the SFIO tried to follow a middle-of-the-road policy by accepting neither the inequities of the imperial system nor the total abandonment of the empire'.[26] Politically, assimilation was this compromise. It was vague enough to offer something to all the different constituencies the Popular Front needed to satisfy. Moreover, with its ideological roots in the revolutionary idealism of 1789, it was, or at least could be presented as being, in the tradition of left republicanism which the French Socialist Party claimed as its own.

Assimilation for everyone was not however affordable. Therefore, what the Popular Front was in effect offering was the carrot of assimilation and a stake in the colonial system to the small élite of French-educated Africans, and association, with its implication of gradual modernization but without a fundamental transformation of traditional society, to everyone else. It was a pragmatic, political 'solution' to the contradiction inherent within the colonial 'problem' confronting the government: how to humanize an essentially repressive and authoritarian colonial regime without changing it so much as to undermine its stability. As a long-term answer to the question of the ultimate aim of colonialism, it was unsustainable, if for no other reason than that it wholly underestimated the force of attraction of the French model for Africans. But it was effective as a holding operation, buying time for the French government by introducing modest reforms while holding out the prospect of further reforms in the future. This was to be a recurring feature of French African policy after the war.

Turning the Colonial Clock Back: The Second World War in AOF

French West Africa on the Eve of War

After the *période des troubles*, which was how many of the European community in AOF perceived the Popular Front years, the colonial order had apparently been restored. The period of colonial questioning that had characterized de Coppet's term of office came to an abrupt halt after he was recalled to Paris in October 1938. On the industrial front, no strikes were reported in 1939 and there were none of any significance in 1940, while on the political front elections in the Four Communes were suspended by decree on 8 September 1939.[27] Moreover, unlike in other parts of the French Empire such as the Levant, the Far East and French North Africa, the defeat of France did not provoke any manifestation of nationalism in AOF. On the contrary, at the outbreak of war pledges of loyalty to France flooded in from throughout AOF and some 100,000 Africans were called up between September 1939 and June 1940. Despite some desertions into British West Africa, the call-up passed off without serious incidents. The promise of citizenship for those who completed their military service, the prospect of a career in the army and sustained anti-German propaganda helped convince many Africans to sign up.[28] At the same time, security was tightened in areas where there had been recent unrest, such as those parts of the Soudan where the Hamallists were active.[29] French West Africa thus gave the appearance of calm as it prepared to make its contribution to the war effort. Events of the next four years were to change all of this irrevocably.

The Vichy Regime in French West Africa

From a metropolitan perspective, following the defeat of France and its occupation by Germany, the empire assumed new importance, as it had done during the First World War, as a source of national self-respect. Unoccupied, it kept alive the hope of national salvation and of France's renaissance as a great power. At the same time, it was important for the Vichy regime's claim to legitimacy because it was thanks to the autonomy of action it enjoyed in the empire that it could claim to exercise sovereignty over French territory without being behoven to a foreign power. It was with the mission to defend the empire against external aggression and maintain its unity that Pierre Boisson was appointed High Commissioner for the whole of French Africa on 25 June 1940.

A First World War veteran, Boisson had lost a leg at Verdun and had subsequently made his career in the colonial service. Anti-German, right-wing and profoundly committed to the French empire, Boisson was no fan of De Gaulle, whom he suspected of being in thrall to the British. Nonetheless, he did not immediately rally French Africa to Vichy, preferring to wait and see whether the Supreme Military Commander of French North Africa, General Noguès, would decide to continue the struggle against the Axis powers or instead rally to the Vichy government. By the end of June, Noguès had decided that Pétain should be supported and any lingering doubts Boisson may have had about which way he should jump were dispelled by the British bombardment of the French fleet in Mers el-Kebir harbour on 3–4 July, which killed 1,285 French sailors. The British attack, which was motivated by the fear that the French fleet might be seized by Germany, was portrayed by the Vichy government as proof of British perfidy. It was thus no surprise that two days later, on 6 July, Boisson announced his decision to rally to Marshal Pétain, thereby extending the Vichy regime to French Black Africa.[30]

Having made his choice, Boisson's first task was to unite the population of AOF behind his administration. While most, although not all, Europeans accepted his decision, as it appeared to keep the colony out of direct involvement in hostilities, it was less readily accepted by many French-educated Africans, who did not understand that France had given up the struggle without a fight and felt that they had much to lose from the defeat of the republican regime. They knew, for example, that the kinds of openings for Africans, albeit limited, which had begun to emerge under the Popular Front, would not be available under the new regime. Also, the fact that much of the French community and most of the colonial administration in AOF rallied to Vichy was a significant portent of a return to a more authoritarian and repressive colonial regime.

The failed Anglo-Gaullist assault on Dakar, which took place on 23–25 September 1940 and which followed an earlier attack on a French naval ship, the Richelieu, on 8 July in Dakar harbour, probably assisted Boisson in his effort to unite the population behind his administration. Codenamed Operation Menace, the objective of the attack, mounted jointly by the British navy and Free French forces in West Africa, was to bring AOF into the Free French camp. According to French army sources, casualties were slight (fourteen dead and thirty-three wounded), but Vichy propaganda put out in AOF after the assault claimed that the death toll was much higher: 184 dead and 379 wounded.[31] Boisson was able to use this to portray the British and Free French as aggressors and Gaullists as traitors to France. Following the failure of Operation Menace, a range of new offences, such as known or suspected pro-Gaullist activity, listening to the BBC and wearing the Croix de Lorraine, was introduced, with penalties varying from expulsion from AOF to imprisonment or a fine. While this did not succeed in ensuring universal or whole-hearted support for the new regime, it certainly served, together with the Administration's propaganda effort, to quell any open expression of opposition to the government.[32]

Meanwhile, Boisson's strategy for maintaining the unity of the empire was running into trouble from another quarter. In late August, most of AEF had rallied to the Free French and Félix Eboué, the Guyanese

Governor of Chad who had led the movement, was appointed Governor-General by De Gaulle. Anxious to prevent any further defections to the Gaullist camp and determined to cement the unity of AOF, an intensive propaganda campaign was launched. Pamphlets, brochures, radio broadcasts and cinema news bulletins sought to spread the ideology of the National Revolution among the African population and praised the populations of the colonies for remaining loyal to France during its darkest hours.[33] In an effort to counter this, an Allied propaganda campaign was directed at the population of AOF from the neighbouring British territories. Resistance networks were also formed in British West Africa, which were joined by some French military personnel and civil servants who crossed the border from AOF. They broadcast Allied propaganda and passed political and military information to the Allies.

Africans suffered more from Vichy's policy of repression than Europeans. Whereas Europeans convicted of acts of resistance might be acquitted, moved to other jobs or, in some cases, sacked, Africans similarly convicted faced possible execution. This was the fate of five Africans in Dakar in 1941–2, while those who were luckier could expect to receive sentences of up to a year in prison or ten years' hard labour.[34] Moreover, the Vichy regime shared none of the Popular Front's qualms about forced labour, which was effectively extended to all African men aged between sixteen and forty. As a result, forced labour recruitment increased dramatically, both for public projects such as the Office du Niger and for work on European plantations. More generally, the Vichy regime in AOF looked forward to 'the abolition of the political regime and the restitution of the rights of custom and tradition',[35] and there was a renewed emphasis on traditional rural society that paralleled the 'return to the land' ideology of the Vichy regime in metropolitan France.[36]

This strengthening of authoritarianism under Vichy represented, in effect, a racialization of colonial rule in French West Africa. Some groups within African society suffered particularly badly from the resulting increased use of the *indigénat* and forced labour. African planters in Côte d'Ivoire, for example, were prevented from benefiting from forced labour, while at the same time being forced to work on European plantations to the detriment of work on their own farms. As for the French-educated élite, the limited advances they had made were threatened by the renewed emphasis on traditional rural society and the effort to bolster the position of village elders and chiefs, and the *originaires* in the Four Communes lost their traditionally privileged position within AOF. Overall, the authoritarian nature of the colonial regime intensified as authority, power and privilege were concentrated in the hands of whites. This had, in practice, always been the case, but its reality had been obscured under the Third Republic by the social stratification that French colonial administration had introduced into African society, dividing it into the categories of *assimilé*, *évolué* and the 'traditional' mass of the population. Under Vichy, such obfuscation was removed and the underlying racist nature of the colonial regime was clearly exposed, since all blacks were now effectively reduced to the same inferior status vis-à-vis whites.

The other important legacy of Vichy in political terms was the way in which it revealed the weakness of the French position in AOF. The Vichy regime in French West Africa lasted a little over two years. It came to an end when, following the success of the Allied landings in Algeria and Morocco, Boisson announced on 7 December 1942 that he would no longer take orders from Pétain but would instead comply with the Marshal's 'true wishes' by declaring for Admiral Darlan in Algiers. In fact, the French army in AOF had no stomach to fight the Americans, so Boisson had no practical alternative but to rally to the north African *bloc*. This was not, however, a decision to rally to De Gaulle. On the contrary, Boisson presented it as in keeping with his original decision of July 1940, which he had justified by the need to maintain the unity of the empire and keep foreign troops out of French West Africa. By avoiding, as he saw it, an Anglo-Saxon/Gaullist occupation of French West Africa, he claimed to be safeguarding French sovereignty over AOF.[37] However, while colonial officials put the emphasis on continuity and Boisson's decision was presented as having no implications for internal policy, in practice nothing could hide the fact that, cut off from the métropole and hemmed in by hostile territories to the north, east and south, French West Africa was now militarily and economically dependent upon the Allies. British West Africa and AEF were already in the Allied camp, and the fall of north Africa to the Allies consummated the isolation of AOF. As we shall see below, this further indication of the weakness of the French position, after the capitulation of 1940, together with the increase in authoritarianism under Vichy, were to have a significant impact on political developments in French West Africa once the republican regime was restored in 1943.

From Vichy to the Free French

Early December 1942 to mid-July 1943 was a period of uncertainty in French West Africa. It began when Boisson declared that AOF was rallying to Admiral Darlan in Algiers and culminated in the appointment of the Gaullist, Pierre Cournarie, as Governor-General in July 1943. Darlan was assassinated on Christmas Eve 1942 and replaced by General Henri Giraud who, unlike his predecessor, supported the Allies. However, he did not bring any Gaullists into his administration and made no immediate attempt to repeal Vichy colonial legislation. This period of wavering in Algiers was paralleled in Dakar, where Boisson could no longer claim allegiance to Pétain but at the same time refused to rally to the Gaullist cause. Indeed, during the first three months of 1943, continuity and stability were the watchwords. Rather than encourage a return to a more normal political life, the Vichyite administration that Boisson had established continued to function much as it had for the previous two-and-a-half years. Gaullist 'agitators' continued to be pursued; it was 26 February before Allied pressure obtained the release of the last political prisoners in AOF and it was 14 March before Giraud, again under Allied pressure, finally issued decrees restoring republican liberties, repealing anti-Jewish legislation and the ban on freemasonry, and dissolving the Service d'Ordre Légionnaire in AOF.[38] It seemed that the Governor-General and many of his officials, blinded perhaps by their anti-Gaullism, refused to acknowledge the enormous significance of recent external developments for AOF, a point that is confirmed by the first despatches from the newly appointed British Consul-General in Dakar in January 1943. The picture he painted of AOF was not an edifying one: the Governor-General, he reported, was an unpopular figure in Dakar, defeatism was widespread, censorship by French officials of war propaganda being broadcast from British West Africa continued, and he suspected most colonial officials of being unwilling to put themselves out for the war effort. As for the French community in AOF, the Church, the military and much of the business community remained strong supporters of Pétain and equally strongly opposed to De Gaulle.[39]

During this period, resistance networks in French and British West Africa put pressure on Boisson by organizing propaganda campaigns criticizing him and supporting De Gaulle: Gaullist pamphlets came into AOF from British West Africa, posters appeared throughout the colony in support of De Gaulle's leadership, and patriotic associations, such as the Amis de Combat, the Croix de Lorraine and the Groupement d'Action Républicaine, were formed in AOF. This pressure helped make Boisson's position untenable. He was forced to resign and was replaced as Governor-General on 17 July by Pierre Cournarie, who had until then been Governor of Cameroun.

The Free French Regime in French West Africa

Cournarie's appointment raised expectations of a new policy, but the wartime situation imposed severe constraints on the new Governor-General's political freedom for manoeuvre, as he could not take any action that might further destabilize French authority or undermine AOF's contribution to the war effort.[40] He was well aware of France's weakened position: the Armistice, the dependence of AOF on the Allies since the end of 1942, and the fact that the colonial administration was divided between Vichyites and Free French supporters were all factors here. The colonial personnel working under him were for the most part the same people as had served under Vichy and their entrenched attitudes and practices did not change as a result of the change of Governor-General. In late 1943, the British Consul-General reported that they were used to severe measures of oppression against natives and that 'the average French administrator, planter or merchant is still inclined to regard the native as little more than a slave'.[41] As a result, the new Governor-General's arrival did not herald any abrupt improvement in the situation of most Africans in AOF. On the contrary, for many Africans living conditions were actually more difficult under the Free French than under Vichy because of the increased demands made upon them for the war effort.[42] Despite the fact that African resentment against the practice was widespread and growing, forced labour inevitably made a significant contribution to the achievement of production targets, provoking renewed migration into British West Africa from the border regions of French West Africa. Moreover, the unrealistic demands and the lack of sensitivity to local conditions with which production quotas were set further fuelled African resentment. The now infamous telegram from a *commandant de cercle* to his superior, in response to the quota for honey production for his *cercle*: 'Agreed honey. Stop. Send bees', has gained notoriety as an illustration of the absurdity of the quota-setting process.[43]

It was against this background that political activity in the colony resumed during 1943. Initially, this mainly took the form of patriotic associations which demanded a purge of Vichyites within the Administration.[44] However, this was not possible because of the lack of availability of replacement personnel, with the result that even some top-ranking colonial officials, such as the governors of Mauritania, Soudan and Niger, retained their posts, and further down the administrative hierarchy virtually everyone remained in post, although there were some demotions.

The tendency of these associations to focus on what they saw as score settling between Europeans rapidly disillusioned their African members, who left to form their own autonomous, all-African groups. The war had sharpened tensions between Africans and the French to the point where the former no longer wanted to belong to associations controlled by whites. The main interest of French-educated Africans was in any case not in the purge, but rather in preparing for the resumption of politics in AOF after the war.[45] They wanted the right to elect their own representatives, equality with Europeans and a share of power. The re-formed Union Républicaine Sénégalaise, it was reported, had chosen to position itself 'on the field of racial conflict'. In November, native associations (*associations indigènes*) were reported to be invoking 'republican liberties' to press their demand for 'assimilation', and discontent was noted among Dakar-Niger railway workers because of the differences in salary between Europeans and Africans. In December, soldiers who were subjects were reported as demanding equal pensions with soldiers who were citizens.[46] The common theme underlying all of these demands was a rejection of racial discrimination. As for the aspiration to create autonomous bodies, controlled by Africans to represent African interests, this would extend after the war to a whole range of organizations, from political parties to trade unions and youth organizations. In this respect, they were a foretaste of future political developments in French West Africa.

One group that felt especially aggrieved was Ivoirian coffee and cocoa planters. They produced some 80 per cent of Côte d'Ivoire's coffee harvest and nearly 90 per cent of its cocoa beans, but were not allowed access to forced labour and were often requisitioned for work on European plantations at the very moment when their own crops were ready for picking; they were subject to stringent quality controls and sometimes ordered by agricultural inspection teams to destroy their crops, which they saw as a mechanism for reducing African output; and they were paid a lower price for their produce than European planters on the grounds that their material needs were less than those of whites. In July 1944 they finally decided enough was enough: no longer prepared to accept such blatant economic discrimination, they left the European-dominated planters' organization (to which they had only recently been admitted) and set up their own representative body, the Syndicat Agricole Africain (SAA) at an inaugural meeting in Abidjan. Led by Félix Houphouët-Boigny, a former medical assistant who had since become a canton chief and planter, its first priorities were to put an end to forced labour and to the economic discrimination to which African farmers were subject. The SAA grew quickly to over 20,000 members and within a year formed the nucleus of Côte d'Ivoire's first political party, the Parti Démocratique de la Côte d'Ivoire (PDCI).[47] The SAA was supported by the newly appointed Free French governor, André Latrille, but the measures he tried to introduce to improve the lot of African planters were consistently thwarted by Governor-General Cournarie.[48]

Members of the French-educated élite also began to organize themselves into various political and quasi-political groups at this time, well before the right to freedom of association was officially restored in 1946.[49] African branches of the patriotic associations, ostensibly established to support the Free French, rapidly became politicized; Groupes d'Etudes Communistes (GEC) were set up in the main urban centres of AOF from the end of 1943, providing political education and training for trade union and political activists;[50] and the first Comité d'Etudes Franco-Africaines (CEFA: Franco-African Study Committee) was formed in Dakar in February 1945. The GECs and CEFAs spread rapidly to other towns in AOF and became a focus for anti-colonial activity; they will be discussed in more detail in the next chapter. The important point to underline here is that the backcloth to all of these initiatives was the intensification of anti-colonialism and the growing rejection of the French colonial regime by Africans as a result of the racialization of colonial rule during the Vichy period and the continuing hardships of the Free French period.

The Tirailleurs Return Home

Some 100,000 Africans were recruited from AOF into the French army between September 1939 and June 1940. After the Armistice, approximately 75,000 were demobilized. Allowing for casualties during the 1940 campaign, this left some 15,000 African soldiers in Europe, many of whom spent time in German prisoner of war (PoW) camps before being returned to France. Once back in France, they were assembled in camps while they waited to be shipped home. Tirailleur Sénégalais units were also involved in fighting after the Armistice and it has been estimated that perhaps as many as 100,000 Africans served in the years 1943–5. Sometimes, as in Syria, they were to be found on both the Vichy and Free French sides. They also fought elsewhere in Europe, taking part in the Italian campaign for example, and in the Liberation of France.[51] The repatriation and reintegration into African society of these African soldiers created a major headache for the Free French regime in AOF in 1944–5.

The first contingent of 1280 African ex-PoWs arrived back in Dakar in November 1944, by which time they had good reason to feel they had been badly treated. Having spent up to four years in German camps and then been rounded up in camps in France to await embarkation, they contrasted their treatment with that of their French colleagues, who were given a warm welcome on their return home, received better food rations and housing, plus their pay arrears. Moreover, as the Liberation of France progressed, the French army underwent a deliberate process of *blanchiment* ('whitening'), as black and north African troops in combat units were replaced by white French soldiers from the French Forces of the Interior, in order to enable De Gaulle to claim that the Liberation of France was the result of action by internal French forces, rather than the product of external intervention.

The question of pay arrears was a particular source of discontent among the first contingent of ex-PoWs to be repatriated, as they had been promised that their arrears and demobilization allowances would be paid when they arrived in Dakar. But on arrival they were taken to another camp, at Tiaroye just outside Dakar, to wait for their money before being sent back to their home villages. When the payments were still not forthcoming, and afraid that they were not going to be paid at all, they organized a protest and on 1 December took the French officer in command of the camp hostage. In the ensuing chaos, French troops opened fire on the African soldiers, leaving 35 of them dead and a further 35 injured. The colonial authorities in Dakar presented this as a mutiny by undisciplined African troops who had been influenced by German propaganda, which succeeded in defusing any immediate African political reaction to the massacre.[52] The incident did, however, seriously worry the Governor-General, who cabled Paris that the use of force 'could not be permitted to be repeated, under any pretext whatever'.[53] In order to avoid further protests, improved arrangements were made for the settlement of back pay and other monies owing, so that subsequent consignments of African PoWs arriving back in AOF were quickly returned to their home villages.

Despite Tiaroye, it is notable that war veterans remained some of the most consistent supporters of the maintenance of *la présence française* in Africa right through to independence: an army pension, their contacts with ordinary people in France who were neither colonialists nor racists and their military discipline all seem to have played a role here. Not all former soldiers were so compliant, however: one group, for example, was responsible for creating the first African independence movement in AOF after the war. Called the Mouvement Nationaliste Africain, it had no mass following, but did produce a monthly newspaper, *La Communauté*, for two years, before ceasing publication at the end of 1947.

Impact of the Second World War

From the French perspective, the outbreak of war reinforced the image of the 'loyal African', ready to come to the assistance of the motherland in its time of need. The image had its roots in the First World War, when some 180,000 black African soldiers had been called up for service in Europe. The role played by Africans in the First World War conditioned French attitudes to empire throughout the inter-war period and, when France was again led to call on the empire to come to its rescue in 1939, this cemented the imperial link for many French people. The image of the 'loyal African' became a powerful myth that helped shape French attitudes to empire in post-war France.[54]

The empire was also important as a symbol of French grandeur. This notion predated the First World War but gained currency as a direct result of the imperial contribution to France's war effort between 1914 and 1918. It became a recurrent theme in school textbooks after the war and entered popular consciousness in the inter-war period as a justification for the possession of empire.[55] The Colonial Exhibition of 1931 helped to anchor this view in the public mind so that when, nine years later, France was occupied by Germany, the notion of the empire as a symbol of French grandeur struck a powerful chord with public opinion. For the Vichy regime, however, it was more than that, because the empire was the only part of French territory over which it could claim to exercise unrivalled sovereignty. This was equally true, if not more so, for De Gaulle. Not only was the colonial empire central to his claim to be the leader of Free France, but it was the launching pad for the liberation of metropolitan France: the first significant colonies to rally to De Gaulle were in Africa; he chose Brazzaville, the capital of AEF, to launch the Conseil de Défense de l'Empire in October 1940; and by 1943 the whole of France's African empire was under Free French administration. Against this background, it is not surprising that Africa, and especially Black Africa, occupied a peculiarly important place in public affections and in the mindset of a whole generation of leading French politicians from right across the political spectrum after the war. To take just two examples, the attitudes to Africa of both De Gaulle and Mitterrand were shaped by the contribution of France's Black African empire to the war effort.

At the same time, the defeat of 1940, the fragmentation of the empire, and what Martin Thomas has characterized as its piecemeal re-fashioning under the pressure of external interventions over the next two and a half years, together with the dependency of the empire on the Allies for supplies after 1942, all served to underline the fragility of the French colonial presence.[56] By 1940, most Africans in AOF, with the exception of the very elderly, had never known anything except French rule, which was imbued with an aura of inevitability. After 1940, this was no longer the case. Although France emerged on the side of the victors, this was only thanks to Allied help: the fragility of French power had been exposed and the assumption of *de facto* French superiority had been dealt a severe blow.

Against this background, the war acted as a catalyst for members of the French-educated élite to define for themselves an identity and a political role within African society. Partly separated from their own society by their acquisition of a French education, yet at the same time not admitted to full membership of European society, they were often considered and treated by French officials as *déclassés*. Hitherto, they had also to some extent perceived themselves in this way, as 'outsiders', unable to define for themselves a group identity or a role *within* African society. The experience of war provoked a fundamental change in the self-perception of this French-educated élite. They began to forge a new sense of identity, and to redefine their role, no longer simply as auxiliaries of French colonial power but as representatives of their people. They were helped in this by the reforms introduced at the end of the war: not only were they the first beneficiaries of the new liberties granted to Africans by the Free French, but as French speakers they were the obvious candidates to represent their people in the various elected bodies that were established in the *métropole* and French West Africa at the end of the war.

The racialization of colonial rule under Vichy had another important impact on African attitudes. One distinguishing feature of the colonial regime in French West Africa up to 1940, compared to that in British West Africa, was the possibility for Africans to obtain full French citizenship. There were two ways in which this could be achieved: one was through being a resident of the Four Communes and the other was by earning it through the acquisition of 'Frenchness'. In each case, French citizenship provided Africans with a powerful model to which they could aspire and served to reinforce the belief that French colonialism opened the door to progress and modernity to deserving Africans. This door was closed under Vichy. The prize of citizenship was taken away and the racial discrimination between whites and blacks became more stark. This fuelled a new anti-racist politics which, unlike before the war when it had been largely confined to the Four Communes, now spread throughout French West Africa.

However, in a somewhat perverse way, the open racism of the Vichy regime actually helped republicans because it made it possible for the Free French to portray the Vichy period as an aberration by contrasting Vichy colonial policy with their own approach, which accorded political rights to Africans. This kept many French-educated Africans on board the French colonial boat for longer than might otherwise have proved possible, by re-creating the notion that French colonialism, republican style, was progressive and modernizing, and suggesting that it was through integration into 'the one and indivisible Republic' that African liberation would ultimately be achieved. This notion had first found political expression under the Popular Front and it is not therefore surprising that French-educated Africans looked to the return of a republican regime to restore their rights and privileges. The notion involved a political sleight of hand, since all Africans would in practice never be able to achieve liberation through assimilation and integration into a 'one and indivisible France', if for no other reason than that there was no realistic prospect of the métropole funding it. But the important point from the French point of view was that it succeeded once again in buying time for the French government, which it desperately needed if it was to restore French colonial authority.

Nevertheless, the Free French period saw an unprecedented upsurge in anti-colonial activity. Both the Provisional Government and the colonial administration in AOF appear to have been largely oblivious to the profound changes that were taking place within African society at this time. Preoccupied with their own struggles that set Vichyites against resisters, concerned to establish their own legitimacy, and faced with the practical difficulties of carrying out any significant purge, even of prominent Vichyites, without further undermining French authority, the Free French regime in AOF fell into the trap of interpreting African reactions from the perspective of their own internecine conflict. Thus, for example, the Free French held the repressive nature of the Vichy responsible for acts of opposition or expressions of dissent by Africans, in the apparent belief that, once a more liberal, reformist regime had replaced it, these problems would cease. As David Gardinier has suggested: 'Propaganda on both sides tended to interpret all African actions in light of the Vichy-Free French conflict and never on their own terms.'[57] What they failed to see was that these expressions of dissent were often actually acts of resistance to the French colonial regime itself and that the repression of the Vichy period, followed by the exactions of the Free French period, provoked intensified resistance to French rule in AOF. This took a multiplicity of forms: migration into neighbouring territories to avoid conscription or recruitment for forced labour; the murder of Europeans, as happened at Bobo-Dioulasso in August 1941; mass resistance to the expropriation of crops, as in the case of the Floups who refused to give up their rice stocks to the Administration in Casamance (Senegal) in 1943; and the creation of organizations to defend African interests, of which the formation of the SAA in Côte d'Ivoire is the best-known example. Among the French-educated élite, this took the form of what the security services termed increasing 'separatist' tendencies: 'There is a need to keep a close eye on the development of this state of mind which is best described as independent rather than "autonomist" and which represents a new stage in the process of emancipation from European influence'.[58] Yet colonial officials, as the archival records of the time show, failed to report on this rising tide of anti-colonial feeling to their superiors, perhaps partly out of weariness, perhaps because they were unaware of the scale of the upsurge, or perhaps because they were afraid to admit to the existence of unrest on their 'patch'. As a result, the Comité Français de la Libération Nationale (CFLN) and subsequently the Provisional Government, preoccupied by more pressing concerns and partly taken in by their own propaganda images of the 'loyal African', also either failed to notice the rising tide of anti-colonial opposition, or at the very least did not fully appreciate the significance of what was happening.

However, if the government was unaware of the depth and political significance of the changes taking place in French West Africa, it was nonetheless well aware that the diminution in French imperial prestige and the sacrifices made by Africans for the war effort made the continuation of the same kind of colonial regime as before the War impossible. It recognized that changes were essential if colonial rule was to be maintained. Thus, even before the end of the War, the CFLN took the decision to organize the Brazzaville African Conference in January–February 1944 in order to signal its reformist intentions. It is to this that we now turn in an effort to uncover the roots of France's post-war imperial policy.

Notes

1. For further details about the territories AOF comprised, see glossary. Because of its distinctive history and status as a UN Trust Territory, the decolonization process in Togo does not form part of the present study.
2. The Four Communes de Plein Exercice, as they were called, were Dakar, Gorée, Saint-Louis and Rufisque, although there were strictly speaking only three of them once Gorée was attached to Dakar in 1927.
3. For a study of politics in the Four Communes, see G. W. Johnson, *The Emergence of Black Politics in Senegal* (Stanford University Press, 1971) and J. Searing, 'Accommodation and Resistance: Chiefs, Muslim Leaders, and Politicians in Colonial Senegal, 1890–1934', 2 vols, PhD thesis, Princeton University, 1985.
4. The William-Ponty School represented the pinnacle of the education system in French West Africa. The Ecole Normale, as it was then called, opened its doors in 1904 in Saint-Louis. It was re-named the William-Ponty School when it moved to the island of Gorée in 1913 and was subsequently transferred to Sébikotane, 42 kilometres from Dakar, in 1938.
5. R. F. Betts, *Assimilation and Association in French Colonial Theory* (Columbia University Press, 1961).
6. A. L. Conklin, '"Democracy" rediscovered: Civilization through Association in French West Africa (1914–30)', *Cahiers d'Etudes Africaines*, 145, 1997, pp. 60–1.
7. For an analysis of the practice of French colonial rule written by a former administrator and director of the Ecole Coloniale, see R. Delavignette, *Service africain* (Gallimard, 1939). See also W. B. Cohen, *Rulers of Empire: the French Colonial Service in Africa* (Hoover Institution Press, 1971).
8. J. Chipman, *French Power in Africa* (Blackwell, 1989), p. 57.
9. Finance Law, 13 April 1900, *Bulletin administratif du Sénégal*, 12, December 1900, p. 908.
10. J. Filipovich, 'Destined to fail: forced settlement at the Office du Niger, 1926–45', *Journal of African History*, 42, 2001, pp. 239–60.
11. B. Davidson, *Modern Africa. A Social and Political History* (Longman, 1994), p. 47.
12. A. Gide, *Voyage au Congo* (Gallimard, 1927).
13. R. Girardet, *L'Idée coloniale en France* (La Table Ronde, 1972), pp. 211–20.

14. Cf. P. Manning, *Slavery, Colonialism and Economic Growth in Dahomey, 1640–1960* (Cambridge University Press, 1982), pp. 267–73; S. C. Anignikin, 'Les facteurs historiques de la décolonisation au Dahomey', in C.-R. Ageron, ed., *Les Chemins de la décolonisation de l'empire français, 1936–1956* (Eds. du CNRS, 1986), pp. 506–7.

15. W. B. Cohen, 'The colonial policy of the Popular Front', *French Historical Studies*, 7, 1971–2, pp. 368–75.

16. Cf. R. Girardet, *L'Idée coloniale*, p. 193; see also T. Chafer and A. Sackur, eds, *French Colonial Empire and the Popular Front* (Macmillan, 1999), p. 16–17 and passim.

17. C. Coquery-Vidrovitch, 'The Popular Front and the Colonial Question. French West Africa: An Example of Reformist Colonialism', in ibid, pp. 161–2.

18. N. Bernard-Duquenet, *Le Sénégal et le Front Populaire*, pp. 65–6.

19. *Paris–Dakar*, 28 September 1936, pp. 5 and 3.

20. See F. Cooper, *Decolonization and African Society*, pp. 92–104.

21. N. Bernard-Duquenet, *Le Sénégal*, pp. 194–9.

22. F. Manchuelle, 'Assimilés ou patriotes africains? Naissance du nationalisme culturel en Afrique Française (1853–1931)', *Cahier d'Etudes Africaines*, XXXV, 2–3, 1995, pp. 335–6.

23. See J. Searing, 'Accommodation and Resistance', pp. 455, 466–9. See also G. W. Johnson, *The Emergence of Black Politics*, passim.

24. W. B. Cohen, 'The colonial policy of the Popular Front', p. 393.

25. Cf. Y. Person, 'Le Front Populaire au Sénégal', *Mouvement social*, 107, 1979, pp. 99–101.

26. W. B. Cohen, 'The colonial policy of the Popular Front', p. 374.

27. The town councils of the other main towns in AOF, the *communes mixtes* as they were called, had restricted African representation and were already effectively administered by the French. These were Cotonou and Porto-Novo in Dahomey, Bamako in Soudan, Conakry and Kindia in Guinea, and fifteen towns in Senegal.

28. Cf. M. Echenberg, p. 4; C. Akpo-Vaché, *L'AOF et la seconde guerre mondiale* (Karthala, 1996), pp. 21–2.

29. For a discussion of the career and activities of Sheikh Hamallah and of French attitudes to the Hamallists, see C. Harrison, *France and Islam in West Africa, 1860–1960* (Cambridge University Press, 1988), pp. 171–82.

30. M. Thomas, *The French Empire at War 1940–45* (Manchester University Press, 1998), pp. 40, 49–51; C. Akpo-Vaché, *L'AOF*, pp. 27–33.

31. Service Historique de l'Armée de Terre, Vincennes, 1P34/D6 EM-Colonies, entry for 26 September 1940, quoted in M. Thomas, *The French Empire at War*, p. 87; C. Akpo-Vaché, *L'AOF*, p. 41, gives the much higher figures published by the Government-General of AOF. See also AAOF 13G16/17, PRO FO371/49266 and 36187.

32. A number of people considered opponents of the regime were arrested immediately after Operation Menace. They included Gaullists and anyone whose previous political activity rendered them suspect, such as known supporters of the Popular Front. Hence, the Mayor of Dakar, Monsieur Goux, was arrested, as was M. Turbé, the President of the Chamber of Commerce, M. Sylvandre, a Dakar notary and SFIO member, M. Graziani, a businessman and prominent Popular Front supporter, and several other colonial officials and businessmen.

33. ANSOM Aff. Pol. 2178/3; R. Girardet, *L'Idée coloniale en France* (La Table Ronde, 1972), pp. 281–3; R. Ginio, 'Marshal Pétain spoke to schoolchildren: Vichy propaganda in French West Africa, 1940–1943', *International Journal of African Historical Studies*, 33, 2, 2000, pp. 291–312.

34. Less than 300 Europeans lost their jobs in the administration, whereas some 2300 Africans were sacked from theirs, C. Akpo-Vaché, *L'AOF*, pp. 67–8 and 138. See also A. K. Diagne, 'La Résistance française au Sénégal et en AOF pendant la guerre 1939–45', undated, p. 42, CAOM (Aix).

35. Rapport Politique Annuel, 1940, AAOF 2G40/2.

36. AAOF 13G34/180. Boisson issued three directives on African colonization on 21 August 1941. All are in 13G34/180.

37. ANSOM Aff. Pol. 895/4 and 872/13.

38. In metropolitan France the Service d'Ordre Légionnaire's main task was to combat freemasonry, Judaism and communism.

39. Reports dated 30 January and 27 May 1943, PRO FO371/36187 and 36189.

40. See P. Cournarie's address: Afrique Occidentale Française, *Conseil de Gouvernement*, session of December 1943, ANSOM 50480, pp. 8–16.

41. Despatch, Meiklereid to Eden, dated 12 January 1944, FO371/42150.

42. N. Lawler, 'Reform and repression under the Free French: economic and political transformation in the Côte d'Ivoire, 1942–45', *Africa*, 60, 1, 1990, pp. 88–110; M. Crowder, *West Africa under Colonial Rule* (Hutchinson, 1968), pp. 497–8; F. Cooper, *Decolonization*, pp. 159–61; M. Thomas, *The French Empire at War*, p. 231.

43. J. Richard-Molard, *Afrique Occidentale Française* (Berger-Levrault, 1956), p. 168.
44. See monthly political reports for 1943–4, AAOF 17G126/17. One list contained the names of 88 Vichyite officials in AOF, see AAOF 17G14/1.
45. Note dated 13 July 1945, AS 11D1/337.
46. Government of Senegal, Political Information Bulletin dated 9 September 1943, AAOF 17G159/28. Cf. also 17G126/17, 17G132/17 and N. Bernard-Duquenet, *Le Sénégal et le Front Populaire* (L'Harmattan, 1985), p. 116.
47. N. Lawler, 'Reform and repression', pp. 99–100.
48. J.-R. de Benoist, *L'Afrique Occidentale Française de 1944 à 1960* (Nouvelles Editions Africaines, 1982), p. 45.
49. Decree on freedom of association dated 13 March 1946, *JOAOF*, 20 April 1946, p. 444.
50. 'Introduction aux cours élémentaires des GEC du Sénégal' and cours no. 1 'Les Communistes et le problème colonial', in J. Suret-Canale, *Les Groupes d'Etudes Communistes (GEC) en Afrique Noire* (L'Harmattan, 1994), pp. 92 and 96–9.
51. Senegal, Annual Political Report, 1940, AAOF 2G40/2; M. Echenberg, '"Morts pour la France": the African soldier in France during the Second World War', *Journal of African History*, 26, 1985, pp. 364–5; A. Clayton, *France, Soldiers and Africa* (Brassey's, 1988), p. 353.
52. Despatches Meiklereid to FO, dated 13 and 20 December 1944, FO371/49258.
53. Quoted in M. Echenberg, 'Tragedy at Tiaroye: the Senegalese Soldiers' Uprising of 1944', in P. Gutkind, R. Cohen J. Copans, *African Labour History*, vol. 2 (Sage, 1978), p. 120.
54. For a discussion of this myth, see R. Barthes, *Mythologies* (Seuil, 1957), p. 201.
55. M. Semidei, 'De l'empire français à la décolonisation à travers les manuels scolaires français', *Revue Française de Science Politique*, XVI, 1966, pp. 56–86. A good example is P. Kaeppelin and M. Teissier, *La Géographie de la France et de ses Colonies* (Hâtier, 1921).
56. M. Thomas, *The French Empire at War*, p. 2.
57. D. Gardinier, 'The Second World War in French West Africa and Togo: recent research and writing', in P. P. Boucher, ed., *Proceedings of the Tenth Meeting of the French Colonial Historical Society, April 12–14, 1984* (University Press of America, 1984), p. 265.
58. Political Information Bulletin dated 7 November 1944, AAOF 17G126/17.

–2–

New Political Context 1944–6

It was in July 1943, at a time when French imperial authority was under threat in a way that it had not been before, that the CFLN in Algiers decided to hold the Brazzaville Conference.[1] Part of the background to this was the crucial role played by the African empire in 1940 in launching the French fightback against the Axis powers, but this was not the whole story. The Atlantic Charter of 1941 had declared the right of all peoples to choose their own government and following this the American Secretary of State, Cordell Hull, had proposed placing the colonial empires under international trusteeship at the end of the war.[2] In response to this, De Gaulle and his Commissaire aux Colonies, René Pleven, were determined to show the US that France had no intention of relinquishing its colonies after the war. At the same time, they wanted to acknowledge the crucial military and economic contribution that French Black Africa had made to the war effort and signal to Africans their intention to reform the imperial relationship once hostilities ended. The overriding priority was the maintenance of France's African Empire.

If we now look at this period from an African perspective, we have seen that for many Africans, the changes of regime, to Vichy and then from Vichy to the Free French, made little difference: faced in most cases with the same colonial officials, who continued to use forced labour and ruled them through the same *indigénat* as before the war, the change to the Free French regime represented just another imposition by whites. At the same time, however, we have seen that the return to a republican regime raised expectations of reform and presented Africans with new opportunities. The authorization of trade unions (7 August 1944); the abolition of the *indigénat* (22 December 1945); the introduction of freedom of association (13 March and 16 April 1946) and of the right to hold meetings (11 April 1946), all these measures granted rights to Africans to participate in French institutions. These reforms created new opportunities above all for the French-educated élite since a knowledge of French language and culture and an ability to operate within a French institutional framework were necessary in order to benefit from them.

The Brazzaville Conference

The Brazzaville Conference has been seen by the French colonial historian, Charles-Robert Ageron, as marking a turning-point in French colonial policy.[3] Yet, as one of the conference's main architects, Henri Laurentie, himself admitted: 'Overall, it cannot be said that the Brazzaville Conference recommendations contained any really startling innovations'.[4] In fact, probably the only points on which all the participants were agreed was that the overriding priority for France was to retain its colonial empire and that to achieve this some changes to the colonial regime would be needed after the war. Beyond this, there was no consensus.

The Conférence Africaine Française, to give it its full official title, brought together sixty participants, which included colonial governors-general, governors and colonial officials, and nine members of the Provisional Consultative Assembly in Algiers were present as observers. The conference programme was prepared by Henri Laurentie, the Director of Political Affairs at the Commissariat aux Colonies in Algiers and Governor-General Eboué's former Secretary-General. It envisaged transforming the colonial empire into a federation, to be governed by a new federal assembly with elected representatives from the *métropole* and each of the associated territories. Within the federation, the colonies would enjoy considerable economic and administrative freedom, and local elected assemblies would afford Africans the opportunity to become involved in the management of their own affairs. He did not rule out self-government *a priori*, but it was made clear that, if this was to happen, it would be the culmination of a very long process of evolution that had barely begun.[5] Thus Laurentie was no radical, in the sense that he did not countenance the possibility of self-government for the colonies in any foreseeable future. He was, however, prepared to envisage far-reaching changes to the structure of the empire in order to maintain French imperial authority and to grant Africans real participation in the management of their own affairs. It should be noted at this point that there were no African representatives at the conference, although two of the governors present, Raphaël Saller and Félix Eboué, were black, albeit of West Indian extraction. However, six reports by Africans were presented to the conference, four from members of the French-educated élite in AEF and two from Fily Dabo Sissoko, a canton chief from Soudan and future *député* to the Constituent Assembly.

The actual recommendations that emerged from the conference were in several respects significantly more conservative in nature than

Laurentie's: the idea of a colonial federation was rejected, it was made clear that political power resided exclusively with the *métropole*, and any future possibility of the colonies governing themselves was emphatically ruled out. As the preamble to the conference's final recommendations put it: 'any possibility of evolution outside the French imperial block' and 'the eventual creation, even in the distant future, of *self-governments* in the colonies, is to be rejected'.[6] Thus, in contrast to Britain, where the Colonial Secretary, Malcolm MacDonald, had indicated in 1938 that, in Africa, 'the ultimate, if distant, aim of British colonial policy was evolution towards self-government',[7] in France there was no sense of preparing for eventual African self-government by cultivating a nationalist élite that was friendly to France, although this would ultimately be the outcome. As for the question of colonial representation in the future Assembly, this was referred to a commission of experts, to be appointed by the government. At one level, these proposals and the reaffirmation of the unity of the empire pointed towards an essentially assimilationist orientation to the conference recommendations in the political sphere. On the other hand, the assertion of the need to respect traditional society and the recommendations in the social sphere, notably with regard to social and family customs, suggested more of an associationist stance: 'Respect for, and the progress of, native life will be the basis of our whole colonial policy, and we must submit ourselves completely to the obligations which this entails'. This reflected the old tension between the 'universalist' claims of assimilation and the particularism of association, which claimed to respect cultural difference. As was often the case in French colonial doctrine, the two co-existed and the conference recommendations represented an uneasy balancing act between the two. Thus, the 'universalism' of assimilation, with its underlying assumption that everyone, African, Asian and European, could ultimately, through education and cultural assimilation, be brought up to the same level, accorded the same rights and governed within the same institutional framework, was tempered by the 'pragmatic' acceptance of the 'particularism' of different peoples that made it difficult, if not impossible, for them to follow the same path of development as Europeans. Moreover, and just as importantly, there remained a deep ambivalence in colonial circles about the creation of a large 'assimilated' African élite, which, having obtained equality with Europeans, would then be in a position to challenge French authority, thus hastening the end of the colonial regime.[8]

Nowhere was this tension between universalism and particularism more striking than in the domain of forced labour. The Commissariat

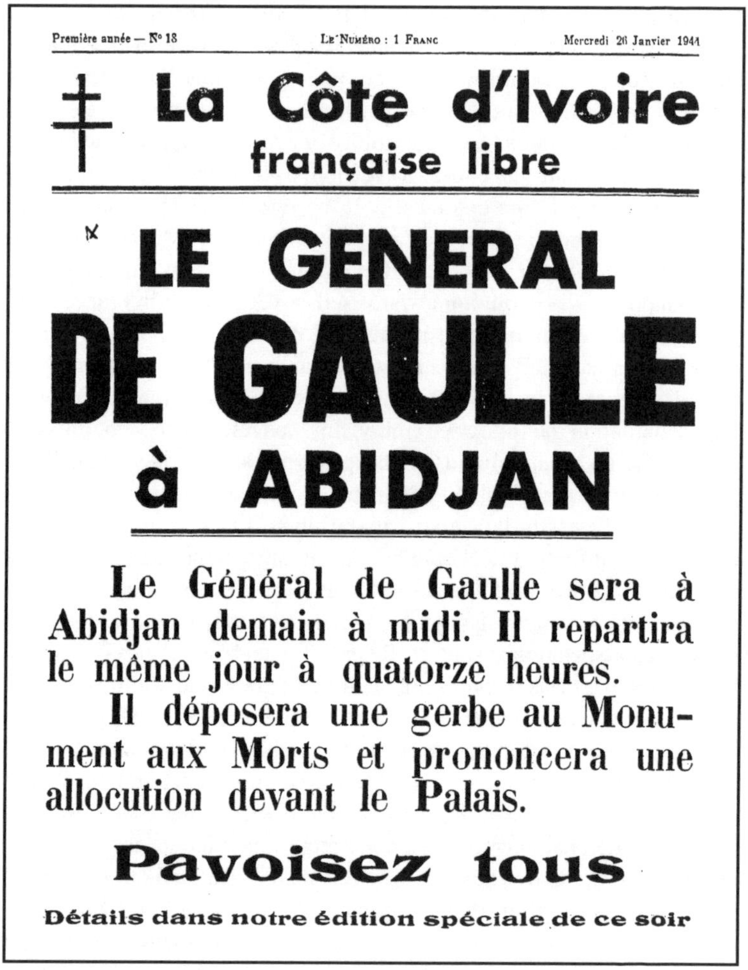

Première année — N° 18   LE·NUMÉRO : 1 FRANC   Mercredi 26 Janvier 1941

✠ La Côte d'Ivoire
française libre

ᴺ LE GENERAL
DE GAULLE
à ABIDJAN

Le Général de Gaulle sera à Abidjan demain à midi. Il repartira le même jour à quatorze heures.

Il déposera une gerbe au Monument aux Morts et prononcera une allocution devant le Palais.

Pavoisez tous

Détails dans notre édition spéciale de ce soir

Général de Gaulle à Abidjan; page 1 of «La Côte d'Ivoire française libre».

Figure 2.1 Poster announcing De Gaulle's visit to Abidjan, en route for the Brazzaville Conference.

aux Colonies worried about the poor image of French colonialism created by the practice of forced labour, recognized the universal superiority of voluntary labour and wanted forced labour abolished. At the same time, it knew that the abolition of forced labour would deprive the Administration of much-needed manpower for public works and would, at least in the short term, reduce agricultural production for the war effort. As a result, the conferees decided on an uneasy compromise: they decided to give themselves five years in which to phase out forced labour, but at the same time to institute a *service obligatoire du travail* of one year for all African men aged between 20 and 21 who were physically fit and had not been conscripted for military service, in order to initiate them into the virtues of work.

The conference recommendations in other areas reflected a similar compromise, representing essentially an agenda for conservative reform. These included the expansion of health and education, although still with no provision for Africans to gain access to secondary or higher education; the progressive phasing out of the *indigénat* once hostilities ended; the promotion of economic development through the adoption of an economic development plan, gradual industrialization and modernization of agricultural methods; an end to discriminatory pay for Africans and Europeans doing the same job; and the opening up of more jobs to Africans, although it was stressed that, while 'emplois d'exécution' (non-managerial posts) were to be open to all Africans, no matter what their status, decision-making and managerial posts would continue to be the preserve of French citizens. Thus, the recommendations adopted by the conference hardly represented the new departure in French colonial policy for which its organizers had apparently hoped. Indeed, the conference's reformism was carefully situated by both Pleven in his opening speech to the conference and by De Gaulle in his closing speech within the continuum of France's *vocation coloniale*. Both paid tribute to the work done by men such as Galliéni, Van Vollenhoven, Lyautey and others in building the empire and sought to portray the work of the conference as continuing their tradition.[9]

However, for the Administration in Dakar, even the conference's relatively modest proposals went too far. Asked about his view before the conference on the proposed abolition of the *indigénat,* Governor-General Cournarie was opposed. Similarly, on the question of local assemblies, Dakar favoured reinstating the old consultative Conseil Colonial, whereas Pleven favoured the creation of elected assemblies composed of both Europeans and Africans.

When it came to implementing the recommendations, the Commissariat aux Colonies asked the Government-General to come forward with proposals. Here again, Dakar dragged its feet. On the question of forced labour, Governor Latrille in Côte d'Ivoire was keen to move quickly to phase out forced labour and to end discriminatory bonus payments to European planters, but Cournarie sided with the planters and rejected this move.[10] With regard to pay, the salary differential between Africans and Europeans remained, provoking a series of strikes among African personnel in 1945–6. Africans also continued to be confined to low level posts as cashiers, postal workers or customs officers, and the only new job opportunities arose largely because of the Administration's concern to reduce the number of illiterate chiefs.[11] Thus, primary school teachers and other French-educated Africans were released from their existing posts in order to enable them to apply for posts as chiefs. In the political sphere, Dakar was concerned above all to retain political control and Cournarie initially proposed a total of four *députés* to represent the 18 million inhabitants of AOF, although in the end it was allocated ten seats, five for citizens and five for subjects.

In their resistance to reform, the authorities in Dakar were reflecting the views of most Europeans in AOF. According to Robert Cornevin, for most officials out in the bush 'the Brazzaville declarations were for external, "American" benefit . . . the African bush would not see any benefit from them for a long time'.[12] As for the *colons,* they were reluctant to give up their privileges, and sought to defend their interests by organizing a colonial conference, the Etats Généraux de la Colonisation, in Douala (Cameroun) in September 1945. So strong was the resistance to change, it seems, that the Minister of Colonies in the Provisional Government, Paul Giacobbi, felt compelled to send a circular to colonial officials to remind them that, since the outbreak of war, the conditions in which they exercised their power had fundamentally changed: 'The truth is that colonialism is condemned and that some forms at least of colonization are outdated. We must therefore substitute a form of association for colonization'. He then went on specifically to warn them against attempts to prevent the promotion and development of the indigenous population: 'Too many French people of metropolitan origin who have settled overseas still display an unfortunate tendency to consider any measure which puts natives on the same level as "Europeans" as a setback for French influence'.[13]

The period that began with the Brazzaville Conference and ended with the election of the First Constituent Assembly in October 1945, was thus a period of back-pedalling, during which top officials in the Government-General and Colonial Ministry sought to limit the impact of the recommendations made at Brazzaville and set 'an agenda of conservative reform in which a limited, advisory role in public affairs would be accorded some colonial subjects within the context of metropolitan supremacy on all questions'.[14] However, events outside French West Africa, such as the Atlantic Charter of 1941 and the challenge to

French authority in Syria and the Lebanon, which were beyond the government's control, forced the Provisional Government to move on its programme of colonial reform. Also, colonial ministers René Pleven then Paul Giacobbi were worried about the impact that the lack of progress would have on colonial opinion. As a result, a number of reforms were implemented, such as the authorization of trade unions, although the colonial bureaucracy was successful in restricting their scope.

Tensions over Policy: A New Framework for Policy making

The significant point to be drawn from the above is the tensions between the metropolitan and the local colonial state that emerge at this time over French African policy making. As the empire moved up the domestic political agenda and the central government began to take a keener interest in colonial matters, the political stakes were raised and these tensions took on heightened political significance. The configuration and dynamics of these tensions were to change over time, with the government sometimes adopting, and attempting to force Dakar to adopt, more radical positions, while at other times it was the Governor-General in Dakar who demanded the implementation of reforms that Paris was either unwilling to deliver or unable to act on because of domestic political difficulties. By late 1944–5, it was the CFLN, shortly to become the Provisional Government, which, with an eye on the wider international context, was pushing a more reformist agenda than Dakar was at this stage prepared to accept.[15]

The Elections to the Constituent Assemblies and the Creation of the French Union

On 20 February 1945, the Colonial Minister, Paul Giacobbi, established a commission under the chairmanship of the Guyanese-born *député* Gaston Monnerville, to study the question of colonial representation in the future Constituent Assembly. Léopold Sédar Senghor and Sourou Migan Apithy were the two Africans from AOF appointed to the commission. At its first meeting, they were amazed to discover that the draft document prepared by officials at the Ministry did not envisage any political representation for France's Black African territories because, unlike the overseas departments and protectorates that would be allowed to elect *députés* to the Assembly, they were classified as subject to a 'policy of domination'. As Joseph-Roger de Benoist has remarked: 'The people who drew up this text seemed not to have heard of the Brazzaville Conference!'[16]

Elsewhere in the Ministry, worries were being expressed about the lack of progress and its potential consequences for French authority. The Director of Political Affairs, Henri Laurentie, sent a memo to his minister, Giacobbi, in June 1945, warning him that: 'We are in the middle of a colonial crisis. Feelings of disaffection, mistrust and hate manifest themselves on so many issues that this forms a dangerous whole. There is little we can do against this: the apathy of the masses is not enough to counter the nationalism which is everywhere beginning to emerge and assert itself'. If France did not respond to these feelings of disaffection among its colonial populations and fulfil the promises it had made, Laurentie told the minister, then the result would be 'anarchy' and the 'eviction' of France from its overseas territories.[17]

In the end, ten seats were allocated to AOF, with five *députés* to be elected by citizens and five by African subjects. Out of the five seats for citizens, only one (Senegal) could be expected to be won by an African, because of the large number of *originaires* who were citizens in the Four Communes. In the rest of AOF, some 8,000 citizens, mostly Europeans, would be represented by four *députés*. In the second college, five African *députés* would represent the mass of African subjects in AOF, although even here the suffrage was extremely restricted, with only some 118,000 Africans (approximately 1 per cent of the population), mainly French-educated Africans and former soldiers, eligible to vote. Compared to the original text presented to the Monnerville Commission, these proposals represented a breakthrough – at least Africans would, after all, be represented in the Constituent Assembly – but they did not go as far as the African *députés* had hoped.

During 1945, there was an effervescence of political activity in preparation for the elections to the Constituent Assembly, which were due to be held on 21 October. In Senegal and Dahomey, the press underwent something of a revival and played an important role in shaping French-educated African opinion. In Senegal, some African members of the Parti Socialiste Sénégalais wanted to assert their autonomy from the SFIO, which they saw as a 'European party', but in the end Guèye's supporters got their way, and both he (first college) and Senghor (second college) were elected on a SFIO ticket in October. In every other territory the elections brought to prominence a new generation of French-educated Africans. In Côte d'Ivoire, where the SAA had begun organizing African planters in September 1944, their leader Félix Houphouët-Boigny was elected. In Dahomey, Sourou Migan Apithy, who had been to secondary school in France between the wars and later graduated from the Ecole Libre des Sciences Politiques in Paris as an accountant, was elected. In Soudan-Niger, the former primary school teacher and canton chief, Fily Dabo Sissoko, was elected, while in Guinea another former teacher, Yacine Diallo, was elected.

The pressure on Dakar from Paris for change increased during the period which lasted from the Constituent Assembly elections of October 1945 until the defeat of the first constitutional draft in the referendum of 5 May 1946. In the October elections, the PCF won the most seats and, together with the Socialists, had an overall majority in the Assembly. The Communists were not in favour of independence for France's colonies, partly out of a belief that they were not yet ready for national independence and partly because they believed that the effect of independence would be to abandon the colonies to the reactionary yoke of American imperialism. But their rhetoric was anti-imperialist, and they were anti-colonial in the sense that they opposed the exploitative nature of the colonial regime and supported the campaigns of colonial populations for equal rights. At the same time, most of the traditional colonial lobby, consisting of planters, settlers, colonial trading companies, and *députés* of the right and centre-right favourable to settler interests, emerged from the Second World War in a considerably weakened position because of the close association of many of them with Vichy.

This period also saw the entry into parliament of a small but significant number of overseas *deputés* with an agenda of colonial reform. In alliance with the reform-minded majority within the Constituent Assembly, they were able during this short period to push through important, and irreversible, changes to the French colonial regime that were to have a profound impact on the subsequent political evolution of French West Africa. Between the Constituent Assembly elections of October 1945 and the publication of the draft constitution on 19 April 1946, the future shape of the proposed French Union and the place of the colonies within it were of crucial importance for overseas *députés*. They won new civil and political liberties, including the acceptance of the principle of equal rights for all within a renovated Greater France, which was henceforth to be called the French Union. Forced labour was abolished by the Houphouët-Boigny law of 11 April 1946 and the creation of the Fonds d'Investissement pour le Développement Economique et Social (FIDES) established the principle of using metropolitan funds for overseas development projects (30 April 1946). Article 41 of the Constitution stated that the union between the *métropole* and its overseas territories was henceforth to be 'freely chosen', while article 44 granted all residents of the French Union the status of citizens and recognized their right to be represented in the National Assembly. Equally radical were the proposals in section VIII of the document, which defined the new administrative arrangements for the Empire: local assemblies, elected by direct universal suffrage, would in future administer France's overseas territories, the colonial governor would be replaced by a resident under-secretary of State in each territory or group of territories, and the 1789 Declaration of Human Rights would be extended to all residents of France's overseas territories. Overall, the *députés* were pleased with what they achieved.

French-educated Africans followed the negotiations closely and, in the referendum on 5 May, the constitutional project was supported by 85 per cent of voters in AOF. It was, however, rejected by a majority of metropolitan voters, for reasons unconnected with colonial matters, and new Constituent Assembly elections were organized for 2 June 1946. Its rejection provoked widespread disappointment among French-educated Africans: they were back to square one on the constitutional front and everything was once again up for negotiation. Moreover, worried that the right would use the opportunity presented by the defeat of 5 May to reverse the citizenship provisions, Lamine Guèye put a short bill before the Assembly on 7 May extending citizenship to all citizens of the French Union. It was passed unanimously. Although the victory was to some extent a pyrrhic one, since it did not stipulate which rights attached to citizenship of the Union and did not mean, for example, that citizens would enjoy the same voting or residence rights as French citizens, it did nevertheless provide a reference point for future campaigns for equality between Africans and Europeans.[18]

Thus, as a result of the reforms introduced between October 1945 and May 1946, a fundamental change in the conditions in which colonial officials exercised their power in French West Africa had taken place. New political actors became part of the policy-making process in the métropole, where African *députés* played an important role in maintaining the momentum for colonial reform both within the National Assembly and sometimes even as government ministers under the Fourth Republic. They also used their function as *députés* to appeal to ministers or metropolitan politicians in Paris for support over the heads of colonial governors. At the same time, the newly created elected assemblies within the colonies afforded Africans new platforms from which to put pressure on the colonial administration to implement reforms.

In the June elections to the second Constituent Assembly, the left lost seats, the centre-right Mouvement Républicain Populaire (MRP) emerged as the largest party and Georges Bidault was charged with forming a new government. Guèye's concerns proved well founded. The colonial lobby used the opportunity presented by the political realignment in metropolitan France to get some of what they saw as the more radical proposals contained in the first constitutional draft reversed. They published a colonial manifesto in June denouncing the constitutional plans prepared by the First Constituent Assembly for having diluted French authority over the empire and demanding the restoration of the double electoral college system, with representation in the National Assembly restricted to French citizens. A second manifesto, published six weeks later, demanded the repeal of the citizenship law of 7 May. Reflecting their increased confidence, the *colons* also decided to organize a second Etats Généraux de la Colonisation Française in Paris. The original plan had been to hold the meeting in Abidjan but it was moved to Paris and took place from 30 July to 24 August. Pressure also came from other quarters for the provisions of the May Constitution to be dropped: De Gaulle made an important speech in Bayeux attacking the constitutional proposals;[19] Edouard Herriot, doyen of the Radical Party, launched a virulent attack on the overseas deputies' proposals in the Assembly on 27 August warning that, if they were adopted, France would become 'the colony of its colonies';[20] and finally, as James Lewis has shown, there was the coordinated campaign by top officials within the Colonial Ministry to scupper the plans for what they regarded as an excessive devolution of French authority which, they believed, would ultimately lead to the secession of France's overseas territories.[21]

Against this coalition of political forces, the African *députés* could do little. Thus, although the commitment to a Greater France, made up of metropolitan France and its overseas territories, was retained, as was a somewhat watered down commitment to 'equality of rights and duties, without distinction based on race or religion', many of the other provisions of the earlier constitutional draft were revised: the reference to a Union 'freely chosen' was dropped, as was the proposal for a resident under-secretary of State in each territory or group of territories; the post of governor was retained; and the number of seats allocated to AOF was reduced from 21 to 13 (this increased to 16 in 1948 when the territory of Haute-Volta was reconstituted and elected three *députés*). The major battle took place over the double electoral college for elections to the National Assembly. The government's refusal to accept the single electoral college caused the overseas deputies to walk out of the constitutional commission on 20 September and in the end a compromise solution was adopted, with the single college adopted for AOF, but the double college retained for AEF, Cameroun and Madagascar. As for the local territorial assemblies, although the plan for them was retained, the issues of the mode of election to them, their composition and powers were left unresolved. These were subsequently defined by the law of 25 October 1946, which modelled them on the metropolitan *conseils généraux* (local departmental councils), after which they were named, except that the electoral system was to be the double electoral college in all the territories of AOF apart from Senegal. The justification given for this was the fear that the single college would eliminate European representation from the local assemblies. As for the local assemblies' powers, these were carefully circumscribed. They were to be consulted, but had no power of decision, on matters pertaining to administrative organization, education, the economy, social affairs and the labour regime; they were also responsible for administering the territory's resources and for voting the annual budget prepared by the governor, but had no right to amend it.[22] Overall, compared to the earlier draft, the effect of the new proposals was to restore power over the empire (now renamed the French Union) to the Colonial Ministry in Paris (now renamed the Ministry for Overseas France) and to the local colonial administrations. Not surprisingly, therefore, in the referendum of 17 October, the constitutional project drawn up by the Second Constituent Assembly was not endorsed with the same level of enthusiasm in French West Africa as the first: although over 80 per cent of those voting supported the proposals, nearly 50 per cent of those eligible to vote abstained.

However, even if the colonial lobby had won an important victory and less had been conceded on the institutional front than looked likely during the First Constituent Assembly, it could not be pretended that the *status quo ante* had been restored. The Provisional Government, then the First Constituent Assembly, had enacted important, and irreversible, reforms, particularly in the areas of human rights and political liberties. And, even if the level of overseas representation in the National Assembly was limited and the local assemblies had restricted powers, they nevertheless provided African elected representatives with a platform from which to conduct, and gain popular support for, their campaigns for equal rights.

One telling indication of the significance of this new political situation was the tensions between the metropolitan and local colonial state that emerged during this period. French-educated Africans began openly to look beyond Dakar, to politicians in Paris, to push forward the process of change. Even before the Brazzaville Conference, the colonial administration, and more generally the French in AOF, were regarded by the educated African élite as die-hard conservatives, committed to blocking

African progress. It was for this reason that Lamine Guèye flew to Algiers in January 1944 to present a petition to General De Gaulle, signed by members of the French-educated élite in Senegal, to enlist his support. In the petition, they complained of the 'racist policy' being pursued in the colony, suggested that the French people responsible were betraying the generous values of republican France and appealed to the CFLN to intervene to put an end to such practices: 'The Comité Français de la Libération Nationale to which we owe the return to republican legality and democracy will certainly wish to put right the situation to which we have drawn its attention'.[23] In the text of the petition, the France of the Liberation represents 'True France'; it is a kind of tribune, defender of the values of liberty and equality and a force for progress, to which French-educated Africans appealed for support over the heads of reactionary colonial officials in Dakar, whom they portrayed as traitors to the cause of republican France. This was to become a recurrent theme in French West African politics during the next two years.

However, it was not always the case that it was reformers in Paris pressing reform on a reluctant administration in Dakar. One of the last acts of the Gouin government, before the defeat of the first constitutional draft in the referendum of 5 May, was to recall the conservative Governor-General of AOF, Pierre Cournarie, and appoint in his place the more liberal René Barthes. This resulted in a reversal of political forces between Paris and Dakar. The Government-General had done its best, both at the Brazzaville Conference and in the two years following, to slow the process of reform. This changed with the arrival of Barthes in AOF, ironically at the very moment when the political tide in colonial affairs was turning in Paris from reform to reaction, and it was during Barthes' short, twenty-one month term of office as Governor-General in Dakar that a number of liberal measures were introduced or set in train, the effect of which was to promote the process of assimilation of AOF with France. The most important of these measures, which brought the education system in AOF more closely into line with that in the *métropole*, will be examined in the next chapter.

The Re-emergence of Trade Union Activity after the War

Trade unions had been authorized and had flourished briefly under the Popular Front, before being banned again during the Second World War. Following their legalization at the end of the war, African workers, particularly in Dakar, rapidly began to organize themselves once more into trade unions. The period 1944–6 was a difficult one for African workers: wages were low, inflation was high and the supply situation, especially for imported goods, remained very difficult. At the same time, the Provisional Government was determined, as in the *métropole*, to keep wages down, believing that this was essential to economic recovery and the revival of production. Coming after the deprivations suffered by African workers during the war, the hardships of the post-war period provided fertile ground for trade union organization. In laying the foundations for an African trade union movement, African unionists were helped by members of the metropolitan *centrales* (trade union federations), who offered both advice and organizational support. It is, however, worth noting that, at their inception, the primary function of the metropolitan unions in AOF was to recruit European workers. Trade union branches were often created on a racial basis and in some cases, such as the construction workers and the railway workers, even made the defence of their European workers' privileges their aim. Moreover, the centralized structure of the unions, imported from France, left little autonomy to the AOF unions. As a result, they were not always well attuned to African needs and demands. However, this organizational structure did have the benefit, from the African point of view, of providing training and financial support, both of which the fledgling African trade union movement sorely lacked in these early days. Leading trade unionists who were trained by the Confédération Générale du Travail (CGT) and were later to play a prominent role in French West African politics included Abdoulaye Diallo and Modibo Keita (Soudan), Djibo Bakary (Niger) and Sekou Touré (Guinea).[24]

Apart from the brief interlude of the Popular Front, it cannot be said that a labour movement existed in French West Africa before the Second World War. There had been strikes, the first of which in Dakar dated back to 1919, and various professional associations – so-called *amicales* – existed, notably in the Four Communes where the *originaires* had citizenship rights and, from 1929, on the Dakar-Niger railway, which took up issues on behalf of their members. It was, however, not possible to build a trade union *movement*, because trade unions were in any case banned and Africans were subject to forced labour conscription. With trade unions once again authorized and French authority weakened thanks to the war, African workers were quick to exploit the new opportunities the situation afforded.

There were a number of strikes by African workers in 1945. Then, in December, French teachers became the first group of French employees to organize a strike in AOF and their success in obtaining a pay increase no doubt served as an example to African workers.[25] The first major post-war strike movement was, however, the general strike of 14–26 January 1946 in Dakar and Saint-Louis, which mobilized between 15,000 and 20,000 workers in both the public and private sectors, from educated Africans working for the government to manual labourers working in the docks. Railway workers and school teachers were the only main groups not to join the strike, the former because their leaders were close to the Socialist Party (Marius Moutet, SFIO, was the Colonial Minister at this time), the latter because they hoped to obtain certain benefits on the back of the strike by French teachers the previous month. Significantly, this first major strike took place in the parts of AOF that had the longest history of contact with, and were thus most assimilated to, France. Moreover, the unions' central demand – 'equal pay for equal work' – reflected the traditional demand in Four Communes politics for racial equality between Africans and Europeans. The unions also demanded equal allowances for the families of African and French civil servants, an increase in the minimum wage and a share of power through union participation in the grading of jobs. The strike effectively shut down the colonial administration and European business in these two towns.[26]

The colonial authorities were unsure how to react in this novel situation. Their first reflex was to attempt to restore authority by conscripting the striking workers into the military, but the workers simply ignored the order. Moreover, aware that French colonial practices were now in the international spotlight and that France was under pressure to prove that its colonial rule was humanitarian and progressive, the recourse to violence to put an end to the strike was not an option. The Administration therefore had no choice but to negotiate, and to oblige employers to do the same. As a result, new contracts were negotiated on a sector by sector basis. Both public and private sector workers made significant gains, with increases in wage levels, the minimum wage and family allowances for civil servants all being conceded. Collective bargaining agreements were also reached with private employers.

The strike had important lessons, both for African social and political movements and for the colonial authorities in AOF. It taught the former that significant improvements in wages and conditions and a share in power could be obtained in the new, post-war colonial situation though coordinated action and negotiation. They also learned that they could turn the French language of assimilation to their own advantage, by using it to justify the demand for equality between Africans and Europeans in the socio-economic field. As for the colonial authorities, top French officials in AOF were deeply worried by the strike, which they saw as representing a serious potential threat to French authority: acknowledging the strikers' organizational success, Inspector Masselot of the Work Inspectorate described it as 'a profound movement of emancipation'.[27] The most important lesson for the colonial authorities, however, was their relative powerlessness, compared to the situation before and during the war. The old-style, authoritarian solutions to colonial social and political problems were no longer an option after the war. The only way forward for colonial rule, therefore, was to identify African leaders who were prepared to talk to the French authorities – what the French were subsequently to call, in the 1950s, 'interlocuteurs valables' (valid representatives) – and then to negotiate the settlement of economic, social, and indeed political, issues with them as they arose. However, whereas this rapidly became the norm in the field of industrial relations, it was to be a number of years before France's governing élites accepted that this was the way forward in the political sphere.

The Emergence of AOF Political Parties after the War

Various political groups, which were subsequently to form the nucleus of, and provide many of the activists for, French West Africa's post-war political parties, began to organize during 1944–5. In a number of cases, the leading figures in these groups had been involved in the Popular Front committees that had sprung up throughout AOF in 1936–7: in Soudan for example, these included Ousmane El Madane Touré, the writer Amadou Hampaté Bâ and the future *député*, Mamadou Konaté.[28]

Among the most important of these groups were the Groupes d'Etudes Communistes (GEC). The French Communist Party's (PCF) official line was that AOF was at that time incapable of existing either economically or politically as an independent nation. Moreover, at its stage of economic development and given the lack of a proletariat, it was not deemed appropriate to create Communist Party sections in French West Africa. Rather, the proper role for African activists was to join with French Communists in the common struggle against the forces of capitalism in the form of metropolitan and colonial trusts. Thus, from late 1943 onwards GECs became active in the main urban centres of AOF. Many of those involved, such as Joseph Corréa and Ousmane Ba (future Malian Minister for Foreign Affairs), were later to play a leading role in AOF's main political party, the Rassemblement Démocratique Africain (RDA).

There were also the Comités d'Etudes Franco-Africaines (CEFA), the first of which was created in Dakar by *originaires* of the Four Communes who seem to have conceived of them as a kind of Franco-African cultural association that would promote a policy of assimilation: 'The CEFAs wish to see this French community come into being under the emblem of the Republic: Liberty – Equality – Fraternity'.[29] The point was underlined in a letter from the Dakar section of the CEFA to Senghor: 'We are neither separatists nor conspirators. We simply want to gain the right to be members of the French family as equals and not as poor relations'. The same letter also proclaimed their intention of working within 'republican legality' for 'the progressive emancipation of Africans' and for 'French nationality . . . which we demand as a matter of urgency'.[30] The fact that Lamine Guèye, was appointed its political director was a further indication of the intended assimilationist stance of the group. Other members of the committees, particularly younger members, seem to have conceived of its objectives in rather different terms, however. Outside Senegal, some CEFAs adopted more explicitly anti-colonial, anti-French positions: in Soudan, for example, two of its activists were arrested for 'anti-French remarks' and imprisoned. One of those arrested, Massene Sene, was reported as having said at a public meeting: 'We must take as our sole motto: "Liberty – Independence" . . . Africa also must unite, demand and obtain its independence'.[31] In Guinea and Haute-Volta, CEFA branches adopted similarly 'anti-French' positions and some openly discussed the idea of African independence, to the consternation of the authorities: 'On the one hand, there are those who stand to gain in material and moral terms from any privileges that are granted generously and without delay. On the other hand, there is a small number of "nationalists" who reject us completely and who believe in the possibility of "sovereign African States"'. The report went on to say that some of the CEFA's leading figures appeared to belong to this latter category.[32] French-educated Africans in other territories also seem to have resented Senegalese dominance of the committees: prefiguring the rivalry that was to emerge within AOF between the territories of Senegal and Côte d'Ivoire, Houphouët-Boigny was reported as criticizing the Bobo-Dioulasso CEFA branch at one of its meetings for its dominance by Senegalese.[33]

CEFAs rapidly spread throughout AOF, reaching Côte d'Ivoire in March, only a little over a month after the first group had been formed in Dakar, and Bobo-Dioulasso in the summer, where the group rapidly grew to 8,000 members and was eventually banned by the authorities in early 1946 when 200 of its members also received prison sentences for alleged fraud.[34] Many of the leading figures in the CEFAs, such as François Gning and Abdoulaye Sadji (Senegal), Makane Macoumba (Soudan) and

Mamby Sidibé (Niger) were later to play a significant role either in the AOF trade union movement or the RDA.

The Founding of the Rassemblement Démocratique Africain

The manifesto drawn up by African *députés* in September 1946 was designed to mobilize African public opinion behind the demand for the rights and freedoms that Africans had been granted in the original constitutional draft that had been rejected in May. It recalled the commitments France had made to equal rights for the people of its colonies at the end of the Second World War, criticized the colonial lobby for its reactionary stance, and set out the objectives of the Africans' struggle. It also called an inter-territorial congress, to be held in Bamako, to work for African emancipation. At this congress, which lasted from 19–21 October, the RDA was founded, and the September manifesto formed the basis of the new party's political manifesto.[35]

Marius Moutet, the Minister for Overseas France, initially hoped that the new movement might join forces with the Socialists. However, when it became clear that this would not happen and suspecting the Communist Party of being behind the manifesto and congress plans, he put pressure on African *députés* who were close to the Socialist Party and had signed the manifesto not to go to Bamako. Lamine Guèye and Léopold Sédar Senghor (Senegal) and Yacine Diallo (Guinea) agreed not to attend, but Fily Dabo Sissoko (Soudan), in whose home territory the congress was due to take place, decided to go, with the intention of denouncing the planned congress as a 'communist plot' and persuading Africans not to attend. He failed in this, and was eventually prevailed upon by his colleagues in the Parti Progressiste Soudanais to take part. As Pierre Kipré has remarked: 'The SFIO lost the battle of Bamako against the PCF' and as a result the RDA was to be allied with the PCF in the National Assembly from 1946–50.[36]

However, despite the radical, anti-imperialist language of some of its leaders, the RDA was not a secessionist party. It favoured instead the foundation of a genuine French Union, which the first draft of the constitution had seemed to promise and was what most of the French-educated African élite in AOF wanted at this time. The manifesto listed as the party's objectives:

- equal political and social rights;
- individual and cultural liberties;
- democratically elected local assemblies;

- a freely chosen union between the populations of Africa and the people of France.[37]

These may be summed up as the political, economic and social emancipation of Africans within the framework of the French Union, based on equality of rights and duties. The words 'autonomy' and 'independence' were deliberately avoided, because leading figures such as Houphouët-Boigny and d'Arboussier believed that talk of autonomy or independence was premature, given the level of economic and social development of Black Africa. Instead, they appealed to Africans to unite in the struggle to create a genuine French Union based on the principles of liberty, political democracy and equality as the key to African emancipation. The following extracts from a text by Ouezzin Coulibaly, future RDA *député* and close collaborator of Houphouët-Boigny, sum up the political ideas of the RDA leadership:

> Our *député* (Houphouët) has always been in favour of union, he only lives for union, firstly between all the Africans of Côte d'Ivoire, then between all the Africans of French Africa and all French people of good-will, who are incapable of betraying France's civilizing mission, but a true union with absolute equality of rights and duties . . .
>
> We do not believe full assimilation to be necessary. Our countries retain their personality within the French Union . . . The most important thing is equality and liberty for all. Our elected representatives have won freedom of the press, freedom of speech, freedom of association, absolute equality in every field. What more do we want? It is up to us to make this equality a reality and to show ourselves to be worthy of the rights we have gained through determined work with our hands and our brains.[38]

French education was seen as the key to achieving this equality. African emancipation meant increasing the number of Africans in executive positions, so that they could take a greater role in the administration of their affairs. In order to compete with Europeans and replace them in such posts, they needed to be educated to the same level. The RDA therefore launched a campaign for a vast expansion and extension of education throughout French West Africa, including the provision of secondary schools in every territory and the immediate creation of a university in Dakar. Without this, they believed, economic, technical and social progress could not take place and the colonial power would always have an argument for delaying the granting of equal rights to Africans. Indeed, the willingness, or otherwise, of France to break with her colonial past in the field of education was seen as an indication of her good faith in wishing to bring about a genuine French Union based on equality of social and political rights. For the RDA, as for most of the French-educated élite, the development of education thus became almost an article of faith and a gauge of political progress towards decolonization.[39] Of course, this priority attached to education may, in part, have been a consequence of the fact that there were so many teachers and former teachers among the Party's founders and early leaders. All those in important positions within the Party would also have received a French education of some sort. However this is not a sufficient explanation, on its own, for the priority given to education. For the RDA, its importance was, above all, a matter of political calculation.

The congress attracted some 1,000 participants, with delegations from every territory in AOF, and the federation's first interterritorial political party was successfully launched. The Bamako Congress failed, however, to achieve one of its key aims, that of realizing African unity. Lamine Guèye and Senghor did not attend the Bamako Congress and did not join the RDA. This was to prove highly significant for the subsequent political development of AOF, since it opened a rift between the main political leaders of Senegal and their counterparts in the rest of French West Africa. Eleven years later, at the inaugural congress of the Convention Africaine in Dakar, Senghor was to admit that his decision not to go to Bamako had been a mistake.[40]

The Beginnings of Modern Nationalism in French West Africa

This was a watershed period for the colonial policy-making process in French West Africa. On the surface, it might have appeared as if little had changed. France's governing élites, of both right and left, remained committed to the retention of empire. In this respect, their mindset contrasted with that of Britain's governing élites, some of whom had for several years been thinking in terms of preparing Britain's colonies for self-government, albeit not in any immediate future. Moreover, the chosen vehicle for keeping the empire together, the French Union, was a compromise between assimilation and association that was fully in keeping with France's traditional approach to colonial rule in French West Africa, which had always represented something of a balancing act between the two. It was a compromise that in different ways suited both France's governing élites and many French-educated Africans. It suited colonial officials and politicians representing the various constituencies in France that wanted to retain the empire. It also offered something –

the promise of progress and a measure of autonomy – to the French-educated African élite. But it was precisely these divergences of perspective that provided fertile ground for the development of the diverse elements of the nationalist movement in French West Africa.

This new policy-making framework played a key role in shaping the political agenda of African political parties, trade unions and the other African political and social movements that emerged in French West Africa after the Second World War. Political action was, of course, not entirely new to AOF. The Four Communes of Senegal had a tradition of competitive politics that dated back to the previous century and they had elected their first African *député* to the French National Assembly in 1916. A small number of Africans from AOF, such as Lamine Senghor (Senegal, and no relation of Léopold Sédar Senghor), Louis Hunkarin (Dahomey) and Tiemoko Garan Kouyaté (Soudan) had also been involved in political activity in the inter-war period during their stay in France, but this had had few repercussions within AOF,[41] and there had been a brief upsurge of mainly trade union activity in AOF during the Popular Front. It was, however, not until after the Second World War that political activity spread throughout AOF and the era of French West African politics can truly be said to have begun. Thus, the period 1944–6 saw the emergence of the federation-wide political parties and trade unions that were to be at the forefront of the anti-colonial struggle in the run-up to decolonization and political independence.

This period shaped the political agenda of the new African political and social movements in a number of ways. Firstly, Paris emerged as a major focus for African political activity. Africans did not expect to gain very much from lobbying the colonial administration in AOF and looked instead to the *métropole*, both to initiate reform and to put pressure on local officials to implement reforms that had been agreed. The creation of the French Union reinforced this pattern, both at an institutional level by admitting a small number of African elected representatives to the National Assembly in Paris, who then allied themselves with metropolitan political parties, and at an ideological level through its implicit assimilationism. The Constitution stated that: 'France forms with its overseas peoples a Union based on equality of rights and duties' and that 'The one and indivisible French Republic' comprises on the one hand, the metropolitan communes and departments and on the other, the overseas territories. This set the pattern for the political action of AOF's political leaders until the eve of independence in 1960. In this respect, it was precisely the ambiguity of the 1946 constitution's provisions, their *implied* assimilationism, that was significant, because it invited Africans, and indeed the residents of France's other overseas territories, to conceive of their future within, rather than outside, the community of Greater France, and to envisage decolonization as taking place through closer association with France, rather than through secession from it.[42] It also provided African political and social movements with a springboard from which to campaign for equal rights between Europeans and Africans, and thereby encouraged them to make this the focus of their campaigns for decolonization, rather than independence. Moreover, the decision to allow a small number of Africans to be elected to the French National Assembly effectively bound them into an essentially assimilationist perspective. This was a result not only of the way in which it focused their political action on the *métropole*, but also of the fact that it gave them the opportunity to climb to the very peak of the French political system. They became members of the French parliament, sat on special commissions and were even on occasion appointed government ministers. France was unique among the colonial powers in offering such openings to representatives from its African colonies and this acted, understandably, as something of a disincentive for them to press for immediate independence. Thus, after the war, it was not only France's governing élites that wanted to maintain the imperial link. It was also Africa's political leaders in the National Assembly who increasingly had a stake in the maintenance of the link.

One result of this was the emergence in AOF of what Videgla has called 'assimilationist nationalism'.[43] This did not mean that Africans wanted literally to become 'black Frenchmen': on the contrary, most French-educated Africans remained deeply ambivalent about assimilation. What it did mean, though, was that the focus of the campaigns of African social and political movements in this period was on the acquisition of equal rights and equal status with French people. This theme was embraced by most French-educated Africans as a way of challenging the racist nature of the colonial regime. The emergence of this form of 'assimilationist nationalism' in French West Africa may be attributed to a combination of two factors. First of all, the old Senegalese political class, led by Lamine Guèye, had a decisive influence in promoting an assimilationist form of nationalism in French West Africa. The long history of contact between France and the Four Communes of Senegal and its tradition of assimilationist politics meant that most of the leading political figures in AOF at this time came from this tradition of Senegalese politics. They used their central position within French West African politics immediately after the war to reject independence and promote the politics of assimilation. Secondly, interventions by French political leaders at crucial moments, such as the visit to AOF by De Gaulle in January 1944 en route to the Brazzaville Conference, the promises of reform he and Pleven made at the conference, the limited reforms implemented by the Provisional Government and, perhaps most importantly, the measures introduced during the first Constituent Assembly, sustained the belief among many French-educated Africans that progress would come through closer association with France, rather than separation from it. They were in no doubt that the colonial regime was exploitative and repressive, but the point was that they ascribed this to the privileges and abuses of France's representatives in AOF, rather than to the fact of belonging to the community of Greater France *per se*. In other words, post-war African nationalism emerged, to an important degree, as a movement of opposition to reactionary French colonial officials in Dakar, rather than in opposition to the French link itself. Colonial officials were held responsible for the problems Africans experienced, as they were seen to be more interested in defending French colonial interests than in promoting African progress,

There was an additional dimension to this in territories other than Senegal, insofar as nationalism in these other territories emerged to a significant degree as a movement of opposition not only to Dakar and its policies but also to the dominant position occupied by Dakar within the federation of French West Africa. This was noticeable in Côte d'Ivoire, for example, where a liberal governor, Latrille, had his progressive policies blocked by a reactionary Governor-General in Dakar. And it was exacerbated by the dominance of Senegalese political leaders over AOF politics at this time. Thus, while 'assimilationist nationalism' was the preferred option of most French-educated Africans, in territories other than Senegal this might also contain a significant element of anti-Senegalese feeling. In these other territories, French-educated Africans wanted direct links with France and chose to exploit these links through their elected *députés* in order to obtain reforms, thus by-passing the Government-General in Dakar and circumventing the perceived dominance of Senegal over French West African politics.

In conclusion, it should not be thought that support for 'assimilationist nationalism' was universal, even in Senegal. For example, the Mouvement Nationaliste Africain, created in 1946 by Abdoulaye Sadji and a group of French-educated Africans and former *tirailleurs*, published an occasional newspaper, *La Communauté*, in Dakar to press for African independence. They rejected all forms of imperialism: 'In this struggle to the death against national oppression, we believe that the colonized peoples of the whole world must learn to know each other and unite against the common enemy: imperialism'. They followed with interest the preparations for Indian independence and demanded 'immediate independence' for Africa.[44] Moreover, as we have already seen, while the Dakar CEFA adopted an assimilationist stance, CEFA members in Côte d'Ivoire, Soudan and Guinea were more favourably disposed to the idea of independence. Thus, even during this early post-war period, there were significant tensions within the nationalist movement in French West Africa. These were destined to take on increased political significance in years to come.

Notes

1. Laurent Gbagbo sees the conference as part of a French tradition of managing national crises by mobilizing colonial resources, in *Réflexions sur la conférence de Brazzaville* (Eds Clé, 1978), p. 15. While this may indeed be true, it ignores the way in which the conference was shaped by the specific wartime circumstances in which it was held.
2. C. Lévy, 'Les origines de la Conférence de Brazzaville, le contexte et la décision', in Institut Charles de Gaulle/Institut d'Histoire du Temps Présent, *Brazzaville, Janvier-Février 1944: Aux sources de la décolonisation* (Plon, 1988), p. 27.
3. C.-R. Ageron, 'Aperçus historiques sur la Conférence de Brazzaville', in ibid, p. 351.
4. 'Cours d'information sur l'Indochine', 22 May 1945, Papiers Laurentie, AN 72AJ535/1. For an analysis of the genesis of what C.-R. Ageron terms the 'myth of the [Brazzaville] Conference marking the beginning of French decolonization in Africa', see Institut Charles de Gaulle/Institut d'Histoire du Temps Présent, *Brazzaville*, pp. 364–8.
5. 'Programme général de la conférence', ANSOM Aff. Pol. 2201/5.
6. *La Conférence Africaine Française*, op. cit., p. 32. The word 'self-governments' was in English in the original French text.
7. J. D. Hargreaves, *Decolonization in Africa*, 2nd ed. (Longman, 1996), p. 44.
8. Cf. R. Betts, *Assimilation and Association in French Colonial Theory* (Columbia University Press, 1961), p. 120.
9. The full text of all the Conference recommendations and speeches is in *La Conférence Africaine Française. Brazzaville 30 Janvier-8*

Février 1944 (Ministère des Colonies, 1945). William Cohen has suggested, in a contribution to a conference on 'Robert Delavignette, savant et politique', organized at the University of Cergy-Pontoise, 17–18 May 2001, that Pleven drew up a report before the Conference indicating what its main conclusions should be. These ideas were broadly reflected in the final recommendations.

10. G. Chaffard, *Les Carnets secrets de la décolonisation*, vol. 1 (Calmann-Lévy, 1965), pp. 39–42.
11. C. Akpo-Vaché, *L'AOF et la seconde guerre mondiale* (Karthala, 1996), p. 216.
12. R. Cornevin, 'Le corps des administrateurs de la France d'Outre-mer durant la 2e guerre mondiale', in Institut d'Histoire du Temps Présent, *Les Chemins de la décolonisation de l'empire français, 1936–56* (Eds, du CNRS, 1986), p. 456.
13. Circular dated 20 October 1945, ANSOM Aff. Pol. 2167/1.
14. J. I. Lewis, 'The French Colonial Service and the issues of reform, 1944–8', *Contemporary European History*, 4, 2, 1995, p. 154.
15. Cf. telegram from the Minister to the Governor-General, 24 March 1946, complaining about the slowness with which Dakar applied new policy initiatives, AAOF 17G413/126.
16. J.-R. de Benoist, *L'Afrique Occidentale Française de 1944 à 1960* (Nouvelles Editions Africaines, 1982), p. 32.
17. Papiers Laurentie, memo dated 20/21 June 1945, AN 72AJ535.
18. For an analysis of the ways in which policy-makers used the distinction between citizenship and nationality to deny Africans the same rights as French people, see C. Coquery-Vidrovitch, 'Nationalité et Citoyenneté en Afrique Occidentale Française: Originaires et Citoyens dans le Sénégal Colonial', *Journal of African History*, 42, 2001, pp. 285–305.
19. C. De Gaulle, *Discours et messages*, vol. 2, (Plon, 1970), pp. 18–23.
20. *Journal Officiel, Débats de la Deuxième Assemblée Constituante*, session of 27 August 1946, p. 3334.
21. J. I. Lewis, 'The French Colonial Service', pp. 171–4.
22. J.-R. de Benoist, *L'Afrique Occidentale Française*, pp. 94–5.
23. The full text of the petition is in ANSOM Aff. Pol. 2098/7.
24. P. Dewitte, 'La CGT et les syndicats d'Afrique Occidentale Française (1945–57)', *Mouvement social*, 117, 1981, pp. 6–7. Djibo Bakary trained as a teacher before founding the Niger section of the RDA, the Parti Progressiste Nigérien. He broke with the RDA after the decision to disaffiliate from the PCF in 1950. Modibo Keita trained as a teacher at the William-Ponty School in Senegal before becoming

involved in politics after the Second World War. In 1945, he founded with Mamadou Konaté the Bloc Soudanais, which became the Union Soudanaise and joined the RDA as the US-RDA in 1946. See chapter 4, note 7, for a biography of Sekou Touré.

25. Letter from AOF Fédération des Syndicats de l'Enseignement Public to Minister of Colonies, dated 1 December 1945, and telegram Governor-General to Minister, dated 4 December 1945, AAOF O267/31.

26. F. Cooper, 'La grève générale de 1946 et la grève des cheminots de 1947-8', *Historiens et Géographes du Sénégal*, 6, 1991, p. 34. See also AAOF 21G20/17 and PRO FO371/60097.

27. Quoted in F. Cooper, ibid, p. 36. This article also contains details of Masselot's role in helping to settle the strike.

28. A. C. Danioko, 'Contribution à l'étude des partis politiques au Mali de 1945 à 1960' (doctoral thesis, University of Paris-VII, 1984), pp. 35–6.

29. Undated circular sent out to all CEFA sections, AAOF 17G526/144.

30. Letter from CEFA, Dakar, to Senghor, 25 February 1944, AAOF 17G127/17.

31. Security Services report of meeting held on 30 June 1945, in ibid.

32. Information bulletin no. 27, 28 July–15 August 1945, marked 'Très secret', dated 16 August 1945, in ibid.

33. Report of a CEFA meeting held on 16 November 1946, in AAOF 17G526/144.

34. Telegram from Houphouët-Boigny to Lamine Guèye, marked 'Très secret', undated (early 1946), ibid.

35. See P. Kipré, *Le Congrès de Bamako* (Eds Chaka, 1989) for a detailed history of the founding of the RDA.

36. Ibid, p. 125.

37. The full text of the Manifesto is in J. Dalloz, *Textes sur la décolonisation* (Presses Universitaires de France, 1989) pp. 35–6.

38. Letter to J. Eyraud, 6 March 1946, Eyraud personal archives.

39. See T. Chafer, 'Decolonisation and the Politics of Education in French West Africa, 1944–58' (PhD thesis, University of London, 1993), especially chapters 1–4.

40. Quoted by R. S. Morgenthau, *Political Parties in French-Speaking West Africa* (Clarendon Press, 1964), p. 89.

41. For a study of the political views and activities of these and other Africans in the inter-war period, see J. S. Spiegler, *Aspects of Nationalist Thought among French-Speaking West Africans, 1921–39* (Nuffield College, Oxford, PhD thesis, 1968).

42. For further discussion of this ambiguity, see M. Michel, *Décolonis-*
    ations et emergence du tiers monde (Hachette, 1993), p. 196; J.-R.
    de Benoist, op. cit., p. 163.
43. M. M. E. Videgla, 'Le rôle des intellectuels dans le mouvement de
    la décolonisation de l'ex-Dahomey' (MA dissertation, University of
    Benin, 1980), p. 79, quoted by C. Akpo-Vaché, *L'AOF*, p. 257.
44. *La Communauté*, 9–10, 30 January 1947.

'Decolonization through Assimilation': The Struggle for Emancipation, 1946–50

The four years from 1946–50 were a period of policy sclerosis in French West Africa. Immediately after the Second World War France had apparently made a good start in laying the foundations for its project of building a 'modern' Africa within a reformed colonial system. Between 1946 and 1950, however, no new policy initiatives of comparable significance were launched. Colonial officials in both Paris and Dakar wanted a period of stabilization and consolidation after the upheavals of the war and its immediate aftermath. But this was to ignore the impact of developments over the previous ten years, the combined effect of which was, on the one hand, to weaken French authority and, on the other, to deepen African resentment towards colonial rule and increase pressure for reform. Although this did not lead to violence and bloodshed in AOF on the scale experienced in Indochina and Madagascar, the period was nonetheless marked by an intensification of opposition to the colonial regime. There were two large-scale strikes (the first of these, the general strike of January 1946, was discussed in the previous chapter) and numerous smaller strikes; the colonial authorities were accused of sabotaging education and a vigorous campaign developed throughout French West Africa for the 'decolonization of education'; the long campaign for the adoption of a new Code du Travail (Labour Code) and for the extension of citizenship rights beyond the political to the economic and social fields, began; and the period culminated with violent protests in Côte d'Ivoire, as a result of which some 20 Africans died, a further 100 were wounded and several hundred were arrested.

Although this was a period of policy inertia in AOF, the policy field cannot be ignored completely. As Kenneth Robinson has stated: 'in the politics of the colonial situation, no less than in other spheres of political action, habits of mind are important even if "policies" are not'.[1] The point here is that, even if new policies were not being made, we still need to understand the mindset of policy makers and officials, as it was this that conditioned their attitudes to African demands and helped determine official discourse. This in turn had an impact on the behaviour and responses of African opposition movements. The process was a dynamic one, in which the government, colonial officials and African political leaders and social movements were constantly interacting and reshaping each other's agendas.

Equally importantly, it is necessary to take into account changes in the policy-making context. The actions of colonial officials were henceforth open to scrutiny and potential challenge at various levels, both within France and in the colony, and this placed limits on their freedom of action and transformed the conditions in which they exercised their authority. Secondly, the balance of political forces in Paris was a significant factor in colonial policy making. As we saw in chapter two, there was a shift to the right between the first and second constituent assemblies and this rightward shift continued in 1947 with the exclusion of the Communists from the government. Since the main political party in French West Africa, the RDA, was affiliated to the PCF in the National Assembly, this inevitably had an impact on AOF politics. Finally, it is necessary to keep in mind the broader international context. The founding of the United Nations, the post-war emergence of the two superpowers, each of which was anti-colonial for its own different reasons, the start of the Cold War, Indian independence and developments elsewhere in the French Empire, notably Indochina and Madagascar, which had serious implications for the future of French imperial power, all these formed part of the backcloth against which politicians and top officials were taking decisions that affected African policy during this period.

The Policy Context

The French 'Colonial Myth' and its Impact on Policy making

A growing body of literature has in recent years shown how republicans of the left and centre-left, having initially opposed the acquisition of colonies, subsequently during the twentieth century became not only reconciled to the possession of colonies but active supporters of empire.[2] Indeed, the 'civilizing mission' became the official imperial ideology of republican France.[3] Behind this change of heart lay the growing conviction that associating the colonies closely with the *métropole* brought benefits to both. For France, the possession of an empire brought enhanced international prestige, guaranteed access to raw materials and new markets and, as two world wars showed, the colonies also represented a reservoir of extra manpower, which was important both militarily and economically for a country in which the birth rate during the first half of the twentieth century remained persistently low. For the people of the colonies, the association with France brought the material and moral benefits of French civilization, including economic development, education and the French republican tradition of democratic politics. It was out of this conviction, that colonialism brought mutual benefits to France and to the people of the colonies, that the French 'colonial myth' emerged.[4]

The myth was, essentially, the belief in an indivisible republic composed of France and its overseas territories. This belief in a republican Greater France was not new. It had underpinned the policy of *mise en valeur* for the colonies after the First World War, which in the end was not implemented, and also the reform projects of the Popular Front.[5] By the beginning of the Second World War, the idea of Greater France was already part of the French political mythology and had become an integral element of the image of France that republican political leaders sought to project, both to domestic public opinion and on the international stage. It gained new force during and immediately after the Second World War when the Empire played a central role in supporting the claim of the Free French to be the authentic representatives of a genuinely 'Free' France. The colonies also provided the springboard from which the campaign to liberate the métropole was launched. Equally importantly, post-war governing élites were convinced that the maintenance of empire was essential if France was to regain its status as a major world power. In a speech in Bordeaux in 1947, De Gaulle expressed a view that was widely shared: 'in a world such as this, and with things as they are, to lose the French Union would be a reduction that could cost us our independence'.[6] The stakes were therefore extremely high, which explains the special importance that France's post-war governing élites attached to the Empire.

The potency of this colonial myth under the Fourth Republic was enormous. It led France to adopt a policy of severe repression in Madagascar that led to the death of some 89,000 Madagascans, and into two hugely damaging colonial wars in Indochina and Algeria.[7] The policy stalemate that it provoked led, ultimately, to the Fourth Republic's demise. And in Black Africa, it meant that the route to gradual decolonization through incremental reform via a liberal French Union was effectively blocked because the spectre of secession was raised as soon as there was any suggestion of giving colonial peoples a greater say over the government of their own affairs.

The colonial myth affected policy making in two crucial ways. Firstly, it forged the mindset within which colonial policy was made in the immediate post-war period. Its effect was to render unacceptable any proposals that seemed to lead to any dilution of French sovereignty over the colonies. Secondly, and perhaps at first glance paradoxically, the colonial myth actually made it more difficult to obtain political agreement for colonial reform. The problem was that, although leading politicians, military figures and colonial officials shared a belief in the colonial myth of a Greater France, they could not agree on what measures were needed to make it workable. This problem was further exacerbated by the polarization of French politics under the Fourth Republic against the backcloth of the continuing divisions within French society resulting from war, the onset of the Cold War and the exclusion of Communist ministers from the government in 1947. The result was that, although leading figures in all the main parties believed it was essential for France to maintain its empire, when it came to obtaining agreement on actual policy measures this consensus evaporated. In French West Africa, the effect of this was to rule out the possibility of decolonization taking place through the gradual planned devolution of authority to elected African leaders.

The Emergence of New Political Actors in the Policy-making Process

During the inter-war period, successive governments were too pre-occupied with domestic affairs to take a sustained interest in colonial policy. Although many French people felt a vague pride in the empire, colonial policy itself aroused little public interest beyond those groups with a particular interest in colonial matters, such as *colons*, colonial trading companies, missionaries and colonial officials, and a small circle of liberal humanists and left-leaning intellectuals who were concerned about the abuses of colonial rule.[8] As a result, the Government-General in Dakar enjoyed considerable autonomy with respect to policy making and implementation, albeit within parameters established by the Colonial Ministry. Inside the colony, apart from in the Four Communes with their long tradition of competitive elections, it exercised largely unchallenged authority, thanks to the *indigénat* that denied political rights to Africans. This changed after the war with the introduction of new political actors into the political process.

The best-known of these new political actors were the African *députés*, who were elected to the Constituent, and subsequently National,

Assemblies from 1945 onwards. They rapidly became astute at using the Assembly as a platform for putting pressure on the government and colonial authorities to implement reform. This worked best when there was a left-wing majority in the Assembly, when the influence of the traditional colonial lobby was diminished and when they had a sympathetic, reform-minded minister at the Colonial Ministry, as was the case during the first Constituent Assembly. Even when this was not the case, the pattern of shifting alliances between parties, which provided governments with small and often fragile majorities in parliament, meant that overseas *députés* could on occasion exert influence disproportionate to their small numbers and, even if their proposals were not adopted, the very fact of bringing issues to the attention of parliament and obtaining the support of metropolitan politicians meant that colonial officials were put on the defensive.

Equally important in terms of changing the policy-making context after the war was the emergence of new political actors within government who were keen to establish their 'sphere of influence' over colonial policy. The constitutional commitment to a 'one and indivisible' French Union, comprising the métropole and France's overseas territories, established the framework for this, since it potentially extended the area of competence of each ministry to the overseas territories. As a result, the Ministry for Overseas France (as the Colonial Ministry was renamed in 1946) now had to share responsibility for policy making in the colonies. This was partly because specialist technical ministries henceforth expected to be consulted about decisions relating to their policy area, and partly because the Ministry for Overseas France increasingly needed their expertise as the areas of government intervention into the economic and social life of the colony expanded and colonial administration became more complex. Thus, the Finance Ministry expected to be involved in decisions about economic development projects; the Ministry of Agriculture expected to be consulted on matters pertaining to agricultural development, the Education Ministry on education matters, and so on. Sometimes, consultation was formalized through the establishment of joint committees, such as the Comité Supérieur Consultatif de l'Instruction Publique in the education field. This sharing of responsibility would not necessarily have been significant, but for the fact that relations between the Ministry for Overseas France and the different specialist ministries were sometimes tense, even conflictual. In the education field, for example, the introduction into the National Assembly by Senghor of a bill to transfer responsibility for colonial education to the Education Ministry from the Ministry for Overseas France, which African *députés* now saw, together with the Government-General in Dakar, as the main bastion of resistance to colonial reform, provoked a bitter battle between the two ministries.[9] As a result of such conflicts, it was more difficult to agree on new policy initiatives, and this exacerbated the policy inertia in the colonial field.[10]

At the same time, the creation in 1946 of the Fonds d'Investissement pour le Développement Economique et Social (FIDES), which established the principle of metropolitan finance for colonial development, introduced another actor into the colonial decision-making process. The fund, which spent substantial sums in AOF up to independence, was administered by a special Commission de Modernisation et d'Equipement aux Territoires d'Outre-Mer. Its decision-making structures were entirely separate from the Government-General in Dakar and outside the control of the Ministry for Overseas France, since it was based in the Commissariat Général du Plan and chaired by the former colonial minister, now deputy in the National Assembly, René Pleven. Representatives from the Ministry for Overseas France, the Ministry of Finance, the Commissariat du Plan, the National Assembly and the Assemblée de l'Union Française sat on the Commission, together with a number of other interested parties, such as for example a delegate from France's main trade union, the CGT. Its existence further complicated the process of policy formulation and implementation in French West Africa.

Finally, in his excellent study of the labour question in French and British Africa, Fred Cooper has shown how the Work Inspectorate played a major role in defining the terms within which the labour question was addressed in French West Africa after the war, which in turn had a profound impact on labour politics in the period leading up to independence. Official colonial discourse up to the end of the Second World War had traditionally conceived of African societies as divided, essentially, into two categories: *paysans* (peasant farmers) and *évolués*. The labour question did not therefore arise in Africa. Of course, the existence of a working class could not entirely be denied, but the African worker was regarded as an essentially transient phenomenon, a peasant farmer or villager only temporarily in an industrial situation. This conceptualization of the African worker came under partial challenge during the Popular Front when 'officials briefly contemplated using European social legislation to mould an urban working population whose numbers they insisted must be kept to a minimum'.[11] The fall of the Popular Front and the repression of the strike movement put a temporary end to such debates. But they surfaced again with renewed urgency at the end of the war, following the legalization of trade unions in AOF and the resumption of strike activity. The general strike of January 1946, which saw French-educated Africans ally with manual workers in a number of different sectors to press their demands for wage increases, was a turning-point. As Fred Cooper has observed: 'The strikes put a very rapid end to the fantasy of reconstructing French Africa through a *politique du paysannat* (policy to promote peasant farming), and French officials – in the very course of the first major challenge of this sort – embraced modernizing solutions, based on the French industrial relations model, with startling rapidity'.[12] The reason for this abrupt change of heart was that official conceptualizations of African society had no place for the labour question and therefore did not provide a basis for understanding, let alone dealing with, labour unrest. It fell to the Work Inspectorate to propose such a strategy.

Inspector Masselot, a colonial inspector who specialized in labour issues, saw that, if such strike movements were to be contained in future, the African worker would have to be recognized as a worker and contracts, based on the French collective bargaining model, would have to be negotiated separately, sector by sector, with each group of workers. This represented a profound change of approach, because it effectively assimilated the African worker to the European worker and treated him in the same way as the latter. It meant acknowledging that he was a 'normal' worker with whom one negotiated over pay and conditions and who responded positively to offers of improvements in wages and conditions. Workers were classified into professional categories and allotted grades within a well-defined hierarchy so that, when labour disputes arose, they could be 'contained' as professional issues suscept-ible to solution via the normal machinery of labour negotiation. In this way, they did not have to be dealt with as colonial opposition movements with a wider political significance, but were instead treated as 'technical' issues, to be resolved with the help of labour specialists from the Work Inspectorate who oversaw the processes of negotiation and collective bargaining. As a result of the 1946 strike, the responsibilities and role of the Inspectorate expanded, its organizational capacity was strengthened and an inspector-general was appointed with responsibility for the whole federation.[13]

The introduction of these new actors into policy making, whose agendas were not necessarily those of the Ministry of Overseas France, made it more difficult for the latter to pursue its conservative reform agenda, and meant that the policy making and implementation process became more conflictual and complex. The potential existed for African political and social movements to play one ministry off against another in an effort to press home their demands, as was to happen, for example, in the increasingly important education field. The emergence of these new political actors also contributed to the colonial policy sclerosis because it was more difficult to reach agreement on policy initiatives, a situation which was exacerbated by the lack of a strong political lead from politicians that was a product of the frequent changes of government under the Fourth Republic.[14] At the same time, policy making became less coherent: the emergence of new political actors drew attention to the deep ambivalence underlying French African policy. At one level, top officials in the Ministry of Overseas France and the Government-General sought to pursue their agenda of conservative reform by reasserting French authority and containing colonial opposition movements while creating the conditions that would allow Africans to continue to evolve gradually within their own societies. The discourse this produced, and the policy that emerged from it, were essentially an updated version of the traditional French approach of association. At another level, in the Education Ministry and the Work Inspectorate for example, the discourse was 'universalist' and the colonial policy that emerged from it assimil-ationist, in the sense that officials in the Education Ministry advocated the extension of full metropolitan-style French education to AOF, and the Work Inspectorate favoured treating African workers like European workers, which entailed establishing labour relations machinery on the metropolitan model in Africa.

The differences between these two discourses, which can be char-acterized respectively as 'traditionalist' and 'modernizing', were not necessarily so stark when it came to actual policy making. Top officials in the Education Ministry and the Work Inspectorate did not believe that all Africans could be assimilated into French metropolitan social structures and institutions, any more than did officials in the Ministry of Overseas France. And assimilation had in any case traditionally co-existed with association in official French colonial discourse. A change had taken place nonetheless. Official French discourse in AOF had accorded pride of place to association over assimilation since the First World War.[15] The return to a discourse of assimilation among parts of France's governing élites was therefore a significant change. While on one level it suggested a degree of confusion at the centre of government over the long-term objectives of French colonial policy, which indeed there was, its crucial importance was that it held out the prospect that there were enough French people of goodwill at the centre of policy making who were committed to the idea of the French Union. In doing this, it once again helped sustain the belief among French-educated

Africans in the idea of a French Union, 'one and indivisible', based on the principle of equality. How this happened, and its influence on the development of the nationalist movement, will be analysed further below.

The International Context

The Second World War opened French colonialism to unprecedented international scrutiny. This came first from the US. The Atlantic Charter of 1941 had established the principle that all peoples should be free to choose the form of government under which they live and President Roosevelt's anti-colonial sentiments were already well-known when the Allied landings in north Africa in 1942 effectively placed the French Empire in Africa under Anglo-American control. His visit to Casablanca in 1943 convinced him of the harmful effects of French colonial rule in Morocco and, later in the same year, he expressed the view that France had achieved little after nearly a century of colonial rule in Indochina. After the death of Roosevelt, growing concerns that newly independent colonies might fall under the thrall of the Soviet Union led the US to soften its position, so that the American priority under President Truman became security for the colonies rather than independence.[16] However, even if the American position on colonial self-government moderated, the international climate with respect to colonial rule had fundamentally changed. The colonial triumphalism that still characterized much of France's governing élite at the end of the Second World War was out of keeping with the new international situation. Italy and Japan were deprived of their colonies at the end of the war and Italy's former colonies would soon become independent. Syria and Lebanon among the former French-administered territories, then India among the former British colonies, became fully independent shortly after the War. At the newly created United Nations, the tide of international opinion was turning against colonialism. The UN General Assembly provided a new and important international forum for the expression of anti-colonial views that could not be ignored. Moreover, following the American change of position after Roosevelt's death, the anti-colonial bloc at the United Nations was led by the Soviet Union, the radical anti-imperialism of which appealed to a number of small nations that were certainly not communist, as well as to many activists in colonial nationalist movements who were not necessarily committed to communist ideology.

The reaction of politicians of the right and centre-right to this was predictable: it led them to interpret manifestations of colonial unrest as having been incited, even instigated, by international communism and to suspect many colonial nationalists of communist or proto-communist sympathies. Their response was to adopt repressive measures both in order to remove the threat to French sovereignty and stamp out the communist menace. The fact that the RDA affiliated to the Communist Party in the National Assembly after the 1946 elections served to corroborate the right's suspicions that the Communist Party was behind what they saw as the RDA's campaign of destabilization in Black Africa and made it all the more determined to eliminate the RDA and reassert French authority. On the left, the political reaction was perhaps less foreseeable. Since the split at the Tours Congress in 1920, French Socialists and Communists had been at daggers drawn. The Popular Front was a rare moment of unity, when they joined together in common cause against the fascist threat, but generally the Communists saw Socialist leaders as moderate reformers and political opportunists who were objective allies of the right, whereas Socialist leaders saw the Communists as Moscow's Trojan Horse, the front line of the international Communist revolution in Western Europe. The outcome of this was that Socialist leaders suspected the Communist Party of seeking to build a power base for itself in Africa and became as enthusiastic as the right in their repression of the RDA and insistence on the need to reassert French authority. The reaction of the Communist Party to these developments, which was to affirm with similar vigour to that of the right and the Socialists the need to maintain French authority over the colonies, was perhaps at first sight even more surprising. However, if one recalls that, at the time of the Popular Front, the PCF had dropped its outright condemnation of French colonialism, asserting that colonial peoples were not yet ready for self-determination, the emergence of what it perceived as an American threat to the French empire after the war only served to reinforce its commitment to keeping the empire French. To grant the colonies immediate independence, it believed, would effectively place them under the reactionary yoke of American imperialism. French tutelage, with its stated commitment to the values of liberty, equality and fraternity, was seen as infinitely preferable to, and more progressive than, domination by American transnational corporations.[17]

Thus, the determination of France's governing élites of both right and left to hold on to empire actually strengthened at this time. Moreover, although France was under increased international pressure to show that it could ensure a better future for its colonial peoples through integration with the *métropole* rather than through the devolution of power leading to self-government, the onset of the Cold War did afford France a space within the international order that allowed it to pursue its policy of integration. In this situation, France was able to portray itself, when the occasion demanded, as the champion of Western interests, preventing swathes of Africa and Asia from falling into communist hands.

The Struggle for African Emancipation 1946–50

The conditions required for the emergence of a sense of national identity, which is the necessary prerequisite for the development of a nationalist movement committed to fighting for self-determination, emerged only slowly in French West Africa. Partly this was the result of repressive colonial policies, which until 1944–5 denied any political rights to Africans except for the small minority who enjoyed French citizenship, partly it was the product of limited Western education and the slow pace of urbanization, and partly it was because the fixing of colonial bound- aries that were to constitute the frontiers of future African states was in most cases still too recent to engender among Africans a sense of belonging to a recognizable African state. The priority for most Africans at the end of the war was not therefore political independence, but an improvement in their lot. For the rural masses, their immediate concerns were an end to forced labour, abusive taxation and the often arbitrary punishments meted out under the *indigénat*, and an improvement in their standard of living.

For French-educated Africans and former soldiers, the central issue was equality with Europeans. As a result, 'race politics' played an important role in the early post-war years, as the demand for equality was frequently expressed during this period in explicitly racial terms as a demand for equality with whites. Once the French Union was established, African political activity was directed towards the objective of turning into reality the commitment contained in the constitution to a French Union based on the principle of equal rights. The expansion and extension of education were seen as the key to achieving this because, without education, Africans would not be able to gain access to the same skilled jobs as Europeans, nor earn the same salaries, nor would they have the qualifications and training necessary to replace Europeans in posts of responsibility. Without education, the aspiration to gain greater control over their own affairs would remain a dead letter. At the same time, *négritude*, which had been pioneered by Senghor and the Martiniquan writer, Aimé Césaire, between the wars, was an affirmation of 'black' values and of the intrinsic worth of African art and culture, which had for so long been implicitly, if not explicitly, denied by the French 'civilizing mission'. Although it had no perceptible political impact in

French West Africa before the Second World War, as Senghor's writings became better known after the War *négritude* contributed to a sense of self-worth and racial identity among many French-educated Africans. Edited by the Senegalese Alioune Diop, the foundation of *Présence Africaine* in 1947 as a journal of African culture and ideas also promoted a sense of African cultural identity.

The Campaign for the Decolonization of Education

Education was in a poor state in French West Africa in 1946. The participation rate was low: less than 5 per cent of African children who were eligible actually attended a French school and many of these did not even complete their primary education.[18] Education was largely skills based, with a reduced academic content compared to metropolitan curricula. The emphasis on agricultural production and the importance attached to the acquisition of basic skills had increased further with the introduction of 'rural schools' in the 1930s, with the result that some pupils remembered the regime in these schools as not much different from forced labour.[19] Indeed, when news arrived that forced labour had been abolished, in some parts of Soudan and Guinea schools were deserted by their pupils, who believed that the abolition of forced labour meant that they no longer had to attend school.[20] Also, secondary schools in AOF were effectively closed to Africans, they did not have access to metropolitan qualifications and diplomas such as the Baccalauréat, and there was no higher education in the federation.

The 'decolonization of education' thus became a key demand of the early nationalist movement in French West Africa. Before we go any further, however, a word of explanation is needed in order to avoid any misunderstanding of what was meant by the 'decolonization of education'. It did not signify, as one might have expected in British West Africa for example, the 'Africanization' of the curriculum, so as to gear education more closely to the needs of the indigenous population. On the contrary, reflecting the essentially 'assimilationist' nature of the educated élite's struggle for emancipation in AOF at this time, the demand for the decolonization of education took the form of a demand for the vast expansion of education and the introduction of full metropolitan-style curricula in Africa. This meant an end to what were perceived as watered-down curricula with a reduced intellectual content, an end to the emphasis on manual work and an end to the award of purely local diplomas in AOF that were not recognized in the métropole. In their place, the introduction of metropolitan-style primary and secondary education and the provision of higher education opportunities for Africans were demanded; the metropolitan Certificat d'Etudes Primaires (Primary Education Certificate) and Baccalauréat were to be made available to Africans; grants were to be given to African students to study in France and a university was to be built in AOF. African teachers' unions also campaigned for the introduction of the *cadre unique* (single grade) for all teachers. At that time, there were two *cadres*, the *cadre supérieur*, which was largely reserved for European teachers, and the *cadre secondaire,* to which most African teachers belonged. Teachers in the *cadre supérieur* were far better paid and enjoyed more advantageous conditions of service than those in the *cadre secondaire*. The demand for the *cadre unique* was therefore a demand for equal treatment with Europeans, so that African teachers would enjoy the same salaries, conditions of work and promotion opportunities as their French counterparts.

The campaign was taken up by African *députés* in the National Assembly. In an important speech, Senghor drew a distinction between what had been achieved in the education field in France's 'old' colonies, such as Martinique and Guadeloupe, and the situation in AOF, a situation for which he held the local colonial authorities responsible: 'While we are very happy to praise the work that France has done in the field of education in its old colonies, we cannot but deplore the fact that the local authorities in AOF have not been equal to their mission in this field'. He went on to criticize the Director of Education in AOF, Aubineau, for refusing to develop secondary education and denying Africans access to metropolitan qualifications out of a desire to maintain them in a position of permanent subjection: 'There has been at least one Director-General of Education, who is still in post, who has stated that he does not envisage secondary education for Africans', and he concluded: 'In sum, the intention is to limit education to the primary level, even if it is called "upper primary", and to keep it practical', citing in support the fact that there were at that time only three *lycées* in AOF, that only one out of ten African pupils who applied for a place was accepted and that, with a total of over 700 pupils, only a quarter were Africans. He took this as proof of the institutionalized inequality that existed between African and French pupils and he also cast doubt on the good faith of many of those who now attached priority to developing mass primary education in Africa, because it was often these same people who were responsible for the underdevelopment of education in Africa. He implied that their sudden professed concern for educating the masses, when set alongside their refusal to develop secondary education and their denial of grants to Africans to study in France, derived from a desire to impede African development and prevent the formation of a modern indigenous élite in Africa, as the shortage of qualified Africans could then always be used as an argument for delaying African emancipation.[21] Indeed, it was this concern that lay behind his proposal to transfer responsibility for colonial education from the Ministry for Overseas France to Education.

His tactic here is clear: if such problems existed and France had not fulfilled the promise of its 'civilizing mission' in Africa, if Africans have been denied access to secondary and higher education, it was the colonial administration in AOF that was responsible for this state of affairs. In doing this, he was appealing for support over the heads of reactionary French colonialists and officials in Africa, who had proved unworthy representatives of the mother country, to the generous traditions of republican France, to the 'true France' represented by all French people of goodwill both inside and outside Parliament.[22] As a tactic it was astute, because it did not blame France or French people in general for the problems in Africa. Instead, it separated 'good' French people who genuinely believed in the values of liberty, equality and fraternity, from 'bad' French people who did not, or who only paid lip service to them, and it held out the possibility of an alliance with French people of goodwill to promote the cause of African emancipation and create a genuine French Union based on the principle of equality.[23]

The campaign for the 'decolonization' of education was significant because of the way in which it was conducted, the broad support it gained and the wider issues in relation to the decolonization process that it raised. First of all, its significance lay in the way in which Africans exploited to the full the new political openings provided by the institutions of the French Union. The campaign was waged on a number of different fronts, all of which were opened up by the new constitution. African elected representatives in the National Assembly in Paris, the Grand Conseil in Dakar and the local assemblies (*conseils généraux*) in the different territories all took up the issue. Even if the latter did not have legislative powers, they did provide French-educated Africans with platforms from which they could gain publicity and wider public support for their demands. At the same time, taking advantage of the law authorizing trade unions, the new African teachers' unions led an effective campaign, occasionally backed up by strike action, which linked their demands for better pay and conditions and improved status for their members to the broader political campaign for the decolonization of education. In this, they could count on support not only from African elected representatives, but also from the new political parties in AOF and from most parents whose children attended a French school. They also used the press to good effect and the RDA's own newspaper, *Le Réveil*, carried regular articles on the education issue during this period, reflecting the special importance the party attributed to education in the struggle for African emancipation.[24] Even if, at the end of the day, there was no chance of these reform proposals being accepted, because the cost of implementing them was way beyond what the government was either willing or able to invest in education in Africa, the campaign did put colonial officials on the defensive.

The broader significance of the campaign for the decolonization of education lay in the way in which it highlighted both the ambiguity at the heart of post-war French policy and the ambivalence of the nationalist response. On the one hand, self-government was rejected as an option for the overseas territories, yet the alternative that was apparently proposed in the constitution, assimilation, was not a viable one. A weakened France, emerging economically and militarily diminished from the war, simply did not have the resources to finance a massive expansion of French education in Africa, as a genuine policy of assimilation would have required. The cost of such a project would, quite simply, have been unacceptable to metropolitan taxpayers. However, it could not reject outright the demand for a vast expansion and extension of the education system, because the constitutional commitment to a one and indivisible Union based on the principle of equality clearly required that Africans should have access to the same educational opportunities as French people. To have rejected outright the demand would have provoked a hostile reaction from French-educated Africans at precisely the moment when France needed to win over this group, and would have risked turning them to the other alternative, secession, which was unacceptable to the government. The only politically acceptable option for the government, therefore, was to buy time by displaying goodwill and delay the implementation of projects until money was available, while at the same time holding out the carrot of assimilation as a potential reward to deserving individuals. But, given the continent's enormous development needs, it could realistically only extend such privileges to a small, restricted élite of Africans. The conflicts over education exemplify this ambiguity.

A second level of ambiguity derives from the conflicting aims of the French government and African nationalists with regard to education. On the one hand, France viewed the provision of metropolitan education as a means of binding France and Africa more closely together and, if not actually of creating 'black Frenchmen', then at least of creating an élite of loyal French-educated Africans that was profoundly *francisé*. Africans, on the other hand, saw French education as central to their struggle for emancipation. It was their means of achieving equal status with Europeans and greater liberty. Their interest in acquiring a French education was therefore fundamentally different from the French interest in providing it. Through education, they did not want to become French, but rather to gain equal rights with French people. Calling the French government on its apparent commitment to assimilation, they invested a great deal of effort into both showing where France was falling down on its promise and campaigning for a genuinely free and equal Union. The campaign for the decolonization of education was central to this strategy. Yet even as Africans were waging a political campaign for the expansion of French education as a means to decolonization, they were being drawn into the French cultural sphere and becoming imbued with French values. Ironically, therefore, *political* success would mean greater *cultural* dependence on France. The nationalist response to the education issue was thus itself a profoundly ambivalent one, insofar as there was a tension between, on the one hand, the demand for more and better French education and on the other, the valorization and promotion of African culture through organs such as *Présence Africaine*.

The Trade Union Movement

By 1948, just over a quarter of the salaried workers in AOF had joined a trade union, making a total membership of just under 70,000, the majority of whom (over 40,000) belonged to the CGT.[25] This was nonetheless a tiny proportion of the total working population, which remained predominantly rural and dependent on agriculture. The unions, in contrast, were overwhelmingly concentrated in the towns and, given the lack of industry in French West Africa, mainly represented those working for the colonial administration and in the few modern sectors of the economy, such as the railways, ports, banks and mines. Even in these sectors, however, union membership was somewhat unstable because of the mobility of the workforce, which tended to migrate from the rural areas when food or money were short and often returned home once they had earned some money or when their help was urgently needed on the farm. This, and the lack of resources, meant that trade unions at this time had a rather precarious existence. This was to some extent overcome by forging links with metropolitan unions, in particular the CGT. The main exception to this was the railwaymen's union, which was 'autonome' and organized into a federation representing all railway workers. In all, some 17,500 workers belonged to unions that were *autonome*.

The links with metropolitan unions brought benefits in terms of resources and organizational capacity to a young trade union movement that desperately lacked both of these, but it also created problems. Trade unions in AOF were originally formed to represent and defend the interests of French workers, with the result that their discourse and their approach to industrial disputes tended to be dominated by their metropolitan counterparts.[26] Thus, the CGT, like the PCF, saw the struggle for independence as inextricably linked with the emancipation of the working class in the *métropole*, which remained the political priority. Although it was anti-imperialist, it did not therefore recognize the autonomy of African workers' struggles and put the emphasis instead on the union of French and African workers in their common struggle against oppression and economic exploitation. As a result, the specifically African dimension of a dispute was not always acknowledged and it was more difficult for workers' movements to feed into, or be seen as expressions of, a nascent African nationalism.

The main campaigns of the union movement during this period were for 'equal pay for equal work' and for the adoption of a new labour code. The campaign for 'equal pay for equal work' represented a rejection not only of the old colonial regime that largely confined African workers to the worst-paid jobs on separate, lower grades from French workers, but also of the attitudes of many French workers in AOF, who remained attached to the old, discriminatory regime.[27] Against this, African workers demanded the creation of a *cadre unique* and, once this principle had been conceded, they campaigned for its honest, non-discriminatory implementation. As we shall see below, this was the issue underlying the railway workers' dispute, and similar campaigns were waged by the teachers' and other white collar workers' unions, culminating in the adoption by the National Assembly of the Second Lamine Guèye Law on 30 June 1950. In theory, this law made discrimination on grounds of race between workers doing the same work illegal, although the victory was in some ways a hollow one because the Administration had various devices by means of which most African workers continued to be denied access to the same *cadres* as French workers, or found it more difficult to reach the higher ranks of the *cadre* once they had gained access to it. The campaign for parity of treatment did not therefore come to an end in 1950.

The second major campaign of this period was for a new labour code. Following the abolition of forced labour in 1946, no new labour code had been adopted to regulate labour in the overseas territories. Within the 'one and indivisible' French Union, there was logically no place for a separate labour code for the overseas territories and it should simply have been a question of extending the metropolitan Code to the colonies. In 1947, two African senators, Ousmane Socé Diop and Mamadou Fodé Touré, introduced a bill to this effect in the Conseil de la République (France's upper house, or Senate), and shortly before leaving office as Minister for Overseas France, Marius Moutet also attempted to get a new labour code, based on the metropolitan Code, adopted. Both attempts failed and the issue was to drag on for another five years. The problem for the government was that it raised broader issues to do with whether or not metropolitan *social citizenship* rights, which included social security and family allowances as well as labour legislation, as opposed to purely *political* rights, should be extended overseas. The language of equal rights contained in the Constitution suggested that they should be. Thus, in this campaign, as in the 'equal pay for equal work' campaign, the trade unions took up and exploited the rhetoric of equal rights to challenge the racial discrimination at the heart of the colonial regime by demanding that these rights be extended to African workers. The government recoiled before the cost of such measures and expressed concern about the practicality of applying them in the context of the traditional African extended family and in a situation where so much of the workforce was unstable. It hesitated and procrastinated for five years before finally, and reluctantly, adopting a new overseas labour code.

The Railway Strike of 1947–8

The most famous strike of the period was the railway strike of 1947–8, which has been dramatized in Ousmane Sembene's novel *Les Bouts de Bois de Dieu* (*God's Bits of Wood*). It began in October 1947, ended in March 1948 and involved almost 18,000 workers in the Fédération des Syndicats des Cheminots Africains. In the dispute that led to the strike, two issues were involved. The first related to the integration of *auxiliaires* (temporary workers) and the second to the *cadre unique*. The great majority of railwaymen (nearly 90 per cent) were *auxiliaires*, which meant that they were employed as temporary workers, despite the fact that many of them had worked on the railway for many years and were highly skilled. They were also paid less than members of the *cadres* and, unlike the latter, had no job security and were not housed. The first demand was therefore for *auxiliaires* to be given permanent jobs. And the second was for all railwaymen, white and black, to be integrated without distinction into a single *cadre* and treated in the same way, with equal pay and benefits.

Figure 3.1 The Dakar-Niger Railway: Bamako Station. © Tony Chafer.

The union's demands were initially submitted to a *commission paritaire* (joint negotiating body) in August 1946. The commission comprised representatives from both sides of the dispute and its task was to discuss the issues separating the two sides with a view to finding a solution. By April 1947, the situation had been made more difficult by the refusal of the unions representing European workers to entertain the idea of a *cadre unique* and their defence of racial privilege. No solution was in sight, so the Fédération decided to stage a strike of African workers to coincide with the visit to Senegal of the French President and the Minister for Overseas France. The Government-General could not be seen denying the principle of equality in the presence of leading government represent-atives from the *métropole* and wanted to avoid a prolonged strike during the visit. The principle of the *cadre unique* was therefore conceded and the commission was left to work out the details. As a result, the strike came to an end after just three days.

By October, the rail company had rejected the commission's proposals for settling the outstanding issues, which included such vitally important matters as how the different *cadres* would be integrated, the points on the new pay scales to which workers would be allocated, and how many *auxiliaires* would be admitted into the *cadre unique*. The strike resumed and lasted five-and-a-half months across most of the network, but less long on the Abidjan-Niger line where Houphouët-Boigny was instrumental in persuading the railwaymen to return to work in January 1948, over two months earlier than elsewhere. Workers on the rest of the network returned to work in March, following an intervention by the new Governor-General, Paul Béchard, a Socialist politician appointed to 'restore order in AOF'.[28] He proposed a number of compromises, backing the company on its refusal to pay the same cost of living indemnity to all workers (this had been introduced to compensate workers for variations in the cost of living in different areas) and insistence on maintaining a hierarchical system, and supporting it in its unwillingness to guarantee housing, or a housing allowance, to all workers, but going part of the way to meet the union's demand for the retroactive integration of *auxiliaires* and its claims concerning the reclassification of workers within the new *cadre unique*. He also decided that no strikers would be punished.

The strike was significant at a number of different levels. Firstly, it showed how, in the new post-war political circumstances, the colonial authorities were no longer able to fall back on the old colonial method of repression to end the dispute, but felt they had to negotiate. They were on the defensive, forced to recognize that the language of assimilation, integration and equal rights, which was the price of maintaining French imperial control after the war, itself had a price, which was that Africans expected France to deliver on the promise of reform that it contained.

Secondly, the strike demonstrated once again how effectively African unions had learnt to exploit the new official colonial discourse of assimilation to their own advantage. The union's new general secretary, Ibrahima Sarr, had showed that he could exploit the commitment to equal rights contained in the constitution to press his members' demands for better pay and treatment. In his first speech, in May 1946, he called for an end to the 'antiquated colonial methods condemned even by *the new and true France* which wishes that all its children, at whatever latitude they may live, should be equal in duties and rights and *that the recompense of labour should be a function solely of merit and capacity*'.[29] Obliged by its own rhetoric to concede the principle of equality, but frightened by the high cost of full implementation of the *cadre unique*, the authorities gave way on the principle but, in order to keep costs down and retain as much control as they could, then sought to implement it in restrictive ways that were ultimately discriminatory. The strike was a victory for neither side, but Africans had obliged the authorities to concede a share of power to the union.[30] The union also knew that they now had a stick – equal rights – with which to beat the colonial authorities and mobilize African support against the colonial regime each time it could be shown that the authorities had not lived up to their promise.

Thirdly, the dispute was significant for the fact that the strike movement remained confined to the rail sector. The railwaymen had not joined the Dakar general strike of January 1946 and now other unions did not come out in solidarity with the railwaymen, although some unions did provide financial support to the striking workers. Similarly on the political front, the main African political party, the RDA, did not become involved in the strike and no African political leader came out openly in support of the strikers. Indeed some, such as Houphouët-Boigny and Fily Dabo Sissoko, actually schemed behind the scenes to get them to return to work.[31] As a result, the strike did not become part of a wider movement for African liberation, in which the forces of labour united and joined with nationalist political parties to promote the cause of African emancipation. There were many obstacles to such a mobilization at this time in French West Africa. The railwaymen's union was *autonome*, whereas most of the other unions in AOF were affiliated to metropolitan unions; collective bargaining procedures were at the time being established sector by sector in AOF, which gave unions in their respective sectors the hope that, by working within these, they would make significant gains for their members; and in Côte d'Ivoire, the main political party, the PDCI-RDA, had its roots in the peasant farmers' union, the SAA, which was worried about the effect of the strike on its business, because it risked preventing the farmers from getting their harvest to market. As a result, the RDA leadership tended to view the dispute as a railway matter, to be settled between the company and the union.

This should not, however, lead us completely to deny the anti-colonial dimension to the strike. Certainly, it was about a range of purely 'professional' issues, but the underlying issue for the strikers was to test the real level of commitment of the company, and beyond it the Administration, to the principle of equal rights. This meant not only agreeing to the principle of equal pay for equal work, but also being prepared to share power with Africans. As Fred Cooper has remarked: 'The real issue [of the strike] was power: who was to control the process by which new modalities of labour organization would be worked out?'[32] In the specific context of this strike, it meant a willingness to negotiate in good faith with the union on crucial questions concerning the implementation of the *cadre unique* and the integration of *auxiliaires*. So when the company rejected outright the proposals put forward by the *commission paritaire* to resolve the dispute, the union felt such good faith was not forthcoming and it was this sense of betrayal that provoked the strike and gave it its anti-colonial dimension. It was in this respect that the strike contributed, albeit indirectly, to a nascent nationalism in French West Africa.[33]

Political Parties

At the beginning of the period under study here, there were two main political groupings in French West Africa: the RDA and the Socialists. This is reflected in the results of the National Assembly elections, which took place on 10 November 1946. Thirteen West African *députés* were elected, six RDA and seven SFIO. By the end of this period, several *députés* had left these parties and joined a new group in the National Assembly, the Indépendants d'Outre-Mer (IOM). By 1950 as a result, the SFIO and RDA each had just four West African *députés*, while six (including three extra *députés* elected from Haute-Volta in 1948) had joined the IOM. Unlike the RDA and SFIO, the IOM were purely a parliamentary group, formed with official encouragement in order to undercut the RDA, and had no party organization in Africa.[34]

Députés of the RDA were not sufficiently numerous to form a separate parliamentary group. In need of an alliance in order to maximize their effectiveness, they decided to affiliate to the Communist Party. However, they were not communists and this decision did not reflect their ideological position. Rather, the PCF was the most consistently anti-imperialist of the French political parties in its doctrine: it had supported the RDA at its founding congress in Bamako and, among the metropolitan parties, it had been the most consistently supportive of the African *députés* in the Constituent Assemblies. It was therefore natural that, in seeking a parliamentary alliance, the RDA *députés* should look to the PCF.

The Party itself was a broad coalition of territory-based parties covering a wide spectrum of political views. Houphouët-Boigny, its leader and also leader of its Ivoirian section, the PDCI, whose main support base was among the Ivoirian coffee and cocoa planters, represented its conservative wing, whereas Gabriel d'Arboussier, one of the party's vice-presidents (he was elected Secretary-General at the Party's 1949 congress), who was a Councillor of the French Union and a member of the Conseil Général of Côte d'Ivoire, represented the current within the party that was closest to the PCF.[35] The PCF for its part had decided not to organize in Black Africa: 'It is certainly not appropriate for the RDA to transform itself into an African communist party. However, in its struggle as an African mass movement opposed to colonialism, it has a reliable ally in the French working class and in the French Communist Party, which is its political expression'.[36] The decision to join with the

PCF was, however, to cost the RDA dear. In May 1947, Communist ministers were forced to leave the government, the PCF went into opposition and France's own internal 'Cold War' started. The PCF was now bitterly opposed by its former partners in the tripartite government, the centre-right MRP and the Socialists. The RDA, which they considered a Communist satellite organization, was vigorously repressed. Ironically, since the PDCI was probably the most conservative of the RDA's constituent parties, the focus for this repressive action was Côte d'Ivoire, which was considered an RDA stronghold. If the Party could be broken there, its opponents believed, the PCF's pernicious influence in the rest of Black Africa would be fatally undermined. Thus, in late 1948, Paul Coste-Floret, the MRP Minister for Overseas France, appointed the Socialist Laurent Péchoux as Governor of Côte d'Ivoire with the specific mission to 'break' the RDA.[37]

The first confrontation was not long in coming. The former RDA senator, Etienne Djaument, having not had his mandate renewed by the Party, decided to launch a rival party and called a meeting to this end at Treichville on 6 February 1949. Activists of the PDCI set out to disrupt the meeting, as a result of which one person was killed, several were injured and property was damaged. Governor Péchoux reacted by arresting and imprisoning several of the PDCI's leading figures. Further incidents ensued throughout 1949, for which the authorities blamed the RDA but which the latter accused the former of deliberately provoking. Then, in December, the RDA leaders who had been imprisoned in February and who were still being held without trial, went on hunger strike. The RDA supported them by launching a boycott of European goods for the Christmas period, which particularly affected French shopkeepers, and the wives of the detainees organized a march on the prison in Grand-Bassam where they were being held, which was supported by thousands of other women. There were more incidents in January 1950, the most serious of which, at Dimbokro, resulted in thirteen deaths. In the midst of the troubles, Houphouët-Boigny himself narrowly missed being arrested, despite his parliamentary immunity as a *député*. By the end of 1950, the accused in the Treichville affair had received prison sentences of three to five years, some fifty Africans had lost their lives, many more had been wounded and some 3,000 had been imprisoned, of whom 274 were in prison in Grand-Bassam alone.[38]

RDA activists elsewhere in AOF were subjected to pressure from the colonial administration, notably in Haute-Volta. Following its reconstitution as a territory in 1947, which was also incidentally part of a strategy for reducing the RDA's influence, the new governor, Mouragues, made it his business to defeat the RDA at the elections for *députés* to represent the territory in the National Assembly and in the elections to the new *conseil général* in 1948. Then, in December 1948, the RDA was banned from holding its second congress at Bobo-Dioulasso (Haute-Volta) and it had to be transferred to Abidjan, where it opened on 2 January. Despite this repression, the Party continued to support the maintenance of close links with France. It held to its line that it was not a secessionist party, but an anti-colonial party committed to the cause of African emancipation through the achievement of equal rights within the context of the French Union. The repression did, however, lead Houphouët-Boigny and his close collaborators in the RDA leadership to reassess the link with the PCF. They had seen a wave of anti-Communism unfurl in France at the same time as repression against the RDA in French West Africa. On the one hand, this appeared to lend support to the Communist Party's line that the interests of the French working class and of colonial peoples were the same and that only the coming to power of a Communist government in France would lead to African emancipation. On the other hand, RDA leaders knew that the Party had lost influence since the departure of the Communists from government. The MRP was the dominant party in government and held the Ministry for Overseas France, the IOM were close to the MRP, and RDA *députés* found that it was difficult to make progress on behalf of their electorates through alliance with a party that was in opposition: 'It is beyond doubt that the overseas *députés* cannot gain anything for their country through system-atic opposition to the government majority'. Houphouët-Boigny also suggested that the link with the Communist Party was an obstacle to African unity and prevented the RDA from cooperating with other French people 'of goodwill' for African emancipation: 'We must unite all Africans, kill off the false pretext, the communist pretext, and cooperate with all men of goodwill'.[39]

The path to disaffiliation was eased by the new Minister for Overseas France in René Pleven's government, François Mitterrand. By relaxing the pressure on the RDA, going to Abidjan to open the new port in February 1951 and, in May, replacing both Governor-General Béchard and Governor Péchoux, Mitterrand also opened the way for the RDA to affiliate to his party, the Union Démocratique et Sociale de la Résistance (UDSR), in January 1952.

The decision to disaffiliate was announced on 18 October 1950. The new line, which was presented by Houphouët-Boigny as a new tactic rather than a change of policy, provoked disbelief on the part of many colonial officials and provoked a split within the Party. In pursuing its new line, the Party leadership was obliged to walk a tightrope between rejection from two diametrically opposed quarters. On the one hand, many colonial officials did not believe that the new policy of cooperation with the Administration represented a genuine change of heart, but simply a tactical retreat to allow the Party to regroup. On the other, a section of the Party, led by the Secretary-General d'Arboussier, believed exactly the opposite, that the new line was not a tactical retreat but represented a major change in Party strategy that betrayed the interests of the African people and broke with the Party's policy of independence vis-à-vis the Administration. This section of the Party developed a radical critique of French colonial policy, believing that it and not the party leadership was remaining loyal to the Party's original stance agreed at Bamako, and it rapidly emerged as a radical movement of internal opposition to the Party leadership. Its political avant-garde, and much of its support, came from a new generation of activists based in the RDA students' association (Association des Etudiants RDA: AERDA) and the Party's youth wing (Rassemblement de la Jeunesse Démocratique Africaine: RJDA). This development was to be profoundly significant for the future political evolution of French West Africa.

The second main political grouping in AOF in 1946 was the SFIO. Its tradition, dating back to before the Popular Front, was assimilationist, and its political stronghold was Senegal, where Lamine Guèye was the party leader. Senghor, who had initially been brought into politics as Guèye's *protégé*, was also an SFIO member, but he increasingly felt that the metropolitan Party exerted too strong an influence over the Party in Africa and that it was too preoccupied by metropolitan matters to pay sufficient attention to the needs of Africa. He resigned from the Party on 27 September 1948 and shortly afterwards announced the creation of a new party, the Bloc Démocratique Sénégalais (BDS), the inaugural congress of which took place from 15–17 April 1949 at Thiès. Senghor also left the Socialist group in the National Assembly and joined the IOM group. He was joined by Apithy of Dahomey and, by 1950, the SFIO was very much in decline, with only four West African *députés* still affiliated to it. In the 1951 parliamentary elections it was also to lose its leading political figure, Lamine Guèye.

Three general points can be made about the nature and action of AOF political parties during this period. Firstly, French West Africa's main political parties emerged after the war as offshoots from, or in alliance with, metropolitan parties. None of the parties with which they were associated supported African independence, although the PCF's language was vigorously anti-imperialist. During this period, African leaders became concerned that their close links with metropolitan parties, while helpful to them in the National Assembly when the party with which they were associated was in power, were not necessarily the best means of furthering the cause of African emancipation. The main focus of metropolitan parties' policies and actions was, naturally, on domestic issues, and, insofar as colonial matters were an issue, the priority, particularly from May 1947 onwards, was the developing crisis in Indochina. Moreover, the alliances with rival metropolitan parties were seen as constituting an obstacle to African unity. African leaders therefore sought to increase the autonomy of their parties – in the case of the RDA by breaking free from the Communist link and in Senghor's case by breaking free from the SFIO. They nevertheless remained committed to working for African emancipation and decolonization within the context of the French Union.

The question of African unity proved a harder nut to crack, however, and the decision to loosen their links with metropolitan parties did not in the end lead to closer cooperation. The main political parties in AOF grew up on a territory-by-territory basis, generally behind strong political leaders who built a base of political support within their own territory. These leaders, all of whom belonged to the small French-educated élite, gained election to the National Assembly in Paris and gradually established their political authority. Apart from a commitment to working for African emancipation within the context of the French Union, which they all shared, the unity of these new political parties was rooted more in loyalty to a particular leader than to a party programme. Although ideology was to be increasingly important, especially for the new generation of activists in the youth and student movements who constituted the main internal opposition to the political leaders of AOF during the 1950s, this personalization of politics had a significant determining influence on the nature of the decolonization process in AOF. In 1950, no one imagined that, within ten years, the whole of French West Africa would be independent. But the pace of events was to accelerate rapidly and, in the turmoil of the rush to independence, loyalty to, and trust in a particular political leader was often more important than a detailed understanding of, or commitment to, what they stood for. In the end, therefore, the historical baggage of personal rivalries, ideological differences and conflicting interests, notably but not only between Houphouët-Boigny and Senghor, proved too burdensome to overcome quickly and was to be a significant contributory factor to the way in which French West Africa ultimately achieved independence as eight separate states rather than as a federation.

Finally, the main political parties and their leaders exploited the colonial myth of a Greater France composed of the *métropole* and overseas territories in their campaign for equality. The language of equal rights and freedoms based on citizenship was a powerful weapon in the context of the French republican tradition with its commitment to liberty and equality, and it was one that African political leaders used to good effect in the first years of the French Union to win reforms and make gains on behalf of their electorate. There were several problems with this strategy, however. Its success depended on political goodwill, and the availability of resources, from the *métropole*, without which the process of reform and modernization in Africa would stall. Such goodwill was more scarce in the period 1947-50 than it had been immediately after the war and the reform process slowed accordingly. As this happened, it became more difficult for the government and African political leaders to keep the lid on more radical African nationalist demands. A further problem was that, given the wide economic gap between France and Black Africa and the latter's enormous development needs, real equality of rights with Europeans was only ever likely to be achieved by a tiny minority of the African population. This was frustrating, especially for the growing number of young French-educated Africans in AOF who rapidly came to see this gradualist approach as an obstacle to the realization of their aspirations for real political change. The strategy therefore carried the risk of African disillusionment, with inevitable political consequences not only for the French Union but also for those African political leaders who favoured maintaining the French link. The problem was that, as advocates of maintaining close ties with France, they became identified, by association, with a colonial policy that many younger French-educated Africans increasingly rejected. This created a political space to their left for political and social movements to emerge that were more critical of the French link, and it was not to be long before a new, more radical, anti-colonial nationalist movement emerged to fill this space.

The Côte d'Ivoire incidents of 1949–50 and subsequent rejection by RDA students and the party's youth wing of the leadership's decision to disaffiliate from the PCF were a watershed in this respect, and also an indicator of the problems that lay ahead. The way in which African political leaders bought into the French colonial myth created problems for them and their parties, as it locked them into the logic, and concerns, of French metropolitan politics. The decision by some African leaders to loosen or break free from their alliances with metropolitan parties was a recognition of this problem, but the fact that they still sat in the National

Assembly, were leading advocates of continuing union with France and depended on metropolitan political support and goodwill to achieve their aims, meant that their autonomy from French politics remained limited. More seriously, it tied their political fortunes to France and implicated them politically in France's colonial policy, thereby associating them with the conduct of France's two colonial wars and running the risk of alienating them from their own supporters in Africa. We shall return to this theme in the next chapter.

Conclusion: The Shaping of the Nationalist Movement in AOF

In this chapter, we have seen how, in order to appreciate why African nationalism took the particular form that it did in French West Africa, it has been essential to understand the historical circumstances and the specific policy context in which it emerged. Thus, a central theme of this chapter has been to show that at the heart of the French Union there was a fundamental ambivalence, which was to have a profound impact on the nature of the nationalist movement in French West Africa.[40] For France's governing élites, the French Union, and the language of assimilation that underpinned it, was a means of cementing the bonds that tied Africa to France. The maintenance of empire was crucial to the re-establishment of France's rank in the post-war world and the 1946 Constitution was intended to cement the link by integrating the colonies more fully with the métropole. This was the policy context, which conditioned French attitudes to empire and set the framework for colonial policy making during this period. African leaders, in contrast, adopted the language of assimilation, not because they wanted to become French, but because their priority was equal rights for Africans and they saw this as a stepping stone to acquiring greater control over their own affairs and eventual African emancipation. As D. Bruce Marshall has aptly remarked: 'The colonial myth provided both metropolitan and colonial deputies with appropriate symbols to justify conflicting constitutional proposals tailored to serve their respective conceptions of unity'.[41] Given this profound difference of perspective with regard to the purpose of the Union, tensions were inevitable and provided fertile ground for the development of the diverse elements of the nationalist movement in French West Africa.

In this respect, the 'universalist' language of assimilation proved a two-edged sword for the government, because it was enthusiastically adopted by post-war African social and political movements to press their demands for real equality of rights with Europeans. The campaigns for the decolonization of education, for equal pay for equal work, for a new labour code modelled on metropolitan labour legislation, and for the extension of social security benefits and family allowances to Africa, were all of a piece insofar as the common theme underlying each of them was the demand for equality. African trade unionists and politicians were able to show how, in each of these different domains, France was failing to live up to its promise of a Union based on the principle of equality. Moreover, given the constitutional commitment to equal rights, it was an argument that the government could not simply ignore. The problem from the French point of view was that, each time it made a concession to African demands, this made the French dream of building a 'modern' Africa within the colonial system increasingly unaffordable.

The emergence of this 'assimilationist' form of nationalism and its focus on achieving equal rights also created problems for the the early post-war nationalist movement in French West Africa, as it tended to 'segment' campaigns within discrete socio-economic sectors. For African railwaymen, the priority was to achieve equality with French rail workers; for teachers, it was to achieve equality with French teachers, and so on. This trend was also encouraged by the growing importance of the Work Inspectorate, which set up metropolitan-style industrial relations machinery on a sector by sector basis in French West Africa. As a result, African unions tended to confine their demands within professional boundaries, because they saw the benefits to their members of working within the collective bargaining procedures that had been established, and the unity of purpose demonstrated by the trade unions in the Dakar general strike of 1946 became more difficult to achieve. Another effect of this segmentation of disputes was that it tended to divide socio-economic issues off from broader political questions. Trade union demands were confined to the socio-economic sphere and not linked to the broader political struggle for African emancipation. The effect of this was to weaken the nationalist movement as a *movement*, since its action was largely confined to the political domain, but conversely to strengthen the position of African political *leaders*, who were able more easily to dominate the weakly structured and often rather diffuse political groupings they headed.

Notes

1. K. Robinson, 'Colonialism French-style, 1945–55: a backward glance', *Journal of Imperial and Commonwealth History*, 12, 2, 1984, p. 38.
2. See in particular R. Girardet, *L'Idée coloniale en France de 1871 à 1962* (La Table Ronde, 1972).
3. See A. Conklin, *A Mission to Civilize* (Stanford University Press, 1997).
4. See D. Bruce Marshall, *The French Colonial Myth and Constitution-Making in the Fourth Republic* (Yale University Press, 1973).
5. The most comprehensive rationale for a policy of *mise en valeur* was provided by Albert Sarraut in his *La Mise en valeur des colonies françaises* (Payot, 1923). For a discussion of the Popular Front's reform projects, see T. Chafer and A. Sackur, eds, *French Colonial Empire and the Popular Front* (Macmillan, 1999).
6. C. De Gaulle, *Discours et messages* (Plon, 1970), vol. 2, p. 81.
7. See A. Clayton, *The Wars of French Decolonization* (Longman, 1994).
8. C.-R. Ageron, *France coloniale ou parti colonial?* (Presses Universitaires de France, 1978), pp. 259–68; J. D. Hargreaves, 'The Africanist International and the Popular Front', in T. Chafer and A. Sackur, eds., *French Colonial Empire*, pp. 74–87. For a general discussion of French attitudes to empire, see T. Chafer and A. Sackur, eds, *Promoting the Colonial Idea: Propaganda and Visions of Empire in France* (Palgrave, 2002), pp. 1–11.
9. The experience of Jean Capelle, who was Rector of Education in AOF from 1947–9 and 1954–7, is illustrative in this respect. Appointed by the Education Ministry, his terms of office were marked by a running battle with officials in the Ministry for Overseas France, who effectively forced him out of office. See J. Capelle, *L'Education en Afrique noire* (Karthala, 1990) and T. Chafer, *Decolonisation and the Politics of Education in French West Africa, 1944–58* (PhD thesis, University of London, 1993), chapter 2. The discussions of the proposed transfer of responsibility for education to the Education Ministry and the Ministry for Overseas France's arguments against the proposal are in MinEd F17bis3298.
10. Cf. report by a 1952 government-appointed mission to AOF in ANSOM Aff. Pol. 2111/1.
11. F. Cooper, *Decolonization and African Society* (Cambridge University Press, 1996), p. 17.

12. Ibid, p. 226.
13. For an analysis of the central importance attached by the Inspectorate to organizing work on a rational basis and to job classification and differentiation, see ibid, pp. 232–3.
14. This is not intended to suggest that I agree with the 'Gaullist' explanation for the failings of the Fourth Republic in the field of colonial policy, which essentially attributed France's problems during this period to the instability of parties and parliamentary coalitions. On the contrary, I am inclined to agree with those historians, such as D. Bruce Marshall, who have suggested that the problem lay with political and bureaucratic élites that were unable to accept and adapt to decolonization. My point here is that, even if decolonization envisaged as a process leading to self-government was not yet on the agenda of any leading politician or bureaucrat, certain reforms could have been introduced earlier and the colonial policy logjam at least partly broken, if governments had been in a position to give a stronger lead. In the end, such reforms had to wait until 1956–8 to be introduced, by which time they were already obsolete.
15. A. Conklin, *A Mission to Civilize*, pp. 187–202.
16. M. Michel, *Décolonisations et émergence du tiers monde* (Hachette, 1993), pp. 86–100.
17. A. Shennan, *Rethinking France* (Clarendon Press, 1989), p. 164.
18. T. Chafer, *Decolonisation*, pp. 378–9.
19. D. Bouche, 'L'école rurale en Afrique Occidentale Française', pp. 276–85, in *Etudes africaines offertes à Henri Brunschwig* (Publications de l'EHESS, 1982).
20. J. Capelle, *L'Education*, p. 81.
21. Session of 21 March 1946, *Journal Officiel Débats Parlementaires (JODP)*, 22 March 1946, pp. 945–7.
22. Cf. article by Doudou Guèye under the headline: 'Jean Rose et ses amis sont de mauvais Français' in *Le Réveil*, 10 October 1946, p. 1. Jean Rose was the *colon* who played the leading role in organizing the Etats Généraux de la Colonisation Française. Letters from Africans intercepted by the security services during 1944–5, copies of which are contained in AAOF 21G159/108, provide an insight into the extent to which such views were held by members of the French-speaking African élite.
23. It won him immediate support from metropolitan politicians of the Left, such as Pierre Cot, see session of 23 March 1946, *JODP*, 24 March 1946, pp. 1044–5.

24. If we take 1947 as an example, *Le Réveil* published front-page articles on education issues once a month on average. A recurring theme was the 'sabotage' of education in AOF by the Administration, cf. 'Sabotage de l'enseignement', 22 September 1947, pp. 1–2.
25. G. Martens, 'Le syndicalisme en Afrique occidentale française de 1945 à 1960', *Syndicalisme et Développement*, numéro spécial. March 1982, p. 12.
26. See P. Dewitte, 'La CGT et les syndicats d'Afrique Occidentale Française', *Mouvement social*, 117, 1981, pp. 6–7.
27. R. Cruise O'Brien, *White Society in Black Africa: The French of Senegal* (Faber & Faber, 1972), pp. 81–2.
28. This was the explanation given for Béchard's appointment by Paul Coste-Floret, Minister for Overseas France at the time. Quoted in J.-R. de Benoist, *L'Afrique Occidentale Française de 1944 à 1960* (Nouvelles Editions Africaines, 1982), p. 87.
29. AAOF K352/26, 'Renseignements', 29 May 1946, quoted by F. Cooper, *Decolonization*, p. 242. For his treatment of the railway strike, see pp. 241–8 in the above and '"Our Strike": equality, anti-colonial politics and the 1947–8 railway strike in French West Africa', *Journal of African History*, 37, 1996, pp. 81–118.
30. According to F. Cooper, 30 per cent of railwaymen were integrated into the *cadre* by 1950, compared to 12 per cent when the strike started, *Decolonization*, p. 247.
31. Ibid, pp. 244–6.
32. F. Cooper, '"Our Strike"', p. 91.
33. For a useful survey of strike movements in AOF, see J. Suret-Canale, 'Strike Movements as Part of the Anticolonial Struggle in French West Africa', in G. Maddox and T. Welliver, *Colonialism and Nationalism in Africa* (Garland, 1993), pp. 106–18.
34. R. S. Morgenthau, *Political Parties in French-Speaking West Africa* (Clarendon Press, 1964), pp. 93–4.
35. For a biography of d'Arboussier, see note 2, chapter 4.
36. R. Barbé, president of the Communist group in the Assembly of the French Union, circular dated 20 July 1948, cited in J.-R. de Benoist, *L'Afrique Occidentale Française*, p. 106.
37. G. Chaffard, *Les Carnets secrets de la décolonisation* (Calmann-Lévy, 1965), vol. 1, p. 107.
38. *1946–1986. Il y a 40 ans naissait le PDCI* (Fraternité-Hebdo Editions, 1997), pp. 83–110. See also report no. 11,348, Commission d'enquête de l'Assemblée Nationale sur les incidents survenus en Côte d'Ivoire, 3 vols, 1950, usually known as the 'Damas report'.

39. *1946–1986. Il y a 40 ans naissait le PDCI* (Fraternité-Hebdo Editions, 1997), p. 115.
40. The ambiguous nature of citizenship of the French Union conferred by the Lamine Guèye Law of 1946, which granted all residents of the Union citizenship but without conferring on them the same rights as French citizens, exemplifies this ambivalence.
41. D. Bruce Marshall, *The French Colonial Myth*, p. 209.

–4–

Building the Nationalist Movement 1950–6: The Trade Union, Student and Youth Movements

The period 1950–6 was the period during which nationalism came of age as a political *movement* in French West Africa. Expanding education, improved literacy, rapid urbanization, better communications, increasing trade union activity and the new opportunities for political participation afforded by the creation of the French Union, all these factors meant that the conditions for the emergence of a modern nationalist movement were now present in French West Africa. It still faced an uphill task, however, as there were many obstacles to overcome before a federation-wide nationalist movement could successfully be established. The 'segment-ation' of workers' struggles, their separation from the political sphere, and the close links that political parties had, and that trade unions continued to have, with metropolitan organizations posed major difficulties for the construction of a cohesive, federation-wide nationalist movement. Even if the main political leaders of AOF had by 1950 broken free from their formal links with metropolitan parties, they continued to work closely with the French government and with metropolitan political leaders. Moreover, the fact that the roots of French West African political parties lay in the separate constituent territories of AOF was a problem. The first inter-territorial party, the RDA, had been created at Bamako in 1946, but its federal structure remained fairly loose and it was in practice, as its name suggested, a *rassemblement* (grouping together) of a number of separate, territory-based parties. Furthermore, the decision by Senegal's political leaders to stay away from Bamako meant that the RDA never had a strong presence in the territory that was the political centre of the federation, Senegal. Personal rivalries also played their part. Taken together, these were major factors militating against the creation of a federation-wide nationalist movement in French West Africa.

A nationalist movement did nonetheless emerge during this period. Although there were no further incidents leading to bloodshed and loss of life, as happened in Côte d'Ivoire in 1949–50, the period did witness an intensification of anti-colonial activity, for which this new, more radical, nationalist movement was largely responsible. The focus of this chapter will therefore be on the different groups that composed the movement, their political activities and ideology, and on the reactions of the French government and African political leaders to it.

The decision of the RDA leadership to disaffiliate from the PCF produced a split within the emerging nationalist movement. On the one hand, there were those, such as Houphouët-Boigny and Ouezzin Coulibaly,[1] who believed that a position of systematic opposition was not the best way forward and that a policy of cooperation with the government would produce more benefits for Africans. The problems they had suffered as a result of the link with the PCF were seen as proof of this. Opposed to this view were those, led within the RDA by d'Arboussier[2] and Cheikh Anta Diop,[3] who believed that the best means of putting an end to the colonial system was through an alliance with the PCF and, through it, with the international forces of anti-imperialism in the Third International. The first view was shared by all the leading political figures of AOF, including those such as Senghor and Sissoko who were otherwise opposed to the RDA, and they led the main political parties, so those who favoured the latter view often combined working within the mainstream political parties with activism in other organizations in an effort to build a broad movement in support of their position. Trade unions, youth and student associations and other groups within civil society became a major focus for their activity. At the same time, they formed quasi-autonomous groups within the main political parties in an attempt to influence their leaders' stance. Within the RDA, these were the Rassemblement de la Jeunesse Démocratique Africaine (RJDA) and the Association des Etudiants RDA (AERDA). The other main parties, such as the BDS and the SFIO, also had youth wings that became a focus for radical opposition to French colonialism and at the same time a radical movement of internal opposition to the ideology and political strategy of their leaders. The groups that composed this new, more radical, nationalist movement thus operated outside the main political parties while at the same time forming groups within them which sought to change the party line. Although more radical than the political leaders of AOF in their critique of French colonialism, they were not initially secessionist. However, this was to change as they rapidly became disillusioned with the painfully slow rate of progress towards African emancipation within the French Union, and they were soon to set their sights on new political horizons by calling for political independence.

Trade Unions and the Nationalist Struggle

Narratives of nationalist success have tended to interpret labour struggles as part of the broader social mobilization in Africa against colonial rule. Yet we have already seen that the link between strikes and labour unrest on the one hand, and the political struggle for African liberation on the other, cannot be taken for granted. The explanation for this lies in the specific historical circumstances in which the trade union movement emerged in French West Africa after the war.

The French project to build a modern Africa within the colonial system, underpinned by the 'universalist' language of assimilation, led colonial officials after the war to seek to treat African workers like 'normal' French workers. Metropolitan-style industrial relations structures were introduced and the Work Inspectorate dealt with labour disputes in French West Africa on a sector by sector basis as purely professional disputes. In response, trade unionists in AOF successfully used the assimilationist rhetoric of official French colonial discourse to deny that there was any justification for treating French and African workers differently and demand equal pay and conditions for African workers. At the same time, the close links between African unions and French metropolitan *centrales* contributed to the downplaying of any potentially nationalist dimension to African labour struggles.

This 'assimilationist' strategy, which was rooted in the 'universalist' claim that African workers were no different from their French counterparts and therefore ought to be treated like them, brought major benefits to African trade unionists. The Second Lamine Guèye Law represented a triumph for this strategy, as a result of which the earnings gap between French and African employees, especially in the civil service, closed considerably, so that by the mid-1950s the latter represented a privileged minority among the AOF workforce.[4] In the private sector, strike action led to a 20 per cent pay increase in 1953. Other victories for this strategy were the adoption of the new Labour Code and the extension of family allowances entitlement to the families of African workers, exactly ten years after it was first mooted by the unions during the Dakar general strike. With these successes under its belt, it is not surprising that the trade unions already represented a third of AOF's waged workers by the mid-1950s.[5]

Part of the success of this strategy was a product of the fact that French colonial modernizers to some extent shared with African trade unions the same objective, which was to build a modern, 'Europeanized' Africa under colonialism after the war. Central to this project was the creation of a modern African working class that was stable, educated, productive and dependable.[6] African trade unionists also wanted to build a modern, productive Africa, and argued that this could only be achieved if the African worker was treated as a modern worker and this meant offering him (it was taken for granted that the African salaried worker was a male) the same wage incentives and the same working conditions as his French counterpart. Thus, although there were, on occasion, major disagreements between African trade unions and the colonial officials with whom they negotiated, for example over the implementation of the principle of equal pay for equal work, these disagreements took place against the back-ground of a shared vision of a 'modern' future for Africa and within a broadly agreed framework for the settlement of disputes. This was an important factor in enabling African trade unions to negotiate significant improvements in pay and conditions for their members during these early years of the AOF trade union movement.

However, although French policy tended to favour the resolution of disputes on a sectoral basis and militated against cross-sector worker solidarity in the pursuit of wage claims, it also, in apparent contradiction to this, fostered a degree of commonality of purpose among African workers. This was partly a product of the chasm between official colonial discourse and colonial reality as the majority of Africans experienced it. The gap between the rhetoric of assimilation and equal rights on the one hand, and the reality of socio-economic discrimination to which Africans were subject under colonialism on the other, encouraged Africans' self-identification on the basis of race. Whatever the sector in which they worked or union to which they belonged, they saw themselves first and foremost as blacks who were discriminated against because of their colour: as blacks, they shared a common experience of discrimination, and thus a common objective to achieve equality with whites. It was this commonality of purpose that made possible the successful general strike of 3 November 1952, which, with the support on this occasion of African *députés* in the National Assembly in Paris, forced the adoption of the new Labour Code and which also lay behind the ultimately successful struggle to have family allowances extended to Africa. At the same time, however, it was a strategy that, as with the campaign for the 'decolonization' of education, implicated its proponents more deeply in the French link. It sucked African trade unionists into an ambiguous position, in which they were demanding that the benchmark for the treatment of African workers should be the French one, while bringing into question the very nature and desirability of the French colonial link.

The Forging of an Autonomous Trade Union Movement

This ambiguity began to pose difficulties for the trade union movement in the early 1950s. Within the CGT, to which more than half of AOF union members belonged, two tendencies emerged. One, led by Abdoulaye Diallo, a former post-office worker and CGT activist from Soudan who was close to the Communist Party, wanted to maintain close links with the metropolitan union, partly for ideological reasons and partly because of the organizational benefits that such links brought. The CGT in French West Africa had also strengthened its links with international communism through the appointment of Diallo as one of the vice-presidents of the Communist-dominated World Federation of Trade Unions (WFTU) in 1949. However, from 1950 onwards, a number of activists within the AOF trade union movement began to seek to loosen the links with metropolitan *centrales*. In the case of the Communist-leaning CGT, this was partly because many of its members supported the RDA, which had recently disaffiliated from the PCF. In the same way, CGT activists in AOF now sought greater autonomy from the metropolitan CGT to which they were affiliated. Led by Sekou Touré,[7] they wanted to create an autonomous African trade union movement that would neither be in hock to metropolitan unions nor dominated by any 'foreign' ideology that did not put African needs first.

The clash between the 'assimilationist' and the 'autonomist' tendencies first emerged at the CGT's Bamako conference in 1951. Although, in the end, a majority of delegates backed Diallo's 'assimilationist' strategy and voted in favour of maintaining the link with the metropolitan CGT, so that an open split was avoided, Sekou Touré returned to the fray at the meeting of the union's coordinating committee in Conakry in July 1955. He proposed a motion in favour of autonomy in order to allow unions to develop in full their 'African personality'. This was opposed by trade unionists from Soudan, but later in that year the CGT in Senegal-Mauritania decided to break the metropolitan link and form a CGT-Autonome (CGTA), which initially cooperated closely with Senghor's BDS. On 1 April 1956, Sekou Touré followed the same path and launched a federation-wide CGTA. A similar aspiration for autonomy was discernible in the Church-dominated Confédération Française des Travailleurs Chrétiens (CFTC), which renamed itself the Confédération Africaine des Travailleurs Croyants (CATC), although in its case this change was also partly motivated by the Christian label which made it more difficult to recruit Muslim workers. In both unions, their leaders wanted greater recognition of the specificity of African labour struggles and the freedom to pursue their own agenda. However, this autonomist strategy created tensions between the union's socio-economic role to defend workers' interests, where the priority was to obtain the best possible deal for their members, and their political ambition to put the labour movement at the service of the struggle for national liberation.

Sekou Touré, as the most prominent trade union leader who sought to use the union movement as a launching pad for his political career, illustrates this tension well. His initial strategy, in his delicate balancing act between the imperative as a trade union leader to defend his members' socio-economic interests and his aspiration to be a nationalist political leader, was to attempt to ride both horses simultaneously. He therefore continued to press the typical AOF union demands for equal pay and conditions through the existing industrial relations machinery and to support strike action when it suited him. At the same time, as an aspiring political leader, he saw the usefulness of the union's organizational strength as a support base for launching his political career as a leader of the Guinean branch of the RDA, the Parti Démocratique de Guinée (PDG).[8] However, trade unionists, as salaried workers with a regular income, were already considered a privileged minority by other Africans. Trade union leaders who hoped to pursue a political career could not therefore afford to become too closely identified with trade union interests because their success as political leaders depended on their ability to build a far wider support base, particularly among the rural majority of the population. Moreover, as an aspiring political leader who was, first and foremost, an African nationalist, association with a metropolitan *centrale* was difficult to justify. The divisions within metropolitan trade unionism, between the CGT and its anti-communist offshoot, CGT-Force Ouvrière, and between the CGT and the CFTC, had been reproduced in AOF and he saw them as an obstacle to African unity.[9] He viewed the Marxist ideology of the CGT as Eurocentric in focus, insufficiently attuned to African priorities and needs, and he was critical of the way in which the CGT prioritized the international struggle of communism against capitalism over the struggle for African liberation. For these reasons, he called for the creation of an autonomous African union movement.

The balance that Sekou Touré sought to achieve between trade union imperatives and political priorities was not an easy or self-evident one. Within the CGT, Touré's strategy brought him into conflict with Abdoulaye Diallo who believed that, given the lack of industry in Africa and the fact that only some 5 per cent of the AOF workforce was salaried, the aspiration to an autonomous African trade union movement was premature and would weaken its effectiveness as a union movement. Diallo's supporters also accused Touré of splitting the working class and of trying to put the brake on some strike movements.[10] At the same time, his strategy created tensions within the RDA. Houphouët-Boigny, who had been instrumental in breaking the RDA's link with the PCF in 1950 and supported his desire for an autonomous trade union movement in AOF, was no fan of the CGT. He therefore sought to prevent 'RDA members from cooperating with the CGT, but agreed that Sekou Touré could do so as long as he kept the RDA out of discussions'.[11]

This position was not sustainable and in the end it was Touré's political ambitions and career that took precedence. While he viewed the labour movement as a key element in the anti-colonial struggle, for him the interests of labour were ultimately subordinate to the political struggle. This meant, first of all, creating an African union movement that was autonomous from the metropolitan *centrales*, then using the union movement's organizational strength to build a broadly-based, anti-colonial front.

For the first part of his strategy, to forge an autonomous trade union movement in AOF, he found an ally in the colonial administration.[12] This alliance of convenience might at first sight seem surprising because the ideological stance of the 'autonomous' unionists represented a fundamental rejection of the very basis of French colonial policy since the war. This policy was 'assimilationist', to the extent that it was driven by the desire to bind the colonies closer to France, whereas Sekou Touré and his trade union supporters who were promoting the idea of an autonomist union movement wanted to loosen the ties with France and were increasingly critical of the French colonial link. The reason why French officials nevertheless decided to support Sekou Touré's efforts was that they thought his initiative would weaken the union movement as a whole in French West Africa, which was giving them so much trouble with its 'culture of demands' based on the claim that African workers should enjoy every one of the benefits accorded French workers. Since the dominant union was the CGT, they also hoped in this way to reduce Communist influence in AOF. Anti-communism had been a significant feature of French colonial policy since Communist ministers left the government in 1947 and the 'autonomists' in the union movement presented the Administration with an opportunity to strike a further blow against 'Communist' influence in the colony.

Initially, the strategy appeared to be working well from the Administration's point of view. The creation of the CGTA further split the AOF union membership, which was now divided between five different organizations. Within months, the new union had almost as many members as the CGT and, at a CGTA federal bureau meeting in Conakry in November 1956, it decided to remain independent from all political parties and not to affiliate to any metropolitan *centrale*. The question of possible affiliation to an international body was left open, to be resolved later. The CGT counter-attacked immediately and called for a unity conference, to which all the unions in AOF were invited. The CGTA was in favour of such a conference, but wanted to delay it in order to allow time for the railway workers, who were still 'autonome', to hold their conference and, they hoped, decide to affiliate to the CGTA, as this would enable the latter to overtake the CGT in membership and go to the proposed unity conference in a position of strength. Instead, the railmen launched an appeal to all the other unions to form an 'independent African *centrale* that was genuinely united'.[13] The resulting conference, which was attended by all the main unions including the CATC and the Autonomes, opened at Cotonou on 16 January 1957 and gave birth to the Union Générale des Travailleurs d'Afrique Noire (UGTAN).

Houphouët-Boigny and his allies in the RDA leadership also had reason to be pleased. Not only had the CGT's unchallenged dominance of the trade union movement in AOF been broken, but one of 'their' men, Sekou Touré, was its leading figure. Moreover, the other two prime movers behind the CGTA, Bassirou Guèye and Seydou Diallo, were Senegalese, which provided the RDA with the hope that the new union might give the party a springboard from which to increase its influence in Senegal.

The creation of the CGTA did not, however, bring any obvious immediate benefits to the rank-and-file trade unionist. From his persp-ective, the adoption of an 'autonomist' strategy involved a radical break from the strategy that had hitherto proved successful for the trade union movement in AOF, of focusing on professional issues and formulating demands for increased pay and benefits based on the principle of parity with European workers. Moreover, although its creation was justified by the need to facilitate trade union unity, the result was actually a union movement that was even more divided than before. In fact, its creation was in no small measure the product of the political jockeying for position of Sekou Touré as there was no obvious pressure for its creation from ordinary union members, who continued to be concerned primarily about issues of wages and working conditions. Thus 1956 saw a major wave of strike activity in AOF. Postal workers were on strike for most of August, health workers and policemen went on strike, as did 4,000 railmen on the Abidjan–Niger line in support of a 30 per cent pay increase. Private sector workers in Abidjan also came out on strike on 20 November in solidarity with the railmen. Moreover, the autonomy of the so-called 'autonomous' union was altogether relative: while it was indeed independent of any metropolitan *centrale*, its relation to African political parties was far more ambiguous, as its best-known leader, Sekou Touré, was also the leader of the PDG and a leading figure in the RDA.

Nevertheless, pressures for the adoption of an 'autonomist' strategy were growing. The reasons for this are to be found in the changing political situation in AOF at the time. By the early 1950s, political, as opposed to specifically industrial, issues were gaining in prominence. Many Africans, especially among the French-educated élite, were becoming increasingly disillusioned with the slow pace of change. In this context, the victory in the campaign for the adoption of the new Labour Code was seen as an example of what could be achieved by a campaign combining political with industrial action. Furthermore, despite growing political pressure for greater African autonomy, the devolution of responsibility for local affairs to Africans had barely got off the ground and the process of Africanization of the civil service in AOF remained painfully slow, so that jobs for the growing number of French-educated Africans remained scarce.[14]

The 'autonomist' strategy brought new problems for the AOF trade union movement, however. If the specificity of African labour vis-à-vis French labour was now to be asserted and African labour struggles were to become part of the broader nationalist political struggle, then it would be much more difficult for trade unions to press for a European benchmark for claims for improved pay and working conditions for Africans. Most of those making such claims worked for the government and, given the economic underdevelopment of Africa, they could only be sustained at the expense of the majority of the population who would have had to pay for them through their taxes. This inevitably led to tensions between the role trade union leaders were expected to play in defence of their members' socio-economic interests and the front-line political role some trade union leaders and activists increasingly sought to play within the struggle for national liberation. These tensions and their significance for the nationalist movement will be explored further in Chapter 7.

The Student and Youth Movements

Following the extension of the right to freedom of association to the colonies at the end of the Second World War, there was a vast expansion in the number of associations in French West Africa. In this upsurge of associational activity, the student and youth movements were especially active and, from 1955 onwards 'in a context of political agitation which was the expression of a more radical challenge to the colonial presence', they played a leading role both in mobilizing opposition to colonial rule and in espousing politically advanced positions.[15] They were the first groups publicly to demand immediate independence in AOF.

African Students in France

The first African student organization was actually created in France immediately after the war. The Association des Etudiants Africains (AEA) campaigned mainly on student welfare issues and for an increase in student grants. It was supported in this both by African *députés* in Paris and by the RDA's newspaper, *Le Réveil*, which ran frequent articles on the hardships endured by African students in France. The students linked the problems they faced to the broader campaign being waged in AOF against the 'sabotage' of education. They accused the colonial authorities of restricting their numbers by preventing students over the age of 23 from applying for grants and of deliberately making their life difficult in order to slow the pace at which Africans could be trained to fill posts of responsibility: 'We do not know if this state of affairs is the result of incompetence, which is becoming increasingly common at the top of the colonial administration which we have the misfortune to be ruled by, or the product of a deliberate plan to do everything possible to deny Africa the qualified personnel it urgently needs . . . we are (inclined) to think that it is the latter'.[16] For as long as their campaigns were concerned with specifically student issues, the students enjoyed the support of African *députés*. Aid committees (*comités de secours*) were even set up in AOF to raise funds for them.[17]

The first clear sign of the politicization of African students in France came on 21 February 1950, when they took part in an 'International Day of Struggle against Colonialism', which was organized by the communist-backed Union Internationale des Etudiants (UIE) in university towns throughout France. Gabriel d'Arboussier's message of support to the students explicitly linked the struggle of African students to that of colonial peoples throughout the world for their liberation:

> To the millions of students grouped together in your great organization, I send my good wishes for the success of the Day of Struggle against Colonialism. I can assure you that the peoples of Black Africa under French rule will greatly appreciate this action and that it will encourage them to pursue with even greater energy and confidence the fight for their liberation.[18]

Shortly after this, an article was published in *Le Réveil* linking the underdevelopment of education in AOF, and more specifically the apparent desire of the colonial authorities to restrict the number of African students in higher education, to the question of national independence: 'We shall never be vigilant enough to thwart the imperialists' plans. Although the student question is just one aspect of the problem of the struggle for national independence, its importance should nevertheless not be under-estimated. Those who have made illiteracy an official policy know this well'.[19] This went well beyond the official line of the RDA at this time and was an early sign of the open conflict that would break out later in the year between the students and African political leaders when the RDA leadership decided to disaffiliate from the PCF. This decision was rejected by RDA students in Paris, who decided shortly afterwards to create their own organization, the AERDA. This new association proclaimed its loyalty to the original line of the RDA, rejecting what was seen as a move to the right by RDA deputies, and in 1952 founded a newsletter, *La Voix de l'Afrique Noire*, to campaign for support for its ideas within the RDA and among potential supporters outside the Party. The radical political orientation of the AERDA can be gauged from the quotation from the Soviet political leader, Zhdanov, which appeared as the headline in the first issue of *La Voix de l'Afrique Noire*: 'The liquidation of the whole colonial system of imperialism is our aim'. It also stated as the association's aim to 'group together all democratic students who wish to defend the African cause under the umbrella of the RDA' and then went on to interpret this in a way that would certainly not have been acceptable to the party's leadership: 'That is to say, despite the distance which separates us, we intend to take part in the struggle of the African peoples for their emancipation from the yoke of colonialism, for political, economic, social and cultural emancipation with a view to national independence'.[20]

The inaugural congress of the Fédération des Etudiants d'Afrique Noire en France (FEANF), which was held in Paris in March 1951, brought the great majority of African students in France together into a single union. Although it was supposed to be a student organization concerned primarily with student issues, it was from the outset overtly political in its orientation. Indeed, its founding conference was notable for a struggle for control between the AERDA and another student group called the Groupement Africain de Recherches Economiques et Politiques (GAREP). The latter had been created in 1948 by a group of students who were influenced by Nkrumah's ideas, did not accept the RDA's strategy of working for equal rights within the French Union, and preferred instead to aim for the creation of 'territorial assemblies with full sovereign powers'.[21] It was this group which won the initial battle for control of the union, but they were replaced in April 1952 at the FEANF's second congress, when AERDA students were elected *en masse* to its executive committee. In 1955, it affiliated to the Prague-based UIE. The students regularly attacked not only the leaders of the RDA but also the leaders of other parties, such as Senghor, for betraying the African cause by cooperating closely with the French government, and the student movement emerged as a movement of radical opposition, not only to French colonialism but also to the political leaders of AOF.

The Beginnings of the Student Movement in French West Africa

There was no institution of higher education, and therefore no student movement, in French West Africa itself until 1950. The Association des Etudiants Africains, bearing the same name as its predecessor in France, was created in 1950, the same year as the Institut de Hautes Etudes de Dakar (IHED) opened its doors, and became the Association Générale des Etudiants de Dakar (AGED) in December 1950. At its inception the IHED was housed in temporary accommodation attached to the Lycée Van Vollenhoven in Dakar. Demands for better accommodation, but above all for better-qualified teaching staff and for an improvement in the standard of education, formed the focus of the Dakar students' early campaigns. Thus, as was the case in the early days of the African student movement in France, its concerns initially related to specifically student issues.

In 1954 came the first signs that this was beginning to change and that a nationalist political consciousness was beginning to emerge in the AOF student movement. Firstly, a problem arose over relations between French and African students within the AGED. According to *Dakar-Etudiant*, French students had left the AGED and were refusing to rejoin unless it merged with the metropolitan students' union, the UNEF, and undertook to remain politically neutral. The AGED, like the FEANF, refused such a merger, as it was felt that the UNEF had not done enough to support African students' demands. The two African unions also wished to retain their identity and they therefore proposed joint actions with the UNEF instead. This the UNEF in turn refused, although it invited the African unions to attend its annual conferences as observers. The problem arose because French students considered the Africans' political views extreme and accused them of excessive nationalism, whereas what the African students claimed they were in fact demanding was the same rights and treatment as metropolitan students, in accordance with the spirit of the French Union, and they accused the French students of being, effectively, closet colonialists: 'The question was now clear for us: our comrades were behaving like *French nationalists* and identifying themselves instinctively with the regime to which we were opposed outside the field of student trade unionism'.[22] The lack of support, and at times hostility, to African students' demands from UNEF members thus actually helped to create a climate in which nationalist sentiments grew among African students. As an article in *Dakar-Etudiant* pointed out: 'the UNEF majority systematically treat any grievance put forward by the overseas students as nationalist and politically motivated, and hence inadmissible. In this way, because of their hostility, they create a climate which is more likely to kindle a latent nationalism in the most apathetic minds'.[23] In short, by refusing the solidarity of joint action, the UNEF was encouraging African students to turn to separatism.

Secondly, international developments, and specifically the situation in Algeria, were beginning to have an impact, particularly on Muslim students in Dakar. As early as 1954, perceiving themselves as a culturally distinct group, they had formed their own association, the Association Musulmane des Etudiants Africains (AMEA), and had started to publish a newsletter, *Vers l'Islam*. Initially intended primarily as a cultural association that would offer students a religious 'anchor' in the cosmopolitan environment of the IHED, the activities of the association became more politically marked during 1955. In particular, the question of discrimination against Muslim students was raised: for example, the colonial administration was attacked as 'anti-Islam' and 'anti-African' for its discriminatory policy on subsidies to private schools, with Christian schools being supported while Muslim ones were not; the fact that the headteacher of the Ecole des Infirmiers d'Etat (State Nursing School) was a nun was deplored; and the term *évolué* was rejected as a 'colonial' word which carried the implication that it was only possible to 'evolve' through the assimilation of French culture. Assimilation in this sense was specifically rejected: 'To be assimilated is to lose everything one possesses that is different without any certainty of gaining anything in return'. The treatment of fellow Muslims, both in the *métropole* and in Algeria, further contributed to the process of politicization of Muslim students and encouraged them to adopt more radical nationalist positions.[24]

By 1956 a number of other developments were pushing the student movement in Dakar towards adopting more radical positions. First of all, the FEANF was beginning ideologically and politically to influence the AGED. This was partly the result of the summer courses that were organized during the summer holidays in AOF by African students returning from France, in which IHED students also participated. They provided a meeting place where the students could come together and exchange ideas, and their activities appear to have reached a peak in 1955.[25] The improved links with students in France were also due to the increasing number of students starting their studies in Dakar then moving to France to complete them, and to a deliberate effort by the FEANF to coordinate its activities with the AGED. One concrete manifestation of this was their joint declaration on Algeria, which was published in *Dakar-Etudiant* in June 1956, asserting the right of all peoples to decide their own destiny: 'The events of the last ten years prove . . . that the idea of, and wish for, independence underpin and legitimate the struggle of oppressed peoples for their liberation'.[26] In 1956 African *députés* were criticized for the first time by the Dakar student association for being cut off from the real aspirations of Africans. The refusal by the colonial authorities to grant the editor of *Dakar-Etudiant* a passport to attend the Congress of the UIE made an impression on many students in Dakar, since African students in France were not subject to this sanction. This underlined the persistence of the colonial regime in AOF and the discrimination to which African students in Dakar were subject. Finally, although they were not yet calling for full independence, the Dakar students were by this time proclaiming 'our complete freedom to administer ourselves' and '(our) right to take initiatives and assume responsibility'.[27]

In 1956, too, the AGED took the decision to change its name to the Union Générale des Etudiants d'Afrique Occidentale (UGEAO). This marked a turning point for the Dakar student movement. The choice of name, which deliberately omitted the word 'Française' and indicated a desire to affirm the autonomy of their movement, caused French students to leave and set up their own association, the Association Générale des Etudiants Français en Afrique Noire (AGEFAN), which affiliated to the metropolitan students' union, the UNEF. Another factor in the radicalization of the Dakar students was events in Indochina and North Africa. As a regular contributor to *Dakar-Etudiant* pointed out, these developments provoked an 'awareness among African students of colonialist repression' and led to a growing 'national consciousness' among them.[28] Having hitherto carefully avoided calling for outright independence, within a month of this article the Dakar students themselves called for African independence.[29]

It seems that Dakar students initially wanted to try to make the French Union work. They demanded 'real' assimilation and campaigned for the provision of a proper metropolitan-style university in AOF. However, the continuing failure to transform the IHED into a university, developments in North Africa, the slow progress of reform generally and the increasing contacts with African students in France, who were more radical than their Dakar colleagues, combined to persuade the students to turn away from assimilation to independence. The early political history of the Dakar student movement was therefore one of gradual evolution towards more radical nationalist ideas and the eventual adoption of the goal of political independence.[30] In this respect its development paralleled that of the youth movement that emerged in AOF at this time.

The Youth Movement

The potential threat to political order represented by the young French-educated élite had been recognized by the colonial authorities as a problem before the Second World War and deliberate efforts had been made to develop the scout movement and sport as ways of channelling the energies of this young élite away from getting involved in political activity, which was in any case banned under the *indigénat*. With the advent of trade unions and political parties this changed and young French-educated Africans outside the Four Communes could become involved in political activity legally for the first time.

In 1952, the colonial authorities set up *conseils de la jeunesse* (youth councils) in most territories of AOF, with a view to establishing an officially sponsored youth movement throughout French West Africa. The youth councils came together within the Conseil de la Jeunesse de l'Union Française (CJUF), which held a meeting at the Lycée Faidherbe in Saint-Louis in July 1952 at which AOF was represented by 32 delegates from the eight territories. Shortly after this, in August 1952, the CJUF welcomed 150 delegates from 24 different countries to the Lycée Van Vollenhoven in Dakar for the Congress of the World Assembly of Youth (WAY). However the movement very rapidly split along political lines: rejecting links with the WAY, which was considered too moderate and too pro-Western in its outlook, the Senegal and Niger councils had left the CJUF by the time of its next annual meeting in Yaoundé in August 1953.[31] Then, in 1954, rather than be associated with the WAY, the Union des Jeunes du Soudan and the RJDA which, like the AERDA, was anti-Houphouët and pro-d'Arboussier, chose instead to send delegates to the Congress of the rival, pro-Communist, international youth organization, the World Federation of Democratic Youth (WFDY), in Peking. There was by this time a strong desire for unity, with the result that, shortly after this, the different territory-based youth organizations, apart from that of Haute-Volta, came together at a congress in Bamako from 23–27 July 1955 and formed themselves into a single federal body, the Conseil Fédéral de la Jeunesse d'AOF.[32] Two months later delegates from the Conseil Fédéral attended the first Congress of West African Youth in Accra at the invitation of Kwame Nkrumah.

The aims of the movement were set out in Article Two of its statutes. They included 'to struggle for better conditions for living, working, studying and leisure, for social progress and for the well-being of their generation through exchanges, information, training courses, holiday camps, parades and study days and fortnights, etc.' and 'to actively involve the youth in the movement for the emancipation of their country'. The radical political tone of the movement was evident from the resolutions adopted at the inaugural congress in Bamako. One deplored the persistence of illiteracy and the lack of measures to combat it; another condemned the lack of funds for education (the motion noted that only 1.79 per cent of the federal budget went on education, while 6.32 per cent was spent on the police force) and the lack of qualified teachers; another attacked the colonial authorities for refusing to grant passports for delegates to attend the Festival of Youth planned to take place in Moscow in 1956; and another expressed support for the right of the Algerian people to self-determination. Although the delegates did not go so far as to demand political independence, the proceedings of the conference provided further evidence of the political gulf separating much of the youth of AOF from the federation's main political leaders.

The movement was led in its early days by locally educated people who for the most part held middle- or lower-level posts in the civil service, mainly as teachers, assistant teachers or clerks. Many of them were active in the trade union movement or at territory level in one of the political parties. Within the latter, they increasingly found themselves in disagreement with the incrementalist approach and constitutional orientation of the leadership, and discovered that they often had more in common with young people in rival movements than with the leaders of their own organization. A typical example of this was the RJDA, which was initially encouraged by the party leadership and published its own newsletter, *La Voix des Jeunes*. However, after the split within the RDA consequent upon the decision to disaffiliate from the PCF, its leaders were less enthusiastic about it, regarding it, like the AERDA, as a focus for opposition to the leadership and a vehicle for the penetration of radical nationalist and Marxist-inspired anti-imperialist ideas into the Party.

The most important political divide thus ceased to be that between different political parties, for example between the BDS and the SFIO in

Senegal, and became instead that within these organizations between, on the one hand, an older generation of leaders, many of whom remained committed to the French Union and to maintaining the link with France, and on the other, the rising generation of 'young Turks' who felt increasingly that their aspirations were not reflected in the political positions adopted by the leaders of AOF and sought a political voice of their own. Given the personal dominance of African political leaders over the main AOF political parties, this meant working outside the mainstream parties, in youth organizations or through the trade union movement, or becoming active in the semi-autonomous youth sections of the political parties. Through these different groups, they launched themes and actions and mobilized people in ways that it was difficult for their leaderships to ignore. Influenced by the Bandung conference, by developments elsewhere in the French Empire and by the prospect of independence in the Gold Coast, they attacked the colonial system, appealed for African unity and discussed increasingly openly the question of independence.

Leaders of the movement had much more in common with people like d'Arboussier and Cheikh Anta Diop than they did with the first generation of African political leaders such as Senghor, Houphouët-Boigny and Apithy. Its leading figures were active at a number of different levels: Amadou Ndene Ndaw, for example, was active in the Senegalese teachers' union, the Association des Parents d'Elèves and the Senegalese section of the RDA,[33] and Kane Aly Bocar, who was active in the youth wing of the SFIO, was also president of the Conseil de la Jeunesse du Sénégal and became president of the Conseil Fédéral de la Jeunesse d'AOF in 1956. In this way, the youth movement became a focus for radical opposition not only to French colonialism but also to the existing political leadership in AOF, whom its leaders saw as allies of France.[34]

The Failure of the 'Centres Culturels' Initiative

Concerned about what they termed the growing 'culture of demands' (*esprit revendicatif*) of young people, the colonial authorities made another attempt to defuse their radicalism by creating *centres culturels* throughout AOF in an attempt to channel their energies away from politics into other, less anti-French, cultural activities such as music and drama. The determinedly non-political nature of the activities envisaged for the centres is indicated by the list of reviews to which it was recommended that they should subscribe – *Paris-Match*, *Bingo*, *Le Chasseur Français* (sic!) and *Constellation* (an illustrated sports magazine) – and by the type of activities that were actually organized – one of the first was a theatre competition between different *centres culturels*. To underline the point, the Governor-General crossed out that part of the draft report that suggested that the best way for the Administration to keep an eye on young people was to allow political meetings to be held in the centres.[35] There was, however, nothing non-political about the centres' intended role, which was the social and political control (*encadrement*) of youth. As the Administrator-in-Chief responsible for Social Affairs emphasized, the Administration was to remain discreetly in control of the centres.[36]

The background to this initiative was the change that the colonial authorities believed had taken place in the nature of French colonial rule since the Second World War and which they held responsible for the gap that had opened up between the French and the French-educated African élite. During the pre-war period, they believed, colonial administrators had relied extensively on their personal relations with local chiefs, whom they used as intermediaries for the exercise of their authority. After the war, with growing urbanization and the advent of African political parties and trade unions, these personal contacts declined. As a result, especially in the towns, colonial rule became more formal and institutionalized. Moreover, the new generation of post-war colonial administrators adopted a less paternalistic, more 'professional' approach than the earlier generation of administrators, so that the personal contact went, and with it the personal sense of loyalty felt by many of the earlier generation of so-called *évolués* to France. The transition from a paternalistic, often personalized, exercise of authority to a more formalized and bureaucratic form of colonial rule was thus seen as part of the backcloth to the transition from political docility to increased political contestation among younger members of the French-educated élite after the Second World War. At the same time, with more and more schools being staffed by African, rather than French, teachers, there were less opportunities for Europeans and Africans to meet and mingle with each other. Direct contact between French people and Africans was increasingly limited, either to the domestic sphere, where Europeans employed Africans as maids or cooks for example, or to when Africans had a problem, for instance with the police or the colonial administration, or when someone was ill. Part of the intention of the *centres culturels* was to remedy this by providing a place where French people could come into contact with Africans: 'The *centres culturels* seem to us to be not only a means of occupying people's free time, but above all, in the debates about the issues that concern us, a means of education, a way of bringing Africans together among themselves and also of bridging the gap between Africans and French people . . .'[37] The colonial authorities in Dakar clearly attached considerable importance to this new initiative, judging by the fact that 157 centres had been opened and 257 million francs spent by the end of 1956. A magazine, *Traits-d'Union*, was also created to publicize the centres' activities and 7,000 copies were printed in the first year.

From the outset they ran into difficulties however. In the first place, judging by the repeated complaints from the Governor-General to governors that the territories were not paying sufficient attention to the *centres culturels*, there was some difficulty in getting the territories to take part. It also seems that a number of centres were frequently not able to function as intended for lack of sufficient *animateurs*. Secondly, and more seriously from the political point of view, the young people whom they were primarily intended to 'control' (*encadrer*) initiated a coord-inated campaign against the centres, which they wanted transformed into *maisons des jeunes* controlled not by the Administration but by them-selves. As early as January 1954 the Conseil de la Jeunesse du Sénégal came out against the centres and, by the second half of 1956, the local administration had responded by transforming some of the centres in Senegal into *maisons des jeunes*. At the meeting of the Conseil Fédéral de la Jeunesse d'AOF held in Conakry in November 1956 the trans-formation of all the *centres culturels* in AOF into *maisons des jeunes* was demanded. A letter from the *commandant de cercle* in Tambacounda, in which he said the local centre was being boycotted by the local youth associations, apparently on instructions from the Conseil de la Jeunesse du Sénégal, highlighted the problem faced by the authorities: the youth of AOF were not prepared to cooperate in a project which was seen as an attempt by the colonial authorities to 'put a brake on the progressive fervour of African youth by maintaining them indefinitely under the colonial yoke'.[38] The language used in the motion suggests that continued participation in the activities of the centre was viewed by young people as a form of collaboration with the enemy. In the end, it seems that the *centres culturels* actually succeeded in achieving exactly the opposite of what was intended. Instead of improving contact with, and the *'encadre-ment'* of, the youth of AOF, the campaign of opposition to the centres was actually one thing that, whatever their other ideological and political differences, was guaranteed to unite all the youth associations in AOF. By the end of 1956 the Governor of Senegal was clearly exasperated with the whole project. He wrote to the Governor-General to point out that they had become a focus for political opposition to French colonial rule and suggested that they should be abandoned: 'I believe that, in the circumstances, it is better for us to change our policy on the *centres culturels* now, without waiting, since it is clear and beyond doubt that the youth do not want to have anything to do with them . . .'[39] Within a few months the colonial administration had given in to the inevitable and itself brought forward a proposal to transform the centres into *maisons des jeunes*.

The failure of the *centres culturels* initiative is significant on two grounds. Firstly, it demonstrates once again the extent to which the colonial authorities had lost control of the political agenda in French West Africa. The *centres culturels* initiative was an attempt to create a network of institutions in AOF, the overt aim of which was to improve the political and social '*encadrement*' of the young. As such it belonged to a phase in the period of colonial rule that had now passed. In the post-war political context it stood no chance of meeting with the acceptance, or even acquiescence, of the educated and politically active youth of AOF, whose aspirations were by now directed towards autonomy and, increasingly, independence. To believe that such aspirations could be met through some renewed form of partnership in the cultural sphere, but with the French remaining firmly in political control, revealed a remarkable inability to move with the times and come to terms with political realities. Secondly, it is evidence of the growing strength of nationalist feeling, particularly among the French-educated youth in AOF. Despite a very considerable injection of funds and a clear determination that they should succeed, the concerted action of the youth movement was sufficient to force the colonial authorities into a humiliating climbdown. In the early 1950s, radical nationalist ideas were largely confined to African students in France. By the mid-50s, political radicalism had spread to young French-educated Africans throughout AOF.

Towards the Convergence of the Student and Youth Movements

The student and youth movements in AOF developed in the early 1950s largely independently of each other. Students at Dakar were drawn from throughout AOF and even from AEF. Their concerns were at the outset primarily with the quality of the education they were getting in Dakar and the thrust of their demands was essentially 'assimilationist' in nature, insofar as they wanted the quality of education provided in Africa to be fully comparable with that in the *métropole*. However, as time went on, they began to articulate demands that were not concerned solely with educational matters but had broader political implications, such as the demand for the Africanization of the civil service or for Algerian self-determination. African students in Dakar were thus anti-colonialist, insofar as they were opposed to the colonial regime in education, but they were not initially separatists. However, seeing the separatist instincts of French students in Dakar, aware of events in other parts of the French Union, particularly Algeria, and influenced by African students returning from France, they began to develop a more radical nationalist consciousness. The creation of autonomous, specifically African student organizations, such as the AMEA and the UGEAO, was a manifestation of this emerging national consciousness.

The youth organizations that were set up throughout AOF during this period were of a different nature. Initially territory-based, although they subsequently came together into an AOF-wide federation, they drew their membership mainly from locally educated young people who were also often active in the trade union movement or at local, grassroots level in one of the political parties of AOF. They provided a forum in which the youth of AOF could meet, discuss their ideas and plan actions with like-minded people.[40] The formation of such alliances was a vital element in the process of building a nationalist movement in French West Africa.

One can therefore see that the student and youth movements developed along parallel paths. From an essentially reformist stance, both movements became politicized and radicalized by a combination of political developments within AOF, international developments and the influence of Marxist anti-imperialist and radical nationalist ideas. Both movements sought to establish their organizational autonomy and began to develop a nationalist consciousness. Both also sought alliances, within AOF with other groups that shared their radical political stance, and at international level with organizations that could provide moral support, financial help and ideological sustenance. The AGED and subsequently the UGEAO increasingly coordinated its activities with the FEANF, while the territory-based youth associations came together into a federal youth council. At the same time both the student and youth movements in AOF were beginning to form international links, the former with the UIE and the latter with the WFDY. Both of these were pro-communist organizations that took a radical anti-imperialist line. In the following two years, as we shall see in Chapter 7, the student and youth movements, in alliance with the trade union movement which was also becoming increasingly politicized, converged in a campaign for political independence.

Notes

1. Born in 1909 in Haute-Volta, Coulibaly was a graduate of the William-Ponty School. He subsequently became a teacher in his home territory before returning to William-Ponty as a pupil supervisor (*surveillant général*) from 1936–42.
2. D'Arboussier was the son of a Soudanese woman and a French colonial governor and a graduate of the Ecole Coloniale in Paris. He became a Vice-President of the RDA in 1947 and subsequently its Secretary-General. He also edited the Party newspaper, *Le Réveil*. Following his disagreement with Houphouët-Boigny over the Party's disaffiliation from the PCF, he was expelled from the RDA in 1955.
3. Senegalese in origin, Diop was active in the AERDA. He is most well-known as the author of *Nations nègres et cultures* (Présence Africaine, 1979), in which he forcefully argued that African civilization was older than European civilization.
4. In 1954, the High Commissioner, B. Cornut-Gentille, 'Les problèmes politiques en AOF', p. 2, referred to them as a 'privileged caste' and pointed out that: 'civil servants in AOF represent 1/60th of the population and share 1/7th of the national income, that is, their income is nine times that of a crop farmer and nineteen times that of a family of livestock farmers'.
5. R. S. Morgenthau, *Political Parties in French-Speaking West Africa* (Clarendon, 1964), p. 414.
6. F. Cooper, *Decolonization and African Society* (Cambridge University Press, 1996), passim, especially Parts II and III.
7. Ahmed Sekou Touré was expelled from technical college in 1937 for organizing a strike. He became a post-office clerk and secretary of the Guinean Union des Syndicats Confédérés in 1946. He was a founder member of the RDA in 1946 and attended the CGT's national congresses in Paris in 1948 and 1950, in which year he also went to the World Peace Congress in Warsaw. He became the General Secretary of the PDG-RDA in 1952.
8. R. S. Morgenthau, *Political Parties*, pp. 227–31.
9. In 1956, members were divided between the unions as follows: CGT 36 per cent, CGTA 30 per cent, CATC (ex-CFTC) 11 per cent, CGT-FO 8 per cent, Autonomes 15 per cent, G. Martens, 'Industrial Relations and Trade Unionism in French-Speaking West Africa', in U. G. Damachi et al., *Industrial Relations in Africa* (St Martin's Press, 1979), p. 35.

10. P. Dewitte, 'La CGT et les syndicats d'Afrique occidentale française, *Mouvement social*, 117, 1981, p. 18.
11. F. Cooper, *Decolonization*, p. 412.
12. Note dated 15 October 1956, AAOF 17G620/152; cf. also ANSOM Aff. Pol. 2264/8 and G. Chaffard, *Les Carnets secrets de la décolonisation*, vol. 2 (Calmann-Lévy, 1967), p. 181. Suspecting administrative support for Sekou Touré's initiative, his enemies within the CGT dubbed the new organization the 'CGT Administratif', Senegal Security Services report dated 31 July 1956, AAOF 21G215/178.
13. J.-R. de Benoist, *L'Afrique Occidentale Française de 1944 à 1960* (Nouvelles Editions Africaines, 1982), p. 373.
14. R. Cruise O'Brien in *White Society in Black Africa: The French in Senegal* (Faber & Faber, 1972), pp. 66–81, shows that the number of European workers in Dakar rose steadily from 1946 to 1955. This influx of so-called *petits blancs* (lower-class whites) meant that the process of Africanization of the lower echelons of the civil service was much less advanced in French West Africa than it was in neighbouring British West Africa at this time.
15. O. Goerg, 'Le mouvement associatif et le processus des indépendances en Afrique occidentale française', in C.-R. Ageron and M. Michel, eds, *L'Afrique noire française: l'heure des indépendances* (CNRS Editions, 1992), p. 89.
16. 'Motion de protestation des étudiants africains de la Métropole contre la carence et le sabotage administratifs', *Le Réveil*, 5 January 1948, p. 1. Cf. also: 'Le scandaleux arrêté des 23 ans', ibid, 13 September 1948, p. 1; D. Michaud, 'Ne laissons pas saboter leurs études', *Le Réveil*, 10 July 1950, pp. 1 and 4.
17. 'Les étudiants africains attendent une aide efficace de toute l'Afrique', ibid, 18 March 1948, p.1 and 'Il ne faut pas sacrifier les étudiants africains. L'avenir repose sur eux', ibid, 13 September 1948, p. 1.
18. 'Message à l'Union Internationale des Etudiants', ibid, 16 January 1950, p. 1.
19. 'Avec les étudiants africains à Paris', ibid, 10 July 1950, p. 4.
20. *La Voix de l'Afrique Noire*, 1, February 1952.
21. K. Nkrumah, *Towards Colonial Freedom* (Heinemann, 1962); *Manifeste du GAREP* (J. Marx et Cie, 1951).
22. *Dakar-Etudiant*, December 1956, p. 6 (emphasis in original letter).
23. 'Leçon d'un congrès', ibid, June 1954, p. 11.
24. *Vers l'Islam*, June–July 1954, pp. 8–9; January 1956, p. 2; May 1955, p. 9; December 1955, p. 10; April 1956, pp. 1 and 5–6. Cf. also

reports on the first congress of the AMEAN in Dakar, 11–15 July 1956, and on the activities of the Union Culturelle Musulmane, in AAOF 17G596/152.

25. Reports on these summer courses are in AAOF O667/31, 17G596/152 and 17G597/152.
26. 'Déclaration commune AGED-FEANF', *Dakar-Etudiant*, June 1956, p. 6.
27. Ibid, January–February 1956, pp. 1–2, June 1956, pp. 10–11.
28. Ly Tidiane Baïdy, 'Notre association à un tournant décisif de son histoire', ibid, December 1956, p. 6.
29. Ibid, January 1957, p. 4.
30. See T. Chafer, 'Students and Nationalism: the Role of Students in the Nationalist Movement in Afrique Occidentale Française', in C. Becker et al., *AOF: réalités et héritages* (Direction des Archives du Sénégal, 1997), pp. 388–407.
31. Security services report, dated 27 July 1956, on Congress of Conseil Fédéral de la Jeunesse, Bamako, 23–27 July 1955, in AAOF 17G596/152.
32. Conseil Fédéral de la Jeunesse d'AOF, 'Travaux du Congrès Con-stitutif', Conakry, 1956, Amadou Ndene Ndaw personal archives. Cf. also reports in AAOF 17G596/152 and 17G612/152. Another meeting of the Conseil was held in Conakry in November 1956, report in AAOF 0655/31.
33. Expelled from the Ecole Blanchot following a pupil strike in 1944, Ndaw became a teaching auxiliary later that same year. He joined the teachers' section of the CGT and took part in the 1946 civil service strike, demanding integration of teaching auxiliaries into the regular assistant teachers' *cadre*. He joined the UDS, the Senegalese section of the RDA, in 1947 and was Vice-President of the Conseil de la Jeunesse du Sénégal from 1955–9.
34. Senghor warned in 1954 that it was necessary to respond to their demands if such opposition was not to become radicalized, leading to a rejection of France and of the gradualist approach adopted by African political leaders, R. Cruise O'Brien, *White Society*, pp. 100–1.
35. It was essentially this thinking that underlay the creation of the *centres culturels* in AOF, as a draft letter written by the Governor-General towards the end of 1953 shows: 'These circles (the title *centres culturels* had not yet been adopted) are a response to three main concerns: to bring together in a fruitful way the French-educated élites which are too often left to their own devices; to give

them the opportunity to come together and work with other natives who are less advanced than them; and to organize the leisure activities of young people who are insufficiently supervised by orienting them discreetly towards certain cultural activities', draft letter from Governor-General to Governors, undated, [early 1953?], in AAOF O655/31. The circular creating the *centres culturels* was dated 14 March 1953 and 120 such centres were created in the first year. See also official reports in AAOF O671/31 and O673/31.

36. 'Confidential' report, dated 12 June 1953, from Poinsot, Administrator-in-Chief responsible to the Governor-General for Social Affairs, p. 22, in AAOF O655/31.

37. 'Le problème des centres culturels en AOF', p. 1, in AAOF O655/31.

38. Letter signed P. Tomasini, dated 7 August 1956 and enclosing a copy of the motion passed by the Tambacounda youth association on 20 July 1956, in AAOF O655/31. The motion went on to demand the immediate transformation of the *centre culturel* into a 'youth and cultural centre where young people will get involved in cultural activities that they themselves have chosen' and to announce the association's intention of withdrawing from the centre's management committee.

39. Letter from Governor of Senegal to Governor-General, dated 13 November 1956, p. 3, in AAOF O655/31.

40. Cf. T. Hodgkin, *Nationalism in Colonial Africa* (Muller, 1956), p. 84; B. Anderson, *Imagined Communities* (Verso/New Left Books, 1983), p. 109.

Policy and Politics 1950–6

The emergence of a radical nationalist movement worried not only the colonial authorities in AOF, but also its political leaders. A rift had opened up by the mid-1950s between, on the one hand, the leaders of the main French West African political parties who for the most part favoured a moderate approach and sought to cooperate with the French government to implement a programme of incremental reform, and on the other, a nationalist movement, based in the student and youth movements and parts of the trade union movement, which espoused more radical anti-colonialist positions and pressed for faster progress towards decolonization. As disillusionment with the slow pace of reform in French West Africa set in and the decolonization process gathered momentum in other parts of the world, this younger generation set a new, more radical, political agenda, to which the leaders of the main political parties were forced to respond. At the same time, the widening of the suffrage at each successive election meant that African political leaders were obliged to pay increasing attention to the concerns of a wider constituency than the French-educated élite, who had comprised the great majority of the electorate in the first post-war elections in AOF. Their continued success as political leaders depended on their ability to carry this wider electorate with them, but increasingly set them at odds with the radical younger generation of activists in the nationalist movement.

Policy Paralysis in France

Growing African disillusionment with the slow pace of change was fuelled by continuing policy paralysis in France. In 1954, Senghor warned the National Assembly: 'The apparent calm of Black Africa should not deceive you; it is growing weary from the unkept promises and from the revival, or rather the continuance, of the "colonial pact" . . . What overseas French citizens want is the loyal application of the Constitution of 1946'.[1] There were many reasons why Africans felt that the Constitution was not being 'loyally' applied. Although the Second

Lamine Guèye Law had established the principle of 'equal pay for equal work' for French and African civil servants, Africans continued to suffer from various forms of discrimination. As a result, the campaign for equal rights intensified after 1950. The initial focus of this campaign was to extend family allowances to the families of African civil servants, which was granted in 1951. Following this success, the trade unions demanded that they be extended to private sector workers, which was initially resisted by the employers, so that it took until January 1956 for regulations to be adopted allowing 350,000 French West African children finally to benefit from family allowances.[2] The marathon discussions of a new labour code for the overseas territories continued in the National Assembly and the new Code was finally adopted by the National Assembly on 23 November 1952. Meanwhile, little progress had been made in devolving responsibility for local affairs to local elected representatives, and economic coordination between the *métropole* and overseas territories, which had been promised in the preamble to the Constitution, also had not happened.[3] New statutes, to replace the provisional statutes governing the operation of the local assemblies (*conseils généraux*) since 1946, had finally been adopted on 23 November 1951, but they were a disappointment to Africans as the double electoral college was maintained (except in Senegal), albeit with a wider suffrage, and the powers of the assemblies remained unchanged. Only their name changed, to Territorial Assemblies. Municipal reform, proposals for which were put before the National Assembly in 1951, took almost as long to be enacted after the Conseil de la République (the Senate, France's upper house) made several attempts to modify the text and reintroduce the double electoral college for the 44 *municipalités de plein exercice* (fully elected town councils) that were being proposed. The Senate finally backed down and the text was adopted by the National Assembly on 18 November 1955.

It was not only African *députés* who were frustrated at the lack of direction from Paris. Governor-General Cornut-Gentille had his ear to the ground and was well aware of the growing frustration in the colony at the lack of progress: 'There is an urgent need to establish a new policy direction which transcends the permanent confusion between a policy of association and that of assimilation or an implicit federalism'.[4] If such a lead was not forthcoming, the Governor-General warned in 1954, the Administration would sooner or later be obliged to improvise its own solutions, with the attendant risks that such a course of action entailed. He knew better than anyone that things could not continue as they were. He was concerned at the unsustainable financial burden that increasing the pay levels of African civil servants to those of their French colleagues and the extension of social citizenship measures to Africans were placing on the federation's budget.[5] He also worried about the fact that these measures only applied to the tiny minority of Africans who were salaried employees and did nothing to improve the lot of the rural majority of AOF who were peasant farmers. What was worse, measures to bring the pay and benefits of African employees up to the level of their French colleagues were bringing no perceptible political advantage to France, since each concession provoked further demands for the particular benefit in question to be extended to more categories of employee. The family allowances campaign illustrated this problem well. Within the system as it was, there seemed to be no end in sight to the continuing spiral of African demands, French concessions, and increasing costs to the federal budget. Something had to be done, but it would not be until the Loi-Cadre of 1956–7 that the government in Paris would address these problems.

International Context

The international situation changed rapidly during this period. Within the French empire, decolonization gathered momentum. The war in Indochina intensified, culminating in France's defeat at Dien Bien Phu and withdrawal from Indochina in May 1954. Serious disturbances in Tunisia in 1952 were followed by the granting of internal autonomy in 1955. Both Morocco and Tunisia achieved independence in March 1956. In the meantime, the Algerian revolution had begun on 1 November 1954. The nationalist movement in AOF followed these developments closely, not least because soldiers from French West Africa fought in substantial numbers on behalf of the French in both Indochina and Algeria.[6]

Outside the empire, 1950 was a turning point, marking the moment when the Cold War extended beyond Europe into Asia and began to impinge directly on the colonial domain. The Soviet model attracted increasing interest from anti-colonial movements, particularly among the young, and the activity of various communist satellite organizations, such as the World Federation of Trade Unions (WFTU) and the World Federation of Democratic Youth (WFDY), escalated in the colonies. They had a significant ideological influence on the emerging nationalist movement in French West Africa. During this period, attacks on the colonial powers at the United Nations also intensified.

The Bandung Conference, which took place from 18–24 April 1955 in the city of that name in the former Dutch East Indies, was especially closely watched by nationalists in AOF. The conference was attended by delegations from 24 newly independent states from the Third World (including the Gold Coast, although it would not actually become independent for another two years). In addition, a number of countries that were not yet independent were invited to send observers, notably Tunisia, Morocco and Algeria, whose presence ensured that there was an anti-French flavour to some of the conference's proceedings. Its final communiqué adopted a stance of non-alignment, in that it condemned European colonialism, with its roots in racial discrimination and segregation, but did not endorse communism. It defended the absolute right of all peoples to self-determination and one paragraph specifically supported the right of the peoples of north Africa to independence and called on the French government to bring about a peaceful solution to the situation. Overall, the conference provided succour, and became a source of encouragement to, the nationalist movement in AOF.[7]

The international context was important, not only because activists in the nationalist movement watched what was happening on the international scene and followed developments elsewhere in the French empire with particular interest, but also because they sought actively to forge international links with anti-imperialist forces outside AOF and were influenced in their thinking by their anti-imperialist ideas. The reasons for cultivating these links were partly ideological and partly strategic. The organizations with which they formed links were strongly influenced by the language of international communism, which placed emphasis on the common interests of the proletariat in the developed world and the peoples of the colonies in the struggle against capitalist imperialism. There was therefore an ideological commitment to internationalism, which was visible in the political line of the RDA before the split from the Communist Party and which continued to dominate the discourse of the d'Arboussier wing of the party and its younger, more radical members after 1950. The political resolution adopted at the RDA's second congress in Abidjan in 1949, which was probably drafted by d'Arboussier, displayed this influence by affirming its belief in 'the alliance of the peoples of Black Africa and the great people of France who, led by the working class and its Communist party, struggle with courage and confidence for national independence against American imperialism'.[8] Also, conscious of the way in which colonial rule had erected barriers between African peoples, and particularly in West Africa between French and British Africa, radical nationalists in AOF were committed to Pan-Africanism and sought to cultivate links with the nationalist movement in British West Africa. But the obstacles to creating and maintaining such links proved too great and these efforts came to little.

Quite apart from these ideological reasons, considerations of strategy underlay the attempts by radical nationalists to cultivate international links. Following the RDA leadership's decision to disaffiliate from the PCF in 1950, radical nationalists were in danger of becoming politically isolated within AOF. Their decisions to forge international links, like their decisions to work within the trade union and youth movements, were motivated by the need to prevent this happening through the formation of new political alliances that bypassed AOF's political leaders.

Parties and Elections

Political life during this period was marked by a constant stream of elections. Elections to the National Assembly took place on 17 June 1951 and 2 January 1956. There were elections to the territorial assemblies on 30 March 1952, which in turn elected representatives to the Grand Conseil the following month.[9] There were also elections to the Conseil de la République in Senegal, Niger and Haute-Volta on 18 May 1952 and in the other territories on 19 June 1955; to the Assemblée de l'Union Française on 10 October 1953; and there were municipal elections on 18 November 1956. Hardly had one election campaign finished than another began. As the suffrage widened with each successive election, the proportion of the population drawn into the arena of competitive politics increased. Universal suffrage was finally introduced in November 1955, but the reform was not implemented in time for the January 1956 legislative elections, with the result that the November 1956 municipal elections were the first to be held under the system of universal suffrage. Nonetheless, the size of the electorate increased enormously in the ten years from 1946 to 1956. To take just one example, in Guinea the electorate increased from 131,000 in 1946 to nearly one million in 1956, and almost 1.4 million in 1957.

For the 1951 elections, AOF's representation in the National Assembly was increased from 16 to 20, with one extra *député* for each of Guinea, Soudan, Dahomey and Haute-Volta. The elections were a defeat for the RDA, mainly because the Administration still did not accept its disaffiliation from the Communist Party as genuine and intervened to ensure, as far as possible, the defeat of its candidates.[10] As a result, apart from Houphouët-Boigny who enjoyed an unassailable position in Côte d'Ivoire thanks largely to his reputation as the man who abolished forced labour, only two other RDA *députés*, the moderate, Mamadou Konaté (Soudan), and Georges Condat (Niger), were successful. The others divided between five political groups, with nine IOM, five SFIO, one

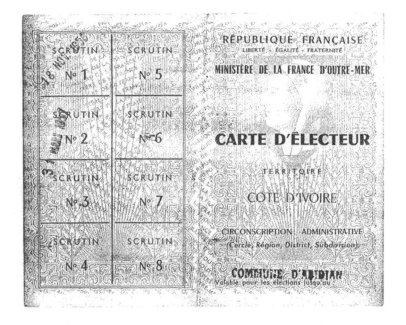

Figure 5.1 Elector's card.

MRP, one RPF (Gaullist) and one independent (Apithy in Dahomey). The other major lesson of the elections was the dramatic decline in influence of the SFIO in French West Africa, which was further confirmed by the results of the territorial assembly elections the following year.

French West Africa was supposed to have been allotted an extra seven *députés* for the 1956 National Assembly elections, but the dissolution of Parliament in the *métropole* came too early for the 1955 electoral reform to be implemented and the election took place under the old law. On this occasion, administrative interference in the elections was much reduced, with the result that the RDA easily won both seats in Côte d'Ivoire, where both Houphouët-Boigny and Ouezzin Coulibaly were elected, and in Niger, where Hamani Diori and Georges Condat were elected; it won two of the three seats in Guinea, with both Sekou Touré and Saïfoulaye Diallo, and two of the four in Soudan, with Modibo Keita and Mamadou Konaté (following the latter's death on 11 May 1956, Barema Bocoum, RDA, was elected to replace him). In Haute-Volta, however, where the Administration had prevented the RDA from winning any seats in 1951, the RDA again failed to make a breakthrough and three of the four incumbents were re-elected in 1956. Nevertheless, with eight out of the twenty seats falling to the RDA, the elections were a resounding victory for the party, underlining its claim to be the only genuinely mass party in French West Africa. *Députés* of the RDA affiliated to the UDSR in the National Assembly. The IOM were left with only four *députés*, Senghor and Mamadou Dia (Senegal), Hubert Maga (Dahomey) and Nazi Boni (Haute-Volta), who affiliated to the MRP, and the SFIO with just two, Sissoko and Hamadoun Dicko (Soudan). The other successful candidates were Sidi el Moktar Ndiaye (Mauritania: MRP), Daiwadou Barry (Guinea: Radical), Sourou Migan Apithy (independent), and Joseph Conombo and Henri Guissou (Haute-Volta: unaffiliated). The IOM presence was thus reduced by more than half compared to 1951 and the Socialists, from being the predominant party in 1946, only avoided a complete rout thanks to the victory of two of its candidates in Soudan. In Senegal, where the elections were marked by violent clashes between SFIO and BDS supporters which left two people dead on election day, the result was a resounding defeat for Lamine Guèye and the Socialist Party.

A number of conclusions can be drawn from this succession of elections. First of all, the decline of the SFIO reflected the loss of influence of the generation of politicians, such as Sissoko and Guèye, who first came to prominence at the time of the Popular Front. Its campaigns, in the assimilationist tradition of Senegalese politics, were focused on the achievement of equal rights between Africans and Europeans and its greatest success was the Second Lamine Guèye Law of 1950. By this time, however, it was already beginning to be challenged by a new generation, many of whom had served their political apprenticeship in the GECs and CEFAs before joining the RDA. This generation was influenced by the radical political language of the RDA in its early days, which was itself coloured by the radical anti-imperialist discourse of the GECs out of which it emerged. A good example of this is Soudan, where the old guard of Sissoko's SFIO was coming under increasing challenge from the local section of the RDA, the Union Soudanaise (US-RDA). After the RDA leadership's change of line in 1950, such radicalism within the RDA was associated mainly with d'Arboussier and his supporters who were concentrated in the party's student and youth sections. However, it also provoked a split within the RDA in Niger, where the 'orthodox' RDA candidate, Hamani Diori, only narrowly beat Bakary Djibo, who was pro-d'Arboussier and whose campaign had the support of the trade unions. It was also reflected in the very different political styles of the two leading figures in the US-RDA, Mamadou Konaté and Modibo Keita. Although this did not amount to a split, the moderate stance and style of the former, whose political apprenticeship dated back to the pre-war period, contrasted strongly with the radical language of the latter, whose ideas had been formed initially in the post-war GECs. In Senegal, where Senghor's BDS was the dominant party and pursued a moderate policy of reform in cooperation with the French authorities, a similar rift opened up between the Party leadership and radical younger members of the urban-based, French-educated élite, many of whom expressed their opposition to the BDS leadership by joining the local branch of the RDA, the Union Démocratique Sénégalaise (UDS). Finally, in Dahomey where the two main political parties, Apithy's Parti Républicain du Dahomey based in the south and Hubert Maga's Groupement Ethnique du Nord, have been described as 'little more than electoral coalitions: once in office they had no firm policy objectives, and accommodated rapidly to the administration's view of reality', the newly formed Union Démocratique Dahoméenne attracted many of the territory's more radical nationalists.[11] Founded in 1955 by Emile Zinsou, Alexandre Adandé and Justin Ahomadegbé, it drew support from every region of the country, was much more critical of the colonial administration than the other parties and, initially at least, had close links with Dahomey's small but powerful trade union movement. In each case, the radical, younger generation of nationalists were more critical of the French colonial administration, they were outspoken critics of French government policy in Indochina and Algeria, and sought to build a broad anti-colonial front of opposition to French colonial rule, spearheaded by the student and youth movement and in alliance with those in the trade union movement and political parties who were prepared to work with them towards this end.

Secondly, these elections confirmed the ideological closeness of AOF's main political leaders to each other at this time. Their political agenda, which they all broadly shared, was a reformist one. All were still publicly committed to reform within the context of the French Union, increased investment through the FIDES, the Africanization of the civil service, and the devolution of more powers to the local territorial assemblies so as to give Africans a greater say over their own affairs. None at this stage favoured independence. The most important ideological split was not therefore between the different political parties which they led, but between the leaders of AOF's main political parties on the one hand, and the younger generation of radical nationalists in the student and youth movements on the other. The ambition of inter-territorial unity remained illusory: personal rivalries and interterritorial tensions remained too strong, as the scattering of AOF *députés* between six different parliamentary groups after the 1956 elections again showed.

Thirdly, relations between the main African political parties and the Administration had greatly improved by the 1956 elections. In Dahomey, it has been suggested that the constant stream of elections since 1946 distracted the press and political leaders from their usual campaigns against the local colonial administration as they increasingly focused on electioneering.[12] Elsewhere in French West Africa, having been worried by the RDA's Communist ties until 1950, the Administration was, by 1956, much more worried about the increasingly radical activities of, and language being used by, the trade union and youth movements, which on the one hand were pushing for full equality of socio-economic rights with Europeans, while on the other adopting more radical nationalist positions than those espoused by the leaders of AOF's main political parties. The government was reliant on AOF's political leaders to contain these 'undesirable elements with their extremist demands', but the Governor-General was not convinced that AOF's political parties possessed the organizational capacity to do this.[13] As a result, he was seriously worried that the BDS leadership in Senegal and the RDA leadership in much of the rest of French West Africa were in danger of being outflanked on the left by radicals, based mainly in their parties' youth organizations, who were dismayed by what they saw as their leaders' conciliatory attitude towards the French government, were highly critical of French policy in Algeria and demanded that the right of all colonial peoples to self-determination be recognized. If the Party leaderships could not contain these radical nationalists, thereby buying time for France to transfer power to 'friendly' nationalists, then France's position in West Africa would be under threat.

This was a difficult political path for the party leaderships to tread, however, since those articulating these demands belonged to the French-educated élite and many of them were civil servants. Although there were just 45,000 civil servants in 1952, out of a total population of some nineteen million, they absorbed over 60 per cent of the Administration's operating budget and were also the social category that dominated the territorial assemblies: at least half of those elected in 1952 were civil servants and this proportion rose to 70 per cent in the case of Niger and Senegal.[14] Despite their small numbers, they therefore exercised a disproportionate influence over AOF politics. This posed a political problem for African political leaders. On the one hand, because of their political importance, they could not afford to alienate this group, whose support and skills they would need once powers were transferred. But on the other hand, because this group was seen by most Africans as a privileged minority, which was already relatively prosperous by African standards, political leaders who hoped one day soon to take over the reins of power could not become too closely identified with them. If they did so, they ran the risk of losing the support of the rural majority of the population, on which their political future increasingly depended as the electorate expanded. The need to win over and retain the support of the rural population was thus a significant factor underlying the growing tension between AOF's main political leaders and the radical nationalists among the French-educated élite. There were exceptions to this. In Guinea, for example, Sekou Touré appealed to both the urban and rural constituencies in that territory by adjusting his message to his audience. Thus, wearing his trade union hat, he continued to press members' demands for equality in the economic arena, while simultaneously building rural support by posing as the champion of the underdog who, in the tradition of Samory, was resisting alien rule.[15] And in Soudan there was no urban-rural political divide, as the main party, the US-RDA, concentrated its organizational efforts on gaining the support of the rural population for its ideology of 'virulent anti-colonialism'.[16]

Factors Shaping the Political Agenda of AOF's Political Leaders

An understanding of the complex factors that led to the rift between the main political leaders and the nationalist movement and of the ways in which it was played out politically are essential to an understanding of the political evolution of AOF in the run-up to independence. To some extent, of course, the configuration of these factors varied from territory to territory and a full appreciation of the political specifics of each situation would require a series of studies on a territory-by-territory basis. A number of such histories have already been written and it is not the intention to summarize their findings here.[17] The purpose of this section is, rather, to focus on three factors that shaped the political agenda during these crucial years that were peculiar to AOF and that differentiated the political evolution of French West Africa from that of neighbouring territories such as, for example, British West Africa.

The first of these was the emergence of Paris as the focus for the political activity of African political leaders after the Second World War. France was unique among the colonial powers in allowing elected representatives from its colonies to sit in the national parliament. This had several consequences. Firstly, it contributed towards the forging of a special relationship between France's governing élites and African political leaders. Their education in French schools, their subsequent employment by the French administration, the fact that they served their political apprenticeship in the National Assembly in Paris and even, in some cases, became French government ministers under the Fourth Republic, all these factors combined to forge a special bond between France and those African politicians such as Houphouët-Boigny, Senghor, Hubert Maga and Hamani Diori who would eventually lead their countries to independence. Had the moderate US-RDA leader, Mamadou Konatë, not died suddenly in 1956, to be replaced as leader by the more radical Modibo Keita, a similar path might also have been followed by Soudan. Moreover, the fact that Africans sat in the French parliament facilitated the formation of close associations with French politicians and drew them into the political networks of French political parties. It discouraged the adoption of positions of outright opposition towards France and generally led them to moderate their political vocabulary and outlook. Perhaps most importantly, as internal autonomy approached and they came under increasing challenge from radical nationalists within AOF, they needed to maintain their political support from France if they were to benefit from the transfer of powers when it came. These factors were crucially important in laying the basis for the maintenance of close relations between France and Black Africa after political independence.

Sending African *députés* to the *métropole* had other important consequences for the development of political life in French West Africa. Their role as *députés* enabled them to consolidate their position of dominance over AOF political life and, in the words of their critics, to become 'stronger than the governor' even before independence.[18] This encouraged the personalization of politics and meant that political parties in AOF emerged largely as gatherings of supporters for particular political leaders, and the other traditional functions of political parties, such as building support for a distinctive political ideology or acting as a training-ground for the exercise of citizenship, were less important. Moreover, African *députés* allied themselves in the National Assembly with different political parties that were in opposition to each other in the context of metropolitan politics. As the ideological differences between them concerning the political future of AOF were at this stage minimal, because all wanted to retain the link with France, this affiliation to rival metropolitan parties tended further to enhance the importance of personal, rather than ideological, rivalries in AOF politics. Finally, because the political activities of African *députés* were centred on Paris, this militated against achieving the objective, which De Gaulle had set at Brazzaville, of guiding colonial populations towards managing their own affairs.[19] This would have meant the decentralization of responsibility, whereas the focusing of political action on Paris tended towards the opposite. More-over, such centralization, together with the key role that the Governor-General and governors still played at federal and territorial level in budget setting, discouraged the development of a sense of political responsibility at lower levels of the political pyramid and fostered instead a 'culture of demands'. This culture of demands emerged at federal, territorial and municipal level, so that the Grand Conseil, territorial assemblies and town councils became fora where demands were discussed and formulated but where responsibility did not have to be taken for the political or financial consequences of decisions. This was one of the issues that the Loi-cadre sought to address, as we shall see in Chapter 6.

Another consequence of the presence of African *députés* in the French Parliament was to convince them that the policy of assimilation was not workable. Logically, this would have meant 300 African *députés* in the National Assembly and France being prepared to grant AOF the status of 'état associé' (associated state) within the French Union.[20] But it was quite clear that neither the government nor metropolitan public opinion were prepared to concede such a far-reaching reform. The difficulties they had experienced in gaining parliamentary support for certain measures, such as the reform of the *conseils généraux*, the introduction of the new Labour Code or the extension of family allowances to African families, were sufficient to convince them of this. They therefore turned their attention to increasing African autonomy, so as to give Africans a greater say over the management of their own affairs. An *intergroupe* of overseas *députés* was formed in early 1953, under the presidency of Sissoko, to work within the French Union for the 'fulfilment, at parlia-mentary level, of real local aspirations'. The increasing importance attached to political autonomy by AOF's main political groupings was underlined by the RDA's communiqué, issued at the end of the meeting of its coordinating committee meeting in Conakry in 1955, which contained no reference to the demand for equality but stressed instead the RDA's aim of achieving African emancipation through greater political autonomy within the context of the French Union.

The second factor to be examined here is the increasing importance of the territory in AOF politics. Although one might have expected Black African *députés* to act in concert in defence of African interests, in practice this happened rarely and was confined to specific issues, such as the Labour Code and family allowances. In every other respect, the political institutions established in AOF after the Second World War militated against such concerted action. Their electoral support was territory-based, so that their success as politicians depended on making gains on behalf of their territory, such as obtaining new investment or having an unpopular governor recalled, which they could then take back to their electorate and present as victories for their action. Where a *député*'s party had a majority in the territorial assembly, he could use his influence in Paris to have its resolutions (*voeux*) implemented. When the metropolitan party to which an African *député* was affiliated was in government, he could use the opportunity to gain advantages for his territory at the expense of colleagues from other territories who were affiliated to rival parties. Thus, both the territorial base of African *députés'* electoral support and the fact that they were affiliated to rival metropolitan political parties militated against enduring cooperation between them.

The defence of territorial interests also emerged as an issue at meetings of the federal Grand Conseil. This manifested itself in two separate, but linked, ways, as resentment against the Government-General for its dominance of the federation and reluctance to devolve responsibilities to the territories, and as competition between territories for federal resources. In each case the underlying motive was economic. The root of the problem was that the Government-General controlled the federal budget, which, in 1951, was nearly double the total budget of the individual territories taken together. This provoked opposition from the territories outside Senegal, which felt they were paying for a top-heavy federal administration, and gave rise to accusations of discrimination in the way that funds were redistributed to the territories. One territory in particular, Côte d'Ivoire, believed that it was less favourably treated than the others. In 1953, for example, its representatives claimed that their territory had contributed 36.5 per cent of the total federal budget but had only received back 22.3 per cent. In fact, only Guinea received back more or less the same amount as it contributed, Senegal and Côte d'Ivoire contributed more than they received back, while the other five territories were net beneficiaries of the federal budget.[21] Such redistribution of resources from the 'rich' territories to the 'poor' ones was done in the name of federal solidarity, but it caused resentment, particularly in Côte d'Ivoire where Houphouët-Boigny suggested that his territory had become the milch-cow of the federation.[22] At least Senegal had the Government-General and benefited from the employment opportunities its services created. It was also, because of the long history of contact between France and the Four Communes and the privileged position of Dakar as the federation's seat of government, more economically devel-oped and enjoyed far better educational facilities than Côte d'Ivoire. Interterritorial tensions over the federal budget were the seed-bed for the eventual break-up of the federation.

The third point that needs to be appreciated because of its significance for the development of nationalist politics in the run-up to political independence is the problematic position occupied by the 'federal' idea in French West Africa. The federation was a colonial construct and, as such, lacked legitimacy in African eyes.[23] Moreover, the federal Government-General continued to be viewed by many of the French-educated élite as a bastion of reactionary colonialism. Towards the end of the war, the idea was launched by French policy-makers of a new, federal structure for the empire, although the proposal was, in practice, not truly federal since real power remained with the central government in Paris.[24] In 1948, IOM *députés* returned to the question of imperial reform and relaunched the idea. A resolution to this effect was also adopted at their Bobo-Dioulasso congress in February 1953. Their idea was that the only way to block the advance of separatist nationalism and maintain an integrated republic, 'one and indivisible', was to make the French Union genuinely federal by decentralizing power within it to the different territories that composed it.[25] In 1954–5, other parties, both in Africa and in the *métropole*, came out in favour of 'federalism'. However, as one commentator has remarked, such an apparent consensus between political groupings who were in other respects politically opposed was probably based on a misunderstanding.[26] In the first place, France would never have accepted a structure within which it was simply a member state and in which the French government would have limited powers. Within AOF, the federation and federalism presented more immediate problems. There were regular complaints from the territories, especially those furthest from Dakar, that the Government-General was too remote, inefficient, and that it stifled local initiative.[27] If we add to this the tensions over the federal budget and the way in which the political institutions set up in 1946 were territory based, we can see that the promotion of the federal idea as the political way forward raised more questions than it answered. Thus, when 'federalism' was subsequently adopted by radical nationalists as a slogan to build support for retaining the unity of the federation and resisting the 'balkanization' of French West Africa into its constituent territories, this rapidly turned into a poisoned chalice, as we shall see in chapter seven.[28]

Conclusion: The End of Assimilation and the Quest for Autonomy

The institutions of the Fourth Republic were a conceit. At one level, they were assimilationist, insofar as they held out to overseas territories the apparent promise of integration into a 'one and indivisible' republic. At the same time, they appeared to offer them the possibility of managing their own affairs through the institution of elected assemblies in the overseas territories.[29] During the early years of post-war AOF politics, African political and social movements became adept at exploiting this tension for their own political advantage. Whether or not they actually believed that full assimilation was possible, or even desirable, the public focus of their action was on making the French Union a reality through greater integration and the achievement of equal citizenship rights. By the mid-1950s, however, disillusionment with what was perceived as the slow pace of reform and French unwillingness to grant equal rights to all but a tiny minority of Africans led many of the French-educated élite to adopt increasingly nationalist positions. Moreover, the local elected assemblies were in practice given limited powers and incremental reform was rendered extremely difficult by the fact that changes to the French Union were made a matter of constitutional revision.[30] The political obstacles to achieving this under the Fourth Republic were enormous and the result was that the possibility for gradual planned evolution towards greater political autonomy was blocked. At the same time, the uphill struggle of African *députés* to gain support for colonial reforms in the National Assembly increasingly convinced them that the 'assimilationist' option was not politically viable. By the end of this period, all the different groups within the emerging nationalist movement were therefore demanding African autonomy. However, they did not all want to move in exactly the same direction or at the same speed, and their visions of what autonomy meant for the political future of AOF were poles apart.

Students and, following them, the youth movement, who were the most impatient for change, wanted to move furthest and fastest. They wanted full educational assimilation, with metropolitan-style French education up to and including university, to be made available to Africans. At the same time, and at the political level in apparent contradiction to this, they were the first to adopt the call for African independence. The trade union movement continued to press for full equality between Africans and Europeans on the socio-economic front, while its leaders simultaneously sought organizational autonomy from metropolitan *centrales* and demanded greater African autonomy. By the end of 1956, the union movement was taking an active role in relation to the major political issues of the day and was on the verge of calling for Algerian independence, which it would do at the inaugural congress of the UGTAN in January 1957. Thus, autonomy was seen as a staging post on the road to independence. However, as trade unions became more politicized from about 1954 onwards, a contradiction emerged between their 'assimilationist' demands for equality with Europeans in the socio-economic field and their 'autonomist', nationalist aspirations in the organizational and political spheres. With the intensification of activity on the political front following the outbreak of war in Algeria and the Bandung conference, this contradiction became more flagrant. For nationalists, who were simultaneously defending demands for a *European* benchmark for wages and benefits and for *African* autonomy (shortly to become a demand for immediate independence), the political difficulties this stance created were acute and ultimately, as we shall see, irresolvable. In contrast, AOF's main political parties and their leaders, such as Senghor, Houphouët-Boigny, Apithy and Konaté, who also wanted greater African autonomy, were content to continue to work for the emancipation of the African territories within the context of the French Union 'through the affirmation of their political, economic, social and cultural personality'.[31] The studied ambiguity of this position evaded the contradictions of the radical nationalists' stance and at the same time offered the prospect of more immediate benefits to a wider cross-section of the population. Thus, in response to the growing radicalism of the nationalist movement, they increasingly looked for political support to the rural population.

This rift which opened up between the political *leadership* of AOF and the more radical nationalist *movement* based in the youth and trade union movements was partly ideological, insofar as the latter's critique of colonialism was influenced by the liberationist ideology of the Bandung Conference and by the language of international communism, which were more radical in both content and tone than that of AOF's main political leaders. It also in part reflected a rift of political generations, between on the one hand those who received their French education before the Second World War and whose political ideas were formed by their experience during and immediately after the war, and on the other those who were educated after the war and whose political ideas were initially formed in the GECs and CEFAs and subsequently consolidated against the background of the outbreak of French colonial wars in Indochina and Algeria and international moves towards decolonization. Crucially from the political point of view, it developed into a rift between two opposing visions for the political future of AOF.

Notes

1. Speech reported in *Marchés Coloniaux*, 26 June 1954, p. 1758.
2. J.-R. de Benoist, *L'Afrique Occidentale Française de 1944 à 1960* (Nouvelles Editions Africaines, 1982), pp. 233–6.
3. Ibid.
4. B. Cornut-Gentille, 'Les problèmes politiques de l'AOF', Roneo, 1954, p. 38. I am grateful to Joseph-Roger de Benoist for providing me with this document.
5. Ibid, p. 4.
6. A. Clayton, *France, Soldiers and Africa* (Brassey's, 1988), pp. 157–60 and 189–91.
7. Interviews with activists from the period confirm this, because many of them specifically mentioned the Bandung Conference as having had a significant influence on their own development: interviews with Iba der Thiam, Dakar, 19 March 1990, Amadou Ndene Ndaw, 31 March 1990. The fact that it had such a significant influence confirms Marc Michel's point that this was the most 'mediatized' international gathering to date, *Décolonisations et émergence du tiers monde* (Hachette, 1993), p. 157.
8. Contained in the RDA's own report on its Second Interterritorial Congress, held at Treichville, 2–6 January 1949.
9. Each territorial assembly elected five representatives to the Grand Conseil.
10. There were many ways in which the Administration could intervene to defeat candidates who were not to its liking, see R. S. Morgenthau, *Political Parties in French-Speaking West Africa* (Clarendon Press, 1964), pp. 201–2 and 240–1, J.-R. de Benoist, *L'Afrique*, pp. 188–90.
11. P. Manning, *Slavery, Colonialism and Economic Growth in Dahomey, 1640–1960* (Cambridge University Press, 1982), p. 278.
12. S. C. Anignikin, 'Les facteurs historiques de la décolonisation au Dahomey', in C.-R. Ageron, ed., *Les Chemins de la décolonisation de l'empire français, 1936–1956* (Eds du CNRS, 1986), pp. 510–11
13. Confidential note drafted by the Governor-General after the 1956 National Assembly elections, quoted in J.-R. de Benoist, *L'Afrique*, p. 287.
14. Report on a speech by Governor-General Cornut-Gentille on 30 October 1952, in ANSOM Aff. Pol. 2200/3; see also J.-R de Benoist, *L'Afrique*, p. 208; R. S. Morgenthau, *Political Parties*, pp. 402–11.

15. The warrior-trader Samory Touré was famous for having organized Mande resistance to French rule at the end of the nineteenth century. Sekou Touré claimed to be descended from him and skilfully used 'Samorism' to build support for the PDG among the descendants of those who had been associated with him, cf. R. S. Morgenthau, *Political Parties*, pp. 231–9.

16. A.C. Danioko, *Contribution à l'étude des partis politiques au Mali de 1945 à 1960* (Thèse de 3e cycle, University of Paris VII), p. 261.

17. For a study covering the politics of French West Africa in general, see R. S. Morgenthau, *Political Parties*. For individual country studies, see for example A. R. Zolberg, *One-Party Government in the Ivory Coast* (Princeton University Press, 1969); J. N. Loucou, 'La vie politique en Côte d'Ivoire de 1932 à 1952' (Thèse de 3e cycle, 2 vols., University of Provence, 1976); S. C. Anignikin, 'Les facteurs historiques de la décolonisation au Dahomey', in C.-R. Ageron, ed., *Les Chemins*, pp. 505–11; M.-A. Glélé, *Naissance d'un état noir* (Librairie Générale de Droit et de Jurisprudence, 1969) (on Dahomey); C. Rivière, *Guinea: the Mobilisation of a People* (Ithaca, 1977); A. C. Danioko, 'Contribution à l'étude des partis politiques au Mali'; G. Gerteiny, *Mauritania* (Pall Mall Press, 1967); F. Fuglestad, F., *A History of Niger 1850–1960* (Cambridge University Press, 1984); A. Ly, *Les Regroupements politiques au Sénégal (1956–70)*. (CODESRIA/Karthala, 1992); F. Zuccarelli, *Un Parti Politique Africain, l'Union Progressiste Sénégalaise* (Librairie Générale de Droit et de Jurisprudence, 1970).

18. *Climats*, 9–15 August 1951, quoted by R. S. Morgenthau, *Political Parties*, p. 123.

19. Opening speech by General De Gaulle to the Brazzaville Conference, *La Conférence Africaine Française. Brazzaville, 30 janvier-8 février 1944* (Ministère des Colonies, 1945), p. 30.

20. *Marchés Coloniaux*, 4 April 1953, p. 1006. In this article he also stated that assimilation was 'stérilisante' and 'hypocrite parce qu'impossible'.

21. J.-R.de Benoist, *L'Afrique*, pp. 198–203.

22. Interview with Joachim Bonny, Abidjan, 18 June 1999. In Yves Person's view, Houphouët also wanted to avoid being part of a federal regime that might be dominated by revolutionary radicals from other territories, see Y. Person, 'French West Africa and Decolonization', in P. Gifford and W. R. Louis, eds, *The Transfer of Power in Africa. Decolonization 1940–1960* (Yale University Press, 1982), pp. 141–72.

23. Cf. interview with Doudou Guèye in *Afrique Nouvelle*, 19 March 1957, p. 6.
24. For a discussion of the complexities and contradictions of Title VIII of the Constitution which set up the French Union, see D. B. Marshall, *The French Colonial Myth and Constitution-Making in the Fourth Republic* (Yale University Press, 1973), pp. 295–301.
25. Cf. L. S., Senghor, 'Contre le courant centrifuge de l'Etat associé, une seule solution: La République Fédérale Française', *Marchés Coloniaux*, 4 April 1953, pp. 1005–7.
26. J.-R. de Benoist, *L'Afrique*, p. 195.
27. Cf. the 1952 session of the Grand Conseil, at which the representative from Dahomey demanded greater decentralization of decision-making away from the Government-General to the territories, *Bulletin du Grand Conseil de l'AOF*, 1952, p. 151.
28. Senghor was the African political leader who took the most prominent role in the fight against the 'Balkanization' of AOF, cf. 'Pour une Fédération de l'AOF', *Afrique Nouvelle,* 6 November 1956, p. 1. *La Balkanisation de l'Afrique Occidentale Française* (Nouvelles Editions Africaines, 1979) is also the title of a book on the history of the break-up of AOF by J.-R. de Benoist.
29. B. Cornut-Gentille, in 'Les problèmes politiques', pp. 24–5, discusses the difficulties this ambiguity created for the colonial administration.
30. D. B. Marshall, *The French Colonial Myth*, pp. 297, 313.
31. This was the RDA's aim, as defined at its inaugural congress in Bamako in 1946. It was broadly shared by the other main political parties in AOF.

–6–

The Loi-cadre and the 'Balkanization' of French West Africa, 1956–60

In the immediate aftermath of the Second World War, major changes were made to the institutional arrangements governing French relations with the empire. However, in the following years, as we have seen, French policy was characterized by inertia. The difficulties encountered over five years in trying to obtain parliamentary approval for the adoption of a new overseas labour code were just one example of the problems confronting those who sought to bring about colonial reform. Moreover, because the institutional arrangements for the French Union were contained within the constitution, any overhaul of the structure of the Union required making changes to the constitution. The political barriers to this under the Fourth Republic were formidable. Constitutional reform had a bad name, having traditionally been a tactic of the extreme right under the Third Republic, and any move towards constitutional revision also risked re-opening the divisive debate about metropolitan institutions.[1] However, by 1955 the pressures for major change had become irresistible and were widely recognized within the Ministry for Overseas France, by colonial officials in Africa and by members of the metropolitan political élite. In France, left-wing critics of French colonial policy, such as Jean-Paul Sartre and the group of intellectuals around the review *Les Temps Modernes*, articulated moral and political concerns about the possession of colonies, while worries about the growing cost of empire to the *métropole* were articulated, notably by the journalist Raymond Cartier in a series of articles for *Paris-Match*.[2] These criticisms found a sympathetic ear among sections of French public opinion. In addition, colonial wars, first in Indochina then in Algeria, and growing international criticism of the colonial powers, notably from the US and from within the United Nations, were putting increased pressure on the government. This combination of domestic and external factors, together with an increasingly difficult political climate in the colonies themselves, forced the government to reassess the imperial link. In 1955, the Minister for

Overseas France, Pierre-Henri Teitgen, therefore convened a group of specialists on colonial affairs, under the chairmanship of the former governor, Robert Delavignette, with a brief to make recommendations about the political future of the French colonies of Black Africa. His report highlighted the ambiguities contained in the constitution of the French Union, which had failed to make a clear choice between assimilation and autonomy: 'It set out to reconcile these tendencies in a vague federation. In fact, it simply juxtaposed them. For too long now we have been promising reforms but failed to implement them'.[3] He concluded that reforms were urgently needed. Another report, written at about the same time, on the problem of how best to maintain the French presence in Africa, had warned: 'nothing is more contagious than the thirst for independence . . . It will spread successively to the Anglophone and Francophone territories'.[4] The problem was how to manage the necessary transition to a 'Franco-African Federation', which would retain France's close relations with Black Africa. But the government in which Teitgen was a minister left office before it was able to act on these reports. This task would fall to his successor, Gaston Defferre.

The main focus of the previous two chapters has been on political developments in AOF. In this chapter, the focus shifts to France, as it was developments in the *métropole* between 1956 and 1958 that finally broke the policy logjam in French West Africa. The Loi-cadre played a crucial role in this respect, by establishing the framework for future relations between France and Black Africa and setting the direction of French policy in the run-up to independence and after. The background to the Loi-cadre, its main provisions, and policy impact in French West Africa will be analysed. The fall of the Fourth Republic two years later and, with it, the end of the French Union, finally opened up the possibility of constitutional reform that had been closed since 1946. On the day of his return to power, on 1 June 1958, De Gaulle announced to the National Assembly that he intended to offer just such an opportunity to the people of the colonies.[5] The setting up of the institutions of the Community, as the restyled French Union was now to be called, and their impact on relations with French West Africa, will form the focus of the second part of this chapter. France was, by this time, well on the way to granting what one commentator has called 'l'indépendance des notables'.[6] The sequence of events leading up to this will be described, and its significance for Franco-African relations analysed, in the final section of the chapter. The referendum campaign and its significance for the nationalist movement will be analysed in the following chapter.

The Loi-cadre

The return of the SFIO to the Ministry for Overseas France in 1956, after an absence of eight years during which the Ministry had been controlled by the centre-right MRP, marked the beginning of a period during which French policy towards West Africa, as indeed towards the rest of French Black Africa, underwent a period of rapid and unplanned change. As Mayor of Marseilles, Defferre was, literally, close to the Algerian problem. He also had personal experience of Black Africa, having worked in his father's law practice in Dakar from 1928 to 1931. On taking office, the spectre of Algeria was very much at the front of his mind. The independence of Morocco (2 March) and Tunisia (20 March), and the rapid progress towards independence of the Gold Coast, which shared borders with French West Africa, added further urgency to the situation. Determined to avoid a second Algeria in Black Africa, he moved quickly to enact reform there.[7] However, conscious of the resistance from certain quarters within the National Assembly to any measure that might be portrayed as a dilution of French authority, he resorted to the constitutionally dubious device of the Loi-cadre, or 'enabling act'. This was essentially a declaration of intent, which set down the guidelines for reform but which made it possible for the actual reforms themselves to be enacted by presidential decree. Thirteen such *décrets d'application* were subsequently issued on 27 March and 4 April 1957.

Once the new government was installed, Defferre's *chef de cabinet*, Fernand Wibaux, resurrected the bill on which his predecessor had been working. They moved swiftly to get the reforms through the National Assembly and on 23 June 1956 the Loi-cadre became law. In a move that was, strictly speaking, unconstitutional, it set out to reorganize the institutions of the French Union without revising the constitution. The key issue was whether to adopt a 'territorialist' approach, by devolving powers to the territories, or a 'federalist' approach, through the devolution of powers to the federal Government-General. The creation of a government council and granting of internal autonomy to Togo in 1955–6 provided a model for the former, but there was no existing model for the latter.[8] Moreover, those advocating reforms of a federalist nature faced a formidable array of enemies: the SFIO, in opposition to Senghor, was anti-federalist; the Communist Party, which was opposed to the Government-General in Algeria, by extension also opposed the idea for Black Africa, despite the clear differences in their situations; and most African *députés*, with the notable exception of Senghor, favoured the transfer of powers to the territories rather than the federation. The territories most distant from Senegal, such as Côte d'Ivoire and Dahomey, were becoming increasingly irritated by the centralization of power in Dakar and Houphouët-Boigny in particular supported the establishment of direct links between the individual territories and France. Indeed, it was at a meeting at which he was present that the idea of transferring powers to a federal executive was finally buried.[9]

However, the Loi-cadre did not simply devolve powers from the Government-General to the territorial assemblies. What actually happened was, in fact, more complicated than this, because a distinction was drawn between 'Services d'Etat' and 'Services Territoriaux'. This was important as the former were to be transferred to Paris and the latter devolved to the territories, but the law itself did not define which services fell into which category.[10] It simply established the principle, which had already been established for Togo, that government councils would be instituted in the territories and that the territorial assemblies would have increased powers. The number and significance of the responsibilities to be transferred to each level were clearly going to be crucial in determining the degree of real autonomy that the territories enjoyed, but this was left to the *décrets d'application*.

The key areas of policy that were to become the direct responsibility of the French government were designated by decree in April 1957. In addition to foreign affairs, they included defence, the police (apart from municipal and rural police), the customs service and certain other areas of policy deemed important for 'maintaining the solidarity of the elements comprising the Republic', such as the financial and monetary regime, communications, the media and higher education.[11] All other public services were designated 'Services Territoriaux'.

The underlying strategy of the French government in introducing the Loi-cadre in this way reflects a classic 'realist' approach to international relations. On the one hand, it sought to maintain French dominance by keeping control of certain strategic areas of 'high' policy deemed central to 'sovereignty', such as foreign affairs, defence and monetary policy. It also maintained French cultural influence. The most important strategic issue here was the French language: if schooling continued to be in French, then the education system would remain within the orbit of French influence. This was achieved by retaining control of examinations (and thus, effectively, of school curricula), teachers' qualifications and higher education. The Institut de Hautes Etudes de Dakar (IHED) was renamed the University of Dakar by decree on 24 February 1957 and designated France's eighteenth university.[12] This was the only university in French West Africa, so any African student who aspired to higher education was forced to pass through the French school and examination system. Also central to this strategy was the decision to retain control of communications and the media.

On the other hand, the Loi-cadre sought to take the French colonial administration out of the political front line by transferring responsibility for unpopular decisions to Africans. This was done by giving the territorial assemblies budgetary responsibility for those areas of policy concerned with African economic and social development that posed the most serious financial, and therefore also political, difficulties for the colonial authorities. Hitherto, the territorial assemblies had essentially been a channel through which grievances were aired and a forum where various groups, such as trade unions and other bodies, could enlist the support of elected members for their cause and exert pressure on the colonial administration and, beyond it, the French government. They did not however take ultimate responsibility for the positions they adopted: in short, they had power without responsibility. The Loi-cadre sought to change this by obliging African elected representatives to abandon their 'culture of demands' (*esprit revendicatif*) and instead think more closely about how the facilities and services they desired would be paid for. Finally, the Loi-cadre set out to reduce the cost of administration by making the civil service in AOF a territorial service, independent of the metropolitan civil service. The government's decision to draw a distinction between Services d'Etat and Services Territoriaux had the major advantage, from the Administration's point of view, of de-linking the metropolitan from the African civil service. Whereas State civil servants would continue to work for the French government and be paid at metropolitan rates, the pay and conditions of territorial civil servants would henceforth be a matter for the local territorial assembly, which would have to find the money to pay them from its own resources. By making this the responsibility of African elected representatives, the government hoped to reduce the escalating cost of administering its Black African colonies.

The Territorial Assemblies and Government Councils

Elections to the new territorial assemblies took place on 31 March 1957. The results meant that the RDA controlled the assemblies of Côte d'Ivoire, Soudan and Guinea, and had a fragile majority in Haute-Volta. It was in a minority in Dahomey, where Apithy's Parti Républicain du Dahomey won a majority of seats, and in Niger, where Bakary Djibo's Mouvement Socialiste Africain won forty-one of the sixty seats. The

Figure 6.1 RDA membership card, displaying the party's symbol, the elephant.

RDA was not represented at all in Senegal or Mauritania: Senghor's Bloc Populaire Sénégalais took forty-seven of the sixty seats in Senegal, against the Socialists' twelve, while in Mauritania Sidi el Moktar Ndiaye's Union Progressiste Mauritanienne won all but one of the seats.

The first government councils were formed in May. The majority of ministers were Africans, over half of whom were civil servants, although Europeans were appointed to a significant minority of posts and in the case of Côte d'Ivoire over 20 per cent of the posts went to Frenchmen.[13] Also worthy of note is the fact that trade union leaders became ministers of labour in several of the government councils and in one case, that of Sekou Touré in Guinea, Vice-President.

As they set about establishing their authority, the new government councils were in a difficult position. On one level, they were in the political vanguard of the movement for African emancipation and, as such, sought to represent the interests of all Africans, including African workers, in their struggle against the colonial regime. On another level, however, they were now employers of African civil servants, teachers and other public service workers, for whose pay and working conditions they were now responsible. They wanted to be seen to be treating their employees at least as well as the colonial power that had employed them previously, yet they could not allow the sectional interests of these workers to take precedence over the wider public interest. Firstly, their demands for salaries on a par with those paid to civil servants in France jeopardized the financial stability of the territory; and secondly, to accede to their demands would further exacerbate existing social inequalities by increasing the gap between them and the rest of society. In fact, the political dilemma confronting them was exactly the same as the one that had confronted the French authorities: where to find the money to pay for civil servants' salaries. And linked to this, how could salary costs in the administration and public services, which absorbed a disproportionate share of public expenditure in the territories, be contained, so as to release funds for development?

The Loi-cadre placed the government councils in an acutely difficult political situation. Decisions about civil servants' pay were henceforth in the hands of government councils formed largely of civil servants and ex-civil servants and answerable to territorial assemblies that were themselves formed largely of civil servants and ex-civil servants, with the result that there was great political pressure on them to respond positively to demands for pay increases in line with those awarded to metropolitan civil servants.[14] If this was refused and it was decided instead to apply the principle of autonomy, by employing African civil servants on local contracts and local rates of pay, then the new government councils risked incurring the wrath of precisely the part of the population that was the most active politically and therefore the most capable of posing them problems: 'The nature of this relationship between the politicians and the civil service is significant: we should not forget that civil servants and others who work for the Administration not only represent the majority of their electorate, but also that it is from among this group that the main organizers of the existing political parties are recruited'.[15] The government councils were in a no-win situation, as there were strong political arguments for maintaining the link between the metropolitan and local civil services, and sound economic reasons for not doing so. Sekou Touré stated their dilemma thus:

> The territorial assemblies soon risk having to confront a heavy burden inherited from successive governments: that of too many legitimate demands not satisfied. They will then find themselves faced with the following dilemma: either to satisfy the civil servants' ambitions by making the peasant farmers pay the price, or to take account of the farmers' difficulties, which their poverty would justify, and reject the workers' demands.[16]

In Côte d'Ivoire it was the political arguments that proved strongest. Without consulting the other territories and without regard for the economic and political consequences for the other territories of AOF, Côte d'Ivoire decided in 1957 to pay all its civil servants the increases that had been recommended by the Governor-General as necessary to keep salaries in French West Africa in line with those in the *métropole*. As the political leaders of Côte d'Ivoire were keen to maintain close links with France, albeit in a renewed form, there was clearly a political argument for doing this. However, by acting unilaterally in advance of the first planned interterritorial meeting of AOF civil service ministers in Dakar on 24 July 1957, which Côte d'Ivoire and Dahomey did not in the end attend, the other territories were presented with a *fait accompli*. With the effective abolition of the Government-General by the Loi-cadre, these meetings were supposed to provide a means of coordinating the action of the different territorial assemblies, something that was seen as particularly important with respect to the civil service since it had hitherto been organized on a federal basis. But this action by Côte d'Ivoire immediately exposed the crucial weakness of the new system: it could only make recommendations. Indeed, Côte d'Ivoire adopted a position of systematic non-cooperation with the interterritorial conferences, abruptly cancelling without explanation the first interterritorial conference of education ministers due to be held in Abidjan on 2 July 1957 and then refusing to attend the meeting of civil service ministers scheduled for 20 March 1958, despite the fact that it was postponed for four days to give its representatives time to arrive. The dispute became public at this meeting after Côte d'Ivoire agreed to pay in full the latest salary increase for civil servants and was condemned by the other territories for breaking ranks and making payments they could not afford.[17]

At a joint meeting of AOF finance and civil service ministers two months later, Sekou Touré complained about the system whereby civil servants' salary levels were decided in Dakar and it was then left up to the territories to find the money. Arguing that Guinea could not continue to pay its civil servants the same as in the *métropole* and that the territories could not expect France to continue to pay many of its civil servants, he declared that from 1958 African and metropolitan salaries should be de-linked.[18] The unilateral action of Côte d'Ivoire in deciding to pay salary increases that other territories could not afford had brought this matter to a head. This was not the only example of the breakdown of interterritorial solidarity following the introduction of the Loi-cadre. Keen to take the political initiative and needing to raise revenue, the new government councils also moved to vary indirect tax rates and customs

Figure 6.2 Grand Conseil, Dakar. Reproduced with kind permission of the Archives Nationales du Sénégal.

duties, thus inhibiting the free circulation of goods within the federation.[19] There were also anti-Dahomean riots in Abidjan in October 1958, provoked by resentment at the number of jobs in Côte d'Ivoire occupied by Dahomeans, which resulted in one dead and 50 injured.[20]

Meanwhile, as the government councils set about establishing their prerogatives in their respective territories, the federal Grand Conseil was left in a kind of limbo because the Loi-cadre made no mention of either it or the Government-General. The *décrets d'application* charged them with 'managing the common interests of the group of territories' and in theory gave them a coordinating role, but they had no executive power. Unlike the territories, which now had their own executives, the creation of a federal executive was not envisaged by the Loi-cadre. The Government-General could organize interterritorial ministerial conferences to discuss matters of common interest, and the Grand Conseil could make recommendations, for the coordination of tax regimes for example, but it had no power to impose them on the territories. Moreover, the position of the federal instruments of government was undermined by the *décrets d'application*, which transferred powers previously exercised at federal level either upwards to Paris or downwards to the territorial assemblies.[21] It is ironic that, in the very year when the Grand Conseil moved into its palatial new building in Dakar, it found itself politically marginalized and without a clear role. The election of Houphouët-Boigny in June 1957 as president of the Grand Conseil was a further pointer to a reduced role for the federal body in future, because he had for long opposed what he felt was the domination of the federation by Dakar. By the time the Grand Conseil officially ceased to exist, just two years later, the disintegration of the federation was already well advanced.

The outcome of the Loi-cadre was thus the political and economic 'balkanization' of French Black Africa. Even those political leaders, such as Senghor and Keita, who were committed to African unity, could do little to prevent this. Their electoral base was the territory and, thanks to the Loi-cadre, they found themselves increasingly locked into the logic of a system that attached political primacy to the territory.

The Fall of the Fourth Republic and the Return of De Gaulle

During the period from February 1956, when Guy Mollet's government was sworn in, to the fall of the Fourth Republic in May 1958, French governments came and went every few months under the spectre of the growing crisis in Algeria. The RDA was represented in every one of these governments by Houphouët-Boigny and the SFIO by Hamadoun Dicko. Modibo Keita and Hubert Maga also served in French governments during this period. The presence of Houphouët-Boigny, initially as Minister delegated to the Présidence du Conseil and subsequently as Minister of State with responsibility for the implementation of the Loi-cadre and for the Overseas Territories, and of Dicko in the 1956–7 governments, ensured the support of the majority of African *députés* for the Loi-cadre because they did not want to be seen opposing a government in which their own party was represented. Their presence also had other advantages from the government's point of view, as it enabled the government to maintain a dialogue at the highest level with Black African elected representatives whom it regarded as 'interlocuteurs valables', it blunted criticism from overseas *députés* to French policy in Algeria, and it ensured that Senghor's rearguard campaign in the National Assembly against the 'balkanization' of AOF from outside government was doomed to failure.

All of this was thrown in the balance by the storm clouds gathering in Algiers and the growing political crisis in Paris. A Committee of Public Safety was formed in Algiers on 13 May 1958, provoking fears among African *députés* that a *coup d'état* might bring to power a government opposed to any progress in the overseas territories. In these circumstances, several of them, including Houphouët-Boigny and Dicko, decided to vote for De Gaulle's investiture as Président du Conseil, whereas others, such as Senghor, preferred to abstain. They were, however, unanimous in supporting the proposal for a new constitutional law to reform the institutional links between France and the overseas territories.

To many Africans, De Gaulle was the 'man of Brazzaville' and, as the leader of Free France, was seen as the liberator of Africa.[22] According to Yves Person, his reputation as a decolonizer was scarcely deserved, but it was nonetheless how he was perceived.[23] Moreover, he had maintained contact with African leaders during his twelve-year 'crossing of the desert' and had made a private visit to Africa in 1953 during which, at the invitation of the Grand Conseil, he had inaugurated a monument in memory of Félix Eboué in Bamako. On this occasion, he had made a speech celebrating the links binding Africa and France and expressing the wish that they should endure for another hundred years: 'to link all the territories to France by means of institutions in which each assumes their rightful place and their future and in which each, while remaining true to itself, also becomes part of an ardent and powerful union . . . this is what the great ambition of the great French Union can and must be'.[24] His return to power was therefore broadly accepted by African political leaders because, after the hesitations and feet-dragging of the Fourth Republic, he represented the hope of renewed political progress. Moreover, his decision to appoint Houphouët-Boigny Minister of State in his government gave them confidence, and the new Minister for Overseas France, Bernard Cornut-Gentille, was well known to them from his spell in Dakar as Governor-General. Pierre Messmer, a close associate of De Gaulle and a future Prime Minister, became the new High Commissioner, as the Governor-General was by this time called, for French West Africa.

The End of the French Union and the Birth of the Community

Shortly after his return to power, De Gaulle began speaking of a new federal or confederal structure for the French Union, based on freely negotiated contracts with the overseas territories.[25] He also received African leaders on 14 July and told them that they would henceforth be presidents, rather than vice-presidents, of their government councils, thus making them effectively prime ministers of their territories. On 18 July, leaders of the RDA and the other main AOF political grouping, the newly created Parti du Regroupement Africain (PRA), held a meeting in Paris to draw up an agreed list of demands: recognition of the right to self-determination, full internal autonomy for all territories, establishment on an equal basis of a federal Republic, freedom for the territories to choose whether to affiliate separately or together to the federation, and economic and financial solidarity based on a major new investment plan for French Black Africa. This 'Front Commun d'Action Africaine', as it called itself, led by Senghor for the PRA and Gabriel Lisette and Philippe Yacé for the RDA, delivered the document to De Gaulle and to the relevant government ministers, Houphouët-Boigny and Cornut-Gentille.[26]

After these favourable initial signs, the draft constitutional reform bill, when it was published at the end of July, was a great disappointment to the *députés*. Not only did it maintain the French president as the head of the proposed new Community, but more seriously, there was no recognition of the right to self-determination. Indeed, De Gaulle made it clear that, if the new form of association between France and the overseas territories being proposed was rejected, then this would be taken to mean that the territories had chosen secession 'with all its consequences'.[27] The decree transforming the vice-presidents of the government councils into presidents was another disappointment, as it did not propose any immediate, real increase in their powers and responsibilities.

On 21 August, De Gaulle set off for a tour of Africa. He stopped briefly at Fort-Lamy (present-day N'Djamena, Chad) before going on to Tananarive and Brazzaville, where he made an important speech offering Africans a third option, in addition to the two – 'Community' or 'Independence' – already on offer. Essentially, he told them that if, having voted 'yes' in the referendum, they decided at some unspecified time in the future that they wanted independence, they could choose to take it without necessarily breaking the French link: 'I guarantee in advance that the *métropole* will not oppose this'. However, he pointed out that France would also retain the right to break its link with the Community 'for it will not have escaped anyone's notice that the Community will place a heavy burden on the *métropole* and it has many such burdens'.[28] His next port of call was Abidjan, where his Minister of State, Houphouët-Boigny, was waiting to meet him, alongside the High Commissioner, Pierre Messmer. He was given a rapturous reception.[29] At Conakry, however, where he arrived on the evening of 25 August, things did not go as planned. Sekou Touré made one of his typically fiery speeches in De Gaulle's presence, in which he made the now famous remark: 'There is no dignity without freedom. We prefer poverty in freedom to wealth in slavery', and went on to proclaim: 'We do not and never shall renounce our legitimate right to independence'. Although he went on to say that he wanted to continue to cooperate with France, this was lost on De Gaulle, who was offended by the tone of the speech.[30] The point of no return between France and Guinea had been reached and, in the following month's constitutional referendum, Guinea would vote 'no' and would not join the new Community.

De Gaulle's final port of call was Dakar. He arrived on 26 August to a hostile reception from the crowds waiting for him in the town's main square, the Place Protêt, where the speeches were to be made. Members of the radical Parti Africain de l'Indépendance, trade unionists and young people chanted 'Down with De Gaulle' and held banners opposed to the proposed French Community and demanding immediate independence.[31] In the absence of both Senghor, who was in France, and the Vice-President of the Government Council, Mamadou Dia, who was in Geneva for a doctor's appointment, the Mayor of Dakar, Lamine Guèye, and the Minister of the Interior, Valdiodio Ndiaye, gave the welcoming speeches. Their message was essentially the same as that delivered by Sekou Touré in Conakry, that Senegal wanted independence but did not wish to break all links with France, but the style was very different. Whereas Sekou Touré's tone was strident, Ndiaye's was courteous and diplomatic. Turning to the *porteurs de pancartes* ('banner carriers'), as he called them, De Gaulle said in his reply: 'If they want independence, let them take it on September 28', but he told the crowds that he hoped they would vote 'yes' in the referendum and work as 'brothers' with France to build the new Community.[32]

The constitutional text, which was made public on 4 September, went some of the way to meet the demands of African *députés* by granting full internal autonomy to the territories. At the same time, it maintained French predominance, because the French President was President of the Community and apparently retained executive powers as Chair of the Community's Executive Council, although this was not made completely clear in the text. Independence was stated to be incompatible with membership of the Community, although the possibility was left open for territories to take their independence at a later date, if they so wished.

The decision to count the referendum votes on a territory by territory, rather than a federal, basis was of critical importance to the political future of French West Africa, because it made it possible for individual territories to take immediate independence, if they so chose, whereas a federal-based count would have ensured that a 'no' vote in one territory would have been drowned in the sea of 'yes' votes of the other territories. The election campaign and its significance for the political evolution of

Figure 6.3 Demonstration to greet General De Gaulle, Dakar, 1958, with placards demanding immediate independence. © Photo ECPAD France.

AOF will be analysed in the next chapter. Suffice it to say here that the effect of this decision was to sound the death knell for the federation of AOF, because Sekou Touré broke ranks with the rest of the RDA leadership, who recommended a 'yes' vote, and decided instead to campaign for a 'no' vote. He won a resounding victory and, on 28 September, Guinea became independent. French officials and ministers continued to maintain that they had no objection to the federations of AOF and AEF joining the Community as federations, rather than individual states, but they also knew that interterritorial rivalries effectively ruled this out. The divisions between African political leaders made agreement difficult and in any case the richest territories in the respective federations, Côte d'Ivoire and Gabon, would never accept it. Thus, just sixty-three years after its creation, the federation of AOF was dead.

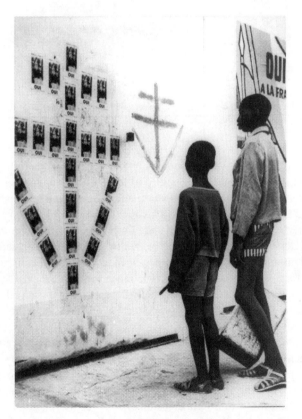

Figure 6.4 Campaign posters for the 28 September 1958 referendum, Dakar. Reproduced with kind permission of the Archives Nationales du Sénégal.

Figure 6.5 Campaign posters for the 28 September 1958 referendum, Dakar. Reproduced with kind permission of the Archives Nationales du Sénégal.

Unlike the RDA, which recommended a 'yes' vote, the other main political grouping, the PRA, decided to leave it to individual territories to make their own decisions. As a result, the political leaderships of Senegal and Dahomey came out in favour of a 'yes', while Bakary Djibo, the Party's General Secretary, decided to campaign for a 'no' vote in Niger. However, he was opposed in this by the traditional chiefs who, suspicious of his radicalism and encouraged by colonial officials, decided to call for a 'yes' vote. This *de facto* alliance between the chiefs and the French administration ensured that only 22 per cent of those voting (just 8 per cent of registered voters) supported Bakary's call for a 'no' vote in the referendum (see Table 6.1).

Overall, the results were a resounding success for the 'yes' campaign in French West Africa. More than 80 per cent of those voting voted 'yes', although the degree of enthusiasm varied enormously from territory to territory. While the official turnout figure was nearly 98 per cent in Côte d'Ivoire and the vote a virtually unanimous 'yes' (a remarkable result when one considers that, just eight years earlier, a number of Ivoirians had been killed in anti-colonial disturbances in the territory), it was only

Table 6.1

Territory	Yes %	No %
Côte d'Ivoire	99.98	0.02
Dahomey	97.84	2.16
Guinea	4.78	95.22
Haute-Volta	99.18	0.82
Mauritania	94.04	5.96
Niger	78.43	21.57
Senegal	97.54	2.46
Soudan	97.53	2.47

56 per cent in Dahomey, 45 per cent in Soudan and went down to just 37 per cent in Niger.[33]

In the following three months, the seven remaining territories decided to become states within the Community. All adopted constitutions with a strong executive, modelled closely on the Constitution of France's Fifth Republic. The first to do so, on 17 January 1959, was the Mali Federation, which at this point grouped together Senegal, Soudan, Dahomey and Haute-Volta. It was followed by the other three territories during the next two months. At this point, Houphouët-Boigny again made it clear that Côte d'Ivoire would not under any circumstances join a 'primary federation' that had either a supra-national assembly or a supra-national government that got in the way of direct relations between individual West African territories and France.[34]

De Gaulle became President of the Republic and the Community on 21 December and appointed Houphouët-Boigny a Minister of State in the new government. The Ministry for Overseas France was abolished and replaced by a Ministry of Cooperation. Raymond Janot was appointed Secretary-General of the Community. His committee, comprising representatives of each of the member states, was responsible for matters of common interest and could theoretically have become a federal executive, had the political will existed to make it so, because its areas of responsibility were foreign policy, defence, the armed forces, the currency, common economic and financial policy, the legal system, external transport links and telecommunications. However, real power lay elsewhere: executive authority for Community affairs lay with the French President and the Senate and Executive Council of the Community had little real power. The President's dominant position was further reinforced by the government's reorganization of economic, social and cultural cooperation with the Community's member states which took place during 1959. An inter-ministerial committee, under the chairmanship of the Prime Minister and including the Finance and Foreign Affairs Ministers, was created to determine French aid and cooperation policy and disburse funds through the newly created Fonds d'Aide et de Coopér-ation, which replaced the FIDES. However, since it was the President who appointed the Prime Minister and who had to sign all ministerial appointments, there was no doubt where effective power lay. It was thus during this period 1958–9 that the French president emerged as the dominant figure in French African policy.

The Rush to Independence

The remaining seven territories of former AOF came together to form the Community, but its unity was, in reality, a surface unity. The priority for Senghor and his PRA supporters was African unity, which they hoped to realize through the reconstitution of the federations of AOF and AEF, followed by independence. Senghor hoped to achieve this without breaking the ties with France, but many in his party were more concerned to move rapidly to independence. Houphouët-Boigny, on the other hand, was implacably opposed to any such 'primary federation'. His priority continued to be self-liberation through economic development and he was in no hurry to move towards independence, although not everyone in the RDA leadership shared Houphouët-Boigny's opposition either to a 'primary federation', or to rapid progress towards independence. The Soudan RDA, under the leadership of Modibo Keita, was in favour of a federal assembly and, despite being in favour of independence, never-theless called for a 'yes' vote in the 1958 referendum because of the overriding priority it attached to African unity as a prerequisite for independence. The RDA leadership in Haute-Volta was in favour of a federation and d'Arboussier, on behalf of the Niger RDA, also favoured the idea. In addition, Dahomey, where the PRA had a majority, was in favour of some kind of federation.

Thus, at the end of 1958, four territories appeared to support the idea of a federation: Senegal, Soudan, Haute-Volta and Dahomey. The position in Niger was unclear following the dissolution of the Territorial Assembly as a result of the defeat of Bakary Djibo's call for a 'no' vote in the refer-endum. And Mauritania, straddling the dividing line between north Africa and Black Africa, hesitated to join any grouping that would anchor it in the Black African camp. The commitment of Haute-Volta and Dahomey to the federal idea was not, however, unequivocal. In Haute-Volta, the Mogho Naba, on behalf of the traditional chiefs, had originally come out in favour of a federation, but he subsequently changed his mind as a result of a visit by a delegation from Niger and Côte d'Ivoire that convinced him that the federal idea was being promoted by extremist groups who posed a serious threat to the stability and prosperity of the territory.[35] Dahomey's leader, Apithy, while in favour of the federal principle, insisted that the federation should be sufficiently flexible to allow his territory at the same time to have relations with its neighbouring territories, Ghana and Nigeria.[36] Nevertheless, delegations from each of these territories met in Dakar from 14–17 January 1959 to agree the Constitution of the new Mali Federation.

Shortly afterwards, the anti-federalists set to work. Pierre Messmer, in his memoirs, claims that the Administration remained neutral throughout this period and did not in any way intervene in what were considered internal African affairs.[37] However, a new High Commissioner, as the governor was called under the new Constitution, was suddenly appointed to Haute-Volta in January 1959 without the local Territorial Assembly

Figure 6.6 De Gaulle, Modibo Keita, Lamine Guèye, Dakar, 1959. Reproduced with kind permission of the Archives Nationales du Sénégal.

even being informed. The appointee, Paul Masson, was a known anti-federalist and used his position to exploit the concerns of some groups within Haute-Volta, notably the war veterans who depended on their army pension from the French government, that federation might lead to secession from France.[38] Côte d'Ivoire's leaders also put pressure on the leaders of Haute-Volta by exploiting their concerns over the territory's economic dependence on Côte d'Ivoire. As a landlocked territory, most of its trade passed through Côte d'Ivoire and the livelihood of many Voltaic families depended on being able to find work on Ivoirian coffee and cocoa plantations. Thus, on 28 February, the Territorial Assembly reversed its previous decision and came out against the federation. The decision was subsequently ratified in a referendum.

In Dahomey, pro-federalists in the PRA leadership were also under pressure. Alexandre Adandé and Emile Derlin Zinsou had gone to the January meeting in Dakar and endorsed the establishment of the federation, but Dahomey's leader and Vice-President of the Territorial Assembly, Apithy, had not gone. On their return from Dakar, Adandé and Zinsou put the federal proposals to the local section of the PRA, the Parti Progressiste Dahoméen (PPD), which adopted them. In the meantime, Apithy, who was by now convinced that the Mali Federation was not in Dahomey's economic interests, came out against the idea of a primary federation.[39] Finding himself in a minority within his own party, he resigned from the PPD and joined forces with the local section of the RDA, the Union Démocratique Dahoméenne, led by Justin Ahomadegbé, which was anti-federalist. This new grouping, with support from elected members from the north of the territory, then went on to win the vote against federation in the Territorial Assembly. The PPD under Adandé and Zinsou refused to take part in the legislative elections that followed and, as a result, pro-federalists were completely absent from the new Territorial Assembly elected on 2 April. The Mali Federation now had only two member states.

However, while Côte d'Ivoire was against any form of primary federation at the political level, it did claim that it wanted economic links with its neighbours. The Conseil de l'Entente, created at the instigation of Houphouët-Boigny, was an attempt to make such economic cooperation a reality by bringing together Côte d'Ivoire, Dahomey, Haute-Volta and Niger in a customs union. Its first meeting was held in Abidjan at the end of May and it came into being at the beginning of July 1959.[40]

The new Community inevitably suffered from these rivalries. Houphouët-Boigny claimed to be committed to it, but his behaviour in sabotaging the Mali federation reinforced the divide between Senegal and Côte d'Ivoire and also turned the RDA leadership in Soudan against him. Shortly afterwards, in September 1959, Modibo Keita and Mamadou Dia, the President and Vice-President of the Mali Federation, announced their intention to exercise the Mali Federation's right to independence. Conscious of the fact that Ghana and Guinea had already become independent and that other African colonies would shortly follow suit, and under pressure from activists in the newly-created Parti de la Fédération Africaine (PFA), they decided to request France to grant independence, although they also made it clear that they wanted to do this by negotiation and that the transfer of power would be followed by the signing of bilateral cooperation agreements between the two countries. At a press conference on 10 November, De Gaulle, who by now apparently saw political independence as a means for France to rid itself of its African colonial 'burden', indicated that France recognized their right to self-determination and would not put any obstacles in the way of states wishing to take their independence 'in friendship with France'.[41] And in a speech that gave a significant indication of the way in which he envisaged French influence being maintained in Black Africa in the post-colonial era, De Gaulle expressed his desire to see created 'a grouping in which they will receive French support and in return for which they will participate in France's activities on the world stage'.[42] This vision of a mutually beneficial relationship, in which independent Black African states would benefit from French support and cooperation in return for their support for France in the global arena, was to be the foundation stone for the maintenance of close Franco-African relations in the post-colonial era.

On 13 December, De Gaulle went to Dakar and gave a speech to the Federal Assembly of Mali in which he recognized their right to independence, but proposed that they should continue to cooperate with France. He reminded them that the world into which Mali would emerge as a sovereign state was a tough one, in which even the most powerful states were increasingly interdependent: 'There is no state, however great or powerful it may be, which can do without others. Nowadays, no policy can be carried out without cooperation'.[43] The government had by this time clearly acknowledged that its key strategic objective – the maintenance of a French 'sphere of influence' in Black Africa – was fully compatible with, and may indeed be facilitated by, the granting of political independence. The language of 'assimilation' and integration thus gave way to the language of 'cooperation' and partnership.

Houphouët-Boigny greeted the news that the Mali Federation was to be granted independence with some bitterness, since it marked the end of his dream of a Franco-African Community. As he put it, somewhat picturesquely: 'I have been waiting in vain on the church steps with my bouquet of faded flowers'.[44] The four members of the Conseil de l'Entente met on 30 December in Abidjan to discuss the new situation. Dahomey in particular was keen to move quickly to independence because its immediate neighbour, Togo, was due to become independent in 1960, nearby Ghana was already independent and its largest neighbour, Nigeria, was not far behind. The Territorial Assembly therefore asked the government to initiate negotiations with France for the transfer of powers.[45] Six months later, the heads of state of the four member states delivered a letter to De Gaulle requesting the transfer of powers without prior signature of cooperation accords with France. By making it clear that they were leaving the Community, whereas the Mali Federation nominally remained a member, and by insisting that the negotiation of cooperation accords with France would only take place after the new states had been admitted to the United Nations, the Conseil states intended to demonstrate that their independence from France was more complete than that of Mali Federation. In this way, they hoped to disarm the attacks of Sekou Touré and Nkrumah, echoed by nationalists within

Figure 6.7 Accession of Mali to independence, 1960: Jacques Foccart reading a message from De Gaulle. Reproduced with kind permission of the Institut Fondamental d'Afrique Noire, Dakar.

their own territories, against their 'so-called subservience to the French government'.[46]

Negotiations with Mali were concluded on 4 April and the Federation proclaimed its independence on 20 June. Negotiations with the four Conseil de l'Entente states were concluded even more quickly than with Mali and the document granting independence was signed on 11 July, on the same basis as the agreement already signed with Mali. They all became independent in August. Mauritania followed on 28 November.

The Mali Federation had, by this time, already collapsed. The declaration of independence brought out into the open fundamental differences between the two states concerning the way in which the federation should be organized, with Soudan demanding a concentration of powers in the federal organs of government, which would have effectively created a unitary state, whereas Senegal favoured a looser structure that would have allowed each country to retain more of its individuality and made it easier for other African states subsequently to join the federation if they wished. This disagreement was rooted in the divergent political traditions of the two states: Senegal's political culture, with its long history of political pluralism and competitive elections, was very different from the communist-influenced political culture of Soudan's RDA which saw the Party as the direct expression of the people. Moreover, there were important differences of both political substance and style between the two leaders, Senghor and Keita: the former moderate and conciliatory, the latter radical and more implacably anti-colonial and anti-French.[47] Tensions increased when Keita began to meddle in internal Senegalese affairs, trying to forge his own links with Senegal's marabouts, who were Senghor's political power base in rural areas, and criticizing Senghor for his lack of radicalism. Matters came to a head over the issue of who was to be President of the Federation, a post both men wanted. No agreement was reached, the Senegalese suspected the Soudanese of plotting a coup, relations soured and a split became inevitable. As a result, Soudan, which retained the name Mali, and Senegal became independent separately.

Conclusion: A Successfully Managed Transition?

After a period of immobilism in French colonial policy, it was only the outbreak of unrest in Algeria and the fear that this might spread to sub-Saharan Africa, combined with the rapid progress towards independence in the Gold Coast, that finally forced the government to review the political institutions of the French Union and establish a new framework for the political evolution of French Black Africa. The Loi-cadre of 1956–7 was the product of this reassessment. It has been described as an 'enlightened' act[48] which helped to avoid major bloodshed in Black Africa, yet this would suggest a degree of foresight and forward planning that simply was not present in French policy making. When it was adopted, it was more a question of the government facing up to the inevitable than skilfully planning for the future. Moreover, the Loi-cadre was by this time already obsolete. What it granted – partial devolution of powers to elected territorial assemblies – might have been acceptable ten years earlier, but in 1956, after the Bandung conference, the granting of internal autonomy to Togo, the Suez crisis and against the background of the rapid march of other African colonies towards independence, it fell far short of satisfying African aspirations.[49] Moreover, even at this stage there was no question of preparing the territories for independence. On the contrary, the Loi-cadre's primary objective was to maintain its Black African territories firmly in the French sphere of influence. The strategy for achieving this was to retain control over areas of 'high' policy such as foreign affairs, monetary policy, defence, higher education and language policy, while conceding political autonomy to Africans in other areas. In this respect, the Loi-cadre prefigured French African policy in the post-colonial period by transferring limited powers to Africans who were loyal and friendly towards France but were nevertheless perceived as the legitimate representatives and leaders of their own people.

The groundwork for this had been laid by the creation of the French Union in 1946, as a result of which they enjoyed legitimacy as the elected representatives of their people, but at the same time were sucked into, and became part of, the French political system. They served their political apprenticeship in Paris, made important and powerful friends, and became familiar with French policy networks and how they functioned. This was a key factor in laying the foundation for the largely peaceful transfer of power to African leaders who were friendly towards France.

However, continuing pressure from radical nationalists and then the fall of the Fourth Republic, within twelve months of the government councils being created and before they had had time fully to establish themselves, reopened the question of the political future of French West Africa. Fortunately for France, De Gaulle's return to power was greeted favourably by most Africans and his return was seen as representing a new opportunity for political progress. However, as in 1946 and 1956, Africans were to be disappointed, because the new Community that was brought into being by the constitution of September 1958 once again fell far short of their aspirations. Even at this late stage there was no question of a real transfer of powers to Africans; on the contrary, power over the key areas of policy remained concentrated in Paris and the institutional arrangements put in place by the 1958 constitution actually represented a step backwards compared to the Fourth Republic, under which, as elected members of the National Assembly, African *députés* had direct access to the centres of power. In contrast, the Community made no provision for African *députés* to be elected to the National Assembly. Henceforth, any lobbying would have to take place outside such official channels, through personal contact with the President and his advisers.

None of this suggests that either the French government or its civil servants were in control of the rapidly evolving political situation in Black Africa, were able to take a long view of policy or in a position to plan for the future. If we now return to the question of France's 'successfully managed transition' in Black Africa, we can see that from the early 1950s, policy making was largely reactive rather than proactive. There is no more powerful illustration of the extent to which the government had lost control of the political agenda in Black Africa than the fact that the Administration was prepared to facilitate the rise of Sekou Touré to lead the CGTA, despite the fact that his anti-colonial discourse and demands for African autonomy represented a complete denial of the vision of a Greater France that had been central to French colonial policy since the Second World War. Although the Loi-cadre and the constitutional reform of 1958 did make changes, they were too little and too late to satisfy African aspirations. Moreover, once the principles on which reforms were to be based were agreed, they were subsequently subject to lobbying, usually from interest groups or politicians for whom the colonial myth remained strong and who saw any kind of imperial reform as tantamount to 'giving away the Empire' (*brader l'empire*). As a result, the final texts that were introduced were invariably a disappointment to Africans. This happened in the case of the *décrets d'application* that followed the Loi-cadre and again in 1958 with the Community. Furthermore, with governments changing every few months and the upheaval caused by a change of regime in 1958, it was effectively impossible for the government to control the decolonization agenda and take a long-term strategic view of French African policy.

Despite this, the outcome in French West Africa was, from the French point of view, very much in line with what France's post-war governing élites wanted to achieve. The transfer of power took place smoothly, to African political leaders friendly towards France, and in such a way as to enable France to maintain a significant and active presence in Black Africa after independence. Its former colonial territories in French West

Africa, excluding Guinea, and in French Equatorial Africa, remained firmly within the French sphere of influence and were to be its most loyal allies on the international stage in the post-colonial period. Although this outcome was not the product of careful planning and successful management on the part of France, nor was it simply a happy accident.

A number of factors were important in laying the foundation for the smooth transition: economic dependency; the institutional structures of the French Union; the personal links that were forged as a result between French politicians and officials and African political leaders; and the ideological underpinning of a progressive, 'assimilationist' discourse that held out the prospect of integration, albeit only for the chosen few, within a 'one and indivisible' republic committed to the values of liberty, equality and fraternity. Thus, economic and political realities ensured that the political options available to African political leaders in the late 1950s – cooperation with, or secession from, France – left them with little real choice about which course of action to take, while the discourse of French republicanism, based on the universal principles of liberty, equality and fraternity, both chimed with their aspiration for African emancipation and served to legitimate their choice for cooperation. Only Guinea took a different course. This was important in determining the nature of the independence granted to the seven remaining territories of French West Africa, and indeed to the rest of French Black Africa, in 1960, as it meant that the process leading to decolonization, and subsequently independence, took place in cooperation with France, rather than in confrontation with it.

Thus, the vision of a successfully managed French decolonization in Black Africa, carefully prepared over many years, is scarcely justified. Nevertheless, it has been a *leitmotif* of French official policy discourse since independence and has played a central role in legitimating the maintenance of an active French presence in Black Africa to both French and African public opinion in the post-colonial era. It was at the centre of High Commissioner Messmer's speech as he left Dakar for the last time: 'My departure is not a sad one, as it marks a new stage in the political development of Africa, preparations for which have been made for many long years, since the end of the Second World War'.[50] Since then, French and African political leaders alike have bought into, and promoted, the idea of 'independence in friendship with France'. For the former, it served to justify France's continuing close involvement with its ex-colonies in Black Africa by suggesting that it recognized some kind of moral obligation to countries that had freely chosen to remain tied to, and friendly towards, France after gaining political independence. For the latter, it provided a justification for their leaders' chosen strategy of negotiating independence with, rather than seizing it from, France, because it enabled their countries to continue to benefit from French support in a vast number of areas, ranging from economic and military support to cultural and technical cooperation. In this way, independence was achieved without any rupture of Franco-African relations. And it was this, in turn, which led to the charge against the political leaders of French Black Africa, from opponents both within and outside their countries, that what they had attained was not real independence from France, but a partial, 'pseudo-' independence.[51] However, in order to be in a position to achieve this, African political leaders first had to defuse and marginalize politically the demands for African unity, secession from France and full and immediate independence that were being articulated increasingly loudly by radical groups within the wider nationalist movement. How this came about will be the subject of the next chapter.

Notes

1. D. Bruce Marshall, *The French Colonial Myth and Constitution-Making in the Fourth Republic* (Yale University Press, 1973), pp. 313.
2. J.-P. Sartre, 'Le colonialisme est un système', *Les Temps Modernes*, 123, March–April 1956; R. Cartier, 'En France Noire avec Raymond Cartier', *Paris-Match*, 11 August, pp. 38–41, 18 August, pp. 34–7, and 1 September 1956, pp. 39–41. See also J. Marseille, *Empire colonial et capitalisme français. Histoire d'un divorce* (Albin Michel, 1984) for a study of the growing rift between French business élites and colonial empire.
3. O. Colombani, *Mémoires coloniales* (La Découverte, 1991), p. 165.
4. 'Réflexions de voyage sur le problème du maintien de la présence française en Afrique', p. 14, unsigned, October 1955, ANSOM Aff. Pol. 2187/6.
5. C. De Gaulle, *Discours et messages*, vol. 3 (Plon, 1970), p. 14.
6. J.-R. Benoist, *L'Afrique Occidentale Française de 1944 à 1960* (Nouvelles Editions Africaines, 1982), title of the conclusion, p. 495.
7. Session of 21 March 1956, *JODP*, 22 March 1956, pp. 1108–9.
8. For a discussion of French policy and its objectives in Togo, see J. Kent, *The Internationalisation of Colonialism* (Clarendon Press,

1992), pp. 259, 298–9. Britain had wanted British Togo's future settled before Ghanaian independence and it was this that had forced France's hand in granting internal autonomy to Togo. It would have been difficult for France to deny the same concession to its other colonies in Black Africa.

9. Fernand Wibaux, quoted in J.-R. de Benoist, *L'Afrique*, p. 298.

10. Article 3 defined the 'Services d'Etat' simply as those services 'responsible for managing the interests of the state' while the 'Services Territoriaux' were those services 'responsible for managing the interests of the territories'.

11. Decree dated 4 April 1957, *Journal Officiel. Lois et Décrets (JOLD)*, 13 April 1957, p. 3952.

12. Its staff were also assimilated into metropolitan staff *cadres* as French civil servants, in accordance with its status as a Service d'Etat, Min Ed F17bis 3273.

13. The proportion of government posts filled by Europeans was: Côte d'Ivoire (3/13 members of the government were Europeans); Mauritania 2/9; Dahomey 2/10; Senegal 2/11; Guinea and Soudan 2/12; Niger 1/10 and Haute-Volta 1/12. See Guillemin P, 'La structure des premiers gouvernements locaux en Afrique noire', *Revue française de science politique*, 9, 3, 1959, p. 675. According to Guillemin, Europeans were concentrated particularly in the financial and technical ministries.

14. Civil servants (which, as in France, included teachers) represented 75 per cent of the Government Council in Haute-Volta, 67 per cent in Mauritania, 63 per cent in Senegal, 50 per cent in Dahomey and Guinea, 42 per cent in Soudan, 40 per cent in Niger and 23 per cent in Côte d'Ivoire, see ibid, p. 669. According to J.-L. Seurin, 'Elites sociales et partis politiques d'AOF', in *Annales africaines*, 1958, p. 154, 235 out of 473 (49.6 per cent) of those elected to the territorial assemblies in March 1957 were civil servants. For a detailed breakdown of their social background, see R. S. Morgenthau, *Political Parties in French-Speaking West Africa* (Clarendon Press, 1964), pp. 401–11.

15. Letter dated 18 January 1957, Governor-General to Minister, in ANSOM Aff. Pol. 2200/3.

16. Sekou Touré, 'Avantages et inconvénients de la Loi-cadre', *Union Française et Parlement*, 71, March 1956, p. 12, in AAOF 17G643/165.

17. Report on the Third Conference of AOF Civil Service Ministers, Dakar, 20–24 March 1958, ANSOM Aff. Pol. 2188/2.

18. Report on a meeting of AOF Finance and Civil Service Ministers, 28–29 May 1958, ANSOM Aff. Pol. 2173/12.
19. Report on Conference of Finance Ministers, Abidjan, 4 July 1958, in *Afrique Nouvelle*, 11 July 1958, p. 10.
20. Report dated 31 October 1958 from Governor Côte d'Ivoire to Governor-General, Dakar, ANSOM Aff. Pol. 2189/12.
21. Decree dated 4 April 1957, *JOLD*, 11 April 1957, pp. 3857–62.
22. Cf. Senghor's poem, written to De Gaulle from a prison camp in 1940. Entitled *Guelowar (The Noble One)*, it contained the lines:

> Your voice speaks of honour, of hope and of the combat, and its wings flutter in our breasts.
> Your voice tells of the republic, that we will build in the City in the blue day.
> In the equality of fraternal peoples and we tell ourselves 'We are present, O Guelowar!'

Quoted by D. S. White, Black Africa and De Gaulle
(Pennsylvania University Press, 1979), p. 190.

23. Y. Person, 'French West Africa and Decolonization', in P. Gifford and W. M. Louis, eds., *The Transfer of Power in Africa* (Yale University Press, 1982), p. 166.
24. C. De Gaulle, *Discours et messages*, vol. 2, p. 579.
25. Ouezzin Coulibaly, Vice-President of the Government Council of Haute-Volta, quoted in *Le Monde*, 22 July 1958, p. 7.
26. *Le Monde,* 22 July 1958, p. 12.
27. Cf. G. Chaffard, *Les Carnets secrets de la décolonisation*, vol. 2 (Calmann-Lévy, 1967), p. 189; J.-R. de Benoist, *L'Afrique*, pp. 412–13; E. Mortimer, *France and the Africans 1944–60* (Faber & Faber, 1969), pp. 310–11.
28. Quoted in D. S. Blair, *Black Africa*, p. 201.
29. P. Messmer, *Après Tant de Batailles* (Albin Michel, 1992), pp. 232–3.
30. Quoted in A. Stanislas, *De Gaulle et les Africains* (Chaka, 1990), pp. 151–2; see also, P. Messmer, *Après Tant de Batailles*, p. 235.
31. See Figure 6.3.
32. C. De Gaulle, *Discours*, vol. 3, p. 38.
33. One should, however, exercise care in interpreting election results from a purely European perspective. In Western liberal democracies, a vote is an expression of an individual preference, whereas in Africa it is often the product of a consensus reached at family, clan or village level, as a result of which everyone votes for the same political option, candidate or party.

34. 'La Côte d'Ivoire refuse toute fédération primaire', *Afrique Nouvelle*, 5 December 1958, p. 1; E. Mortimer, *France*, pp. 344–5.
35. 'Une conférence groupant les partisans d'une fédération primaire en AOF s'ouvre à Bamako', *Le Monde*, 30 December 1958, p. 16.
36. *Afrique Nouvelle*, 19 December 1958, p. 2.
37. P. Messmer, *Après tant de batailles*, p. 245.
38. They were well organized and numbered some 17,000 in the north of the country around Ouahigouya, see J.-R. de Benoist, *L'Afrique*, p. 448.
39. According to J.-R. de Benoist, ibid, p. 449, he only expressed this view in public after he had received assurances from the French government that, if Dahomey left the Mali Federation, it would not withdraw its financial support for the construction of a new port at Cotonou.
40. J.-R. de Benoist, *La Balkanisation de l'Afrique Occidentale Française* (Nouvelles Editions Africaines, 1979), pp. 253–4.
41. A. Peyrefitte, *C'était De Gaulle* (Eds De Fallois/Fayard, 1997), vol. 2, pp. 457–8.
42. 'De Gaulle admet l'évolution de la Communauté', *Afrique Nouvelle*, 13 November 1959, p. 2.
43. Quoted in A. Stanislas, *De Gaulle*, pp. 157–8.
44. P.-H. Siriex, *Félix Houphouët-Boigny: L'Homme de la Paix* (Seghers, 1975), p. 188.
45. *Afrique Nouvelle*, 1 January 1960, p. 7.
46. P.-H. Siriex, *Félix Houphouët-Boigny*, p. 185.
47. For a discussion of the differences between the two men, see J. Vaillant, *French, Black and African. A Life of Léopold Sédar Senghor* (Harvard University Press, 1990), pp. 298–9.
48. M. Kahler, *Decolonization in Britain and France* (Princeton University Press, 1984), p. 197.
49. Africanus, *L'Afrique noire devant l'indépendance* (Plon, 1958), pp. 1–2.
50. 'M. Messmer a définitivement quitté Dakar', *Afrique Nouvelle*, 25 December 1959, p. 1.
51. Cf. Machyo w'Obanda, C., 'Conditions of Africans at Home', in T. Abdul-Raheem, ed, *Pan Africanism* (Pluto Press, 1996), pp. 38–9.

–7–

Nationalist Politics and the Campaign for Independence, 1957–60

By 1956, the emerging nationalist movement was gathering strength: its base of support was broadening, it had successfully forged international links, and the different strands of the movement had begun to converge, ideologically if not organizationally, so that it appeared to be on the threshold of achieving some kind of unity. On the international stage, events were moving fast and increasing pressure on the government to decolonize: in 1956, Morocco and Tunisia became independent and Togo became an autonomous republic within the French Union, the two leading colonial powers, Great Britain and France, were humiliated in the Suez crisis, the Gold Coast was about to gain its independence, and pressure on the French government was increasing because of the deteriorating situation in Algeria. The government had lost control of the decolonization agenda and was on the defensive. On the ground in Africa, the trade unions, student and youth organizations, together with various cultural organizations, which formed the movement's core, were more active than the political parties, which only came to life at election times. As a result, African political leaders were in danger of losing the political initiative to these radical nationalist groups.

Major difficulties still confronted the emerging movement, none-theless. Nationalism, in AOF as in other parts of Africa during the period of decolonization, was, first and foremost, anti-colonial, but beyond this it was multi-layered: people identified with their ethnic group or tribe, with their religious community, with their particular colonial territory, perhaps in some cases with a broader trans-territorial region – the federation of French West Africa, for example – or, in the case of Pan-Africanism, with the dream of a united Africa. At the same time, as teachers or railway workers, for example, they could identify with their trade union colleagues in these professions. Nor were these different identities necessarily mutually exclusive. It was quite possible for a Soudanese teacher to define himself as a Bambara in one situation and a

Soudanese in another, while at the same time seeing himself as part of a wider Black African community and also feeling a sense of professional solidarity as a teacher with other teachers in the colony. Reflecting this, a diversity of organizations existed, operating at different levels, each of which in its own way expressed opposition to colonialism. This diversity did not necessarily pose a problem insofar as these different strands were able to coalesce, or at least fight alongside each other, in a common struggle against the colonial power. In French West Africa, however, these criss-crossing attachments, which were part of a growing nationalist tide, co-existed, in the case of French-educated Africans, with another attachment, described here as 'assimilationist nationalism', which was culturally in fundamental conflict with them. This was an attachment to the national culture and values of the colonial power, of the *French* rather than the *African* nation.[1] Even if this did not mean aspiring to become 'Black Frenchmen', which Africans did not seek, it did entail an attachment to a certain idea of France that projected the values of liberty and equality. This was reflected in the demand for full metropolitan-style education and full entitlement to the rights conferred by French citizenship. These criss-crossing attachments found political expression in a complex of different ways that had created tensions but had not posed insurmountable problems for the emerging nationalist movement before 1956. This changed as the transfer of power approached. The purpose of this chapter is thus to analyse, on the one hand, the growing rift between moderate nationalist political *leaders* and radical nationalist groups based in the student and youth organizations and – increasingly – in the trade unions, which formed the core of the wider nationalist *movement*, and on the other, the tensions within this wider nationalist movement, which were to lead, ultimately, to its defeat.

Impact of the Loi-cadre

The problems confronting the different nationalist groups as they sought to transform the movement into a united political force were exacerbated by the Loi-cadre in two ways. Firstly, it created a situation in which the political momentum was with the territories: this could only lead to political divergence between them, which necessarily occurred at the expense of the pursuit of common, federal interests. By devolving powers to the territory rather than the federation, the Loi-cadre accentuated the tendency for Africans to identify their interests with the former rather than the latter. Although both were, of course, colonial creations, the federation, with its seat of government in Dakar, was – except in the case of Senegal – more remote than the territory. Thus, the territory came to be seen as 'us', representing 'our' interests, against 'them', the federal government, representing external, federal interests in Dakar. These 'external' interests could be those of the colonial power, but could also be portrayed as those of Senegal, which housed the Government-General and was seen as dominating the federation and creating an obstacle to direct links between the other territories and France. This was an ambiguity upon which Houphouët-Boigny was to play successfully in portraying the federation as against Ivoirian interests and advocating instead direct links between Côte d'Ivoire and France.

Secondly, the Loi-cadre transferred financial and political respons-ibility for the civil service, social services, health and education from the colonial administration to the territorial assemblies. This meant that Africans were henceforth responsible for the funding and management of policy in those areas in which the colonial administration had been experiencing the greatest political difficulties. By transferring this responsibility to the territorial assemblies, the Loi-cadre removed the colonial administration from the political front line. Now it was up to African elected representatives, many of whom had in their previous professional lives actively supported the union campaigns for equality with Europeans, to decide how to respond to this demand. In Fred Cooper's metaphor, the fox was put in charge of guarding the chicken coop.[2]

Radical nationalists, with their commitment to keeping the federation of AOF together and, by 1957–8, to 'independence in unity', were increasingly out of step with the trend towards devolution of powers to the territories. The territorial assemblies were keen to increase their prerogatives at the expense of the federation, while radical nationalists waged a bitter battle against the Loi-cadre, accusing the government of a deliberate attempt to 'balkanize' Africa and delay African independence, and branding African political leaders charged with responsibility for applying it 'puppets controlled by the French government'.[3] The fact that the trade union movement had become an important focus for the activities of radical nationalist leaders and that, in the professional arena, trade unions demanded that their members be paid according to a metropolitan benchmark, did not help their cause. The demand for assimilation on the *professional* front, combined with the demand for autonomy and then independence on the *political* front, was easy for its political opponents to exploit. Already a privileged minority compared to the mass of the rural population, this demand looked to many like an attempt to further their own sectional interests at the expense of the mass of the population, and was easily portrayed as such by African political leaders.

From 1957 onwards, therefore, radical nationalists were on the political defensive. The Loi-cadre made their ambition of keeping the federation together more difficult to achieve and its problems were exacerbated by subsequent events. The fall of the Fourth Republic and return to power of De Gaulle, the government's decision to count the votes in the constitutional referendum on a territorial, rather than a federal, basis, and its decision to campaign for a 'no' vote in the constitutional referendum, in opposition to AOF's main political leaders, all these contributed to the process of political marginalization of the nationalist movement.

The Quest for Unity I: Trade Unions, Students and the Youth Movement

Although certain powers had been devolved to Africans by the Loi-cadre, the government did not see this at the time as part of a strategy for eventual French withdrawal. No government spokesman talked, at least not in public, of the eventuality of African independence, and the overriding priority for French governing élites remained the maintenance of the French presence in Africa. If the nationalist movement was to win its battle for secession from France, it needed to be strong enough to mount an effective challenge to this presence. Even more importantly, however, it needed to be able to counter the prestige and influence of AOF's political leaders, who remained committed to working for African emancipation in cooperation with France. To do this, it needed to broaden its appeal beyond its largely urban and trade union bases into the rural areas, which were the main electoral power base of Africa's political leaders. This was the US-RDA's strategy in Soudan and it was also Sekou Touré's strategy in Guinea, where he used the trade union movement as a base from which to construct a wider anti-colonial front under the umbrella of the PDG. The nationalist movement now needed to emulate this strategy if it was to be successful. Until it could do this, it would have little sway over the mass of the population in the other territories. But before it could do this, it needed to make itself into a united, federation-wide political force.

Towards Trade Union Unity: The Creation of the Union Générale des Travailleurs d'Afrique Noire

There were two major obstacles that trade unions needed to overcome if they were to become an effective federation-wide political force in the struggle for African emancipation: their affiliation to different metropolitan *centrales* and the fact that solidarity between the unions' different territorial sections was weak. The creation of the interterritorial Union Générale des Travailleurs d'Afrique Noire (UGTAN) was an attempt to address both of these issues by bringing the AOF unions together into a single organization. Independent of any metropolitan *centrale*, its ambition, as its name suggested, was to bring together into one organization all workers in Black Africa. Its founding conference took place at Cotonou from 16–19 January 1957.

The CGT dominated the conference organizationally and succeeded in getting Abdoulaye Diallo elected as Secretary-General. Its aims – 'emancipation of the African masses' and 'liquidation of the colonial regime' – were such as to unite its different constituent bodies. However, the strength of feeling for autonomy was recognized, so that traditional CGT themes, such as pay and international workers' solidarity, were combined with a new emphasis on the need to promote 'the African personality' and an acceptance of the principle of trade union independence from political parties.[4] Although the demand for African independence was not articulated in public, this new emphasis seemed to suggest that priority was now attached to the *nationalist* struggle over the *class* struggle. This reflected the growing primacy, for the union leadership and many activists if not for rank and file trade unionists, of the *political* campaign for African liberation over the *socio-economic* struggle of African workers for better wages and conditions.

The growing politicization of the AOF trade union movement was the continuation of a trend that was already under way by 1956 but became more pronounced after the Cotonou Congress, which took place against the backcloth of preparations for the first elections to the new territorial assemblies and growing crisis in Algeria. Responding to this intensification of activity in the political arena, the Congress condemned the Loi-cadre for its 'balkanization' of Black Africa and passed a resolution condemning imperialist and colonial wars and demanding Algerian independence.

This new orientation created problems for the union, however. The most important union issue confronting it at this time was the de-linking of African civil servants' pay and conditions from the metropolitan benchmark. Civil servants feared the consequences of this, because it would remove the political justification for their highly privileged position vis-à-vis the rest of the population. The High-Commissioner expressed their fears thus:

> They fear that a break between the metropolitan and local civil services will expose them to an African mass whose standard of living is infinitely lower than that which they have attained, and they are trying to obtain as many benefits as they can in the short term, before the constraints and responsibilities of greater political autonomy place a limit on their social advancement.[5]

A series of strikes took place on the issue in the second half of 1957 and 1958, which put the UGTAN leadership in a difficult position. On the one hand, it wanted to support their claims and sought to pin the blame on France for the territories' financial plight, but at the same time it worried that strikes would provoke splits between Africans and weaken the movement for national liberation.[6] The message it sent out to union members, and indeed to the public generally, was, at best, confused, compared to the clear and unequivocal message sent out by the unions when they were able to use the language of equal rights and entitlements in the pre-Loi-cadre period. In response, African ministers turned the discourse of national liberation against the union by using the language of African unity to warn trade unionists to back off and not press their sectional interests at the expense of the wider national interest.[7] There was a profound irony here: the CGTA and its successor, the UGTAN, had used the argument of national unity to justify the creation of a united, autonomous union movement, but now found the arguments of national unity and autonomy being used against them by African ministers to justify rejecting the retention of the metropolitan benchmark.

For all its proclaimed commitment to unity, the trade union movement faced enormous difficulties in making this a reality. Practical problems included its lack of financial resources or established structures, and the question of how to maintain communications and coordinate actions effectively across such enormous distances. Add to this the personal and inter-territorial rivalries within the union's leadership and the difficulties created by the introduction of the Loi-cadre, and the obstacles to their success were probably insurmountable. Indeed, after the Congress, many of the leading figures at Cotonou returned to their home territories, took off their trade union hats and donned their political hats to campaign for their respective local political parties in the run-up to the March assembly elections. Many did well and, in most of the territories of AOF, either the labour minister or the civil service minister in the new government councils was a leading UGTAN member: Abdoulaye Diallo, for example, became Minister of Labour in Soudan, a leading Senegalese member of UGTAN, Latyr Camara, became that territory's Civil Service Minister, and Sekou Touré became Vice-President of the Government Council in Guinea.

This sudden departure of many of its most seasoned leaders decapitated the trade union movement just at the moment when it was entering a difficult period and desperately needed their skills and experience. Although their departure weakened its effectiveness on the union front, so that union activity was 'very reduced' in 1957,[8] the UGTAN leadership could nonetheless reasonably claim that their strategy had placed the trade union movement at the centre of the political struggle for African liberation. The problem was that this was at the expense of their role as trade unionists, because they were no longer primarily trade union leaders organizing African workers in their struggle against the government or reactionary private employers, but were now territorial assembly members with a mandate to represent the whole of their electorate and government ministers with a ministerial brief to carry out. Moreover, divisions emerged within the union over the participation of trade union leaders in government, with Sekou Touré and his supporters arguing that, because there was no class struggle in Africa, there was no contradiction between belonging to a union and being part of government, whereas others argued that government ministers could not simultaneously support the government and union cause.[9] It was this combining of trade union functions with ministerial responsibilities that the CATC under its leader David Soumah rejected as unacceptable and which led to the latter's refusal to join the UGTAN.[10] Even the organizational unity of the UGTAN was thus only partial.

Those arguing against the dual trade union and ministerial mandate were proved right to the extent that traditional trade union demands about wages and benefits, now given added urgency in the public sector by the de-linking of the local civil services from the metropolitan civil service, continued to be pressed by union members, while their ex-colleagues, now government ministers, lectured the unions on the need for patience given the new governments' lack of resources.[11] In Dahomey, the clash between trade unions and the new government turned nasty when, in January 1958, a series of strike movements culminated in riots that left several people dead and resulted in the imprisonment of a number of others.[12] These developments in turn provoked further divisions within the union movement over the extent to which it was acceptable for unions to pursue these issues against governments that were now run by Africans rather than French colonial officials.[13] The major casualty of the UGTAN leadership's strategy was thus precisely the unity to which the UGTAN was politically and ideologically committed.

The Break-up of the UGTAN

Those advocating that African trade unions under colonialism should give priority to the *political* over the *class* struggle faced their biggest test following the fall of the Fourth Republic and the calling of a constitutional referendum which gave African voters the choice between a 'yes' vote to join the proposed new French Community and a 'no' vote for immediate independence. A 'no' vote would be consistent with giving primacy to the political struggle for African liberation but, given De Gaulle's warning that this would mean forfeiting all French support – taking independence 'with all its consequences' as he put it – many workers worried about the likely economic consequences of a 'no' vote. Consistent with the primacy he now gave to the political struggle and having fallen out with De Gaulle, Sekou Touré called for a 'no' vote and, as a leading figure in UGTAN, succeeded in carrying the union's leadership with him at a meeting in Bamako on 10–11 September. The Ivoirian section of the union immediately denounced the decision and announced its intention to campaign for a 'yes' vote. Many union members in the other territories, worried about the consequences of a 'no' vote, also decided to ignore their leaders and voted 'yes' in the referendum.[14]

This turn of events, with the UGTAN leadership calling for a 'no' vote and immediate independence, in opposition to the RDA leadership, was not quite what Houphouët-Boigny and his colleagues envisaged when they called for union leaders to break free from their metropolitan ties and set up independent unions. In the end, however, the RDA leadership was the beneficiary of this split. The resounding defeat of the 'no' option everywhere except in Guinea left the UGTAN politically weakened and marginalized in the face of the main political leaders of AOF, who had carried the day with their call for a 'yes' vote. Union leaders put a brave face on defeat: meeting in Conakry shortly after the vote, they welcomed Guinean independence, blamed French interference for the defeat of the 'no' vote and vowed to continue the struggle for African independence.

The UGTAN had called, at its inception, for unity in the struggle against colonialism. By the end of 1958, the unity of the AOF trade union movement was looking very fractured indeed. In fact, far from putting an end to union divisions and interterritorial rivalries, the creation of the UGTAN had simply shifted the arena where they were played out. Whereas before 1957 these tensions expressed themselves through disagreements between rival organizations, they now found expression within the UGTAN itself and were tearing it apart. As for interterritorial solidarity, which the UGTAN sought to promote, the union movement had achieved this at key moments and on specific issues – for example, it had held for a time during the 1947–8 railway workers' strike and had been realized at a critical juncture in the struggle to have the new Labour Code applied – but it had always been problematic, as the experience of the rail strike had shown. Now, against the background of territorialization and the break up of the federation following the departure of Guinea, it was effectively impossible to achieve.

A new dispute broke out at the UGTAN Congress in January 1959 between supporters and opponents of union officials participating in government. A compromise was reached, which allowed the dual mandate during the national liberation phase of the struggle, but ruled it out during the class struggle phase. This made it possible for Sekou Touré to be elected president of the union while Abdoulaye Diallo, former Soudan Labour Minister and now Guinea's ambassador to Ghana, became a vice-president. A façade of unity was maintained. However, it was not long before the union started to fragment into its territorial sections. The Senegalese delegation to the Conakry Congress was worried about the politicization of the union movement and opposed the dual mandate. Shortly after its return to Senegal, an UGTAN-Autonome was formed and later in the same year the different Senegalese unions merged into a single organization, the Union des Travailleurs du Sénégal. In August, the UGTAN sections of the Conseil de l'Entente territories split off from the main organization and set about creating a Union Générale des Travailleurs du Conseil de l'Entente. In Niger, the 'orthodox' UGTAN, in which Bakary Djibo who had been defeated in the referendum was a leading figure, was banned, the government having decided that it could not tolerate the activities of a movement that behaved more like an opposition political party than a trade union. Finally, in Soudan, the local UGTAN section broke off from the main organization and became the Union Syndicale des Travailleurs du Mali.

Thus, in the run-up to independence, much of the union leadership was co-opted by the new African governments, while the territorial branches of the UGTAN found themselves increasingly locked in disputes at territorial level with the new government councils. These disputes demonstrated the extent to which trade union autonomy had been compromised, as the movement's leaders struggled to navigate a path between, on the one hand, the demands of African governments for them not to undermine African unity by pressing union demands and, on the other, the demands of their members to protect their standard of living and the rights they had gained. As the leadership struggled with this dilemma, while enjoying the material and other benefits of ministerial status, it could not hold back the militancy of rank-and-file trade unionists, who complained that it had been easier to obtain satisfaction from French colonial officials than it now was from African governments.[15] This put them on a collision course with African governments and was to result, after political independence, in the imprisonment of trade unionists and the repression of an independent trade union movement. Guinea, where Sekou Touré had consistently denied an autonomous space to labour struggles in the name of African unity, was the first territory to travel this road, but the others were to follow not long after.[16]

Students

We have seen how, after 1950, the activities of the student and youth movements began seriously to worry the French government and the colonial authorities in Dakar. African students in France had called for African independence as early as 1952 and, under the influence of the PCF, came to see their struggle against French colonialism as part of a broader international struggle against Western imperialism. However, although their activities worried the authorities in both Paris and Dakar, they could be contained politically for as long as they could be portrayed as the exploits of 'extremists' who were manipulated by external forces, such as 'communists' or the Arab League, or as the actions of a privileged and unrepresentative minority. The students attempted to counter this by claiming it was only they who were prepared to challenge the colonial system at its roots:

> Should those who believe in a doctrine which does not have the support of the Atlantic Alliance be considered as anti-African, whereas in fact they are fighting for a fatherland of their own, which is free and independent? It is in any case significant that it is the young members of the African élite who are putting colonial policy on trial . . . lets us be clear, reformism is not going to satisfy our youth or resolve the crisis which it faces.[17]

Aware of the danger of political marginalization, African students in France made efforts to cement their links with the student and youth movements in French West Africa. This process was well under way by the end of 1956: the students ran summer courses in AOF during their vacations; the FEANF began to coordinate its activities with the AGED; its newsletter, *L'Etudiant d'Afrique Noire*, was circulated in Dakar; and there was an increase in the number of students moving between France and Dakar as more students started their studies in Dakar before transferring to France to complete them. The first of the post-war students also began to return home to AOF from France at this time. Against this background, and that of the intensifying war in Algeria, the student movement in Dakar followed the lead of African students in France and took up the call for African independence.

As one might expect, students were unimpressed by the Loi-cadre. Their reaction was to condemn it as a sop, a device designed to delay African independence and 'balkanize' Africa, without making any provision for the genuine transfer of power.[18] In its place, the students advocated independence for AOF as a federation. Partly for this reason, but also because of its open condemnation of the French war effort in Algeria, the FEANF's newsletter was banned twice within the space of three months. The students also intensified their attacks on African political leaders in the French National Assembly for refusing to recognize the right of all peoples to independence and fight for African independence.[19] Students who returned to AOF in the summer vacation of 1957 were specifically urged to hold meetings 'to expose the current political leaders' who could no longer be trusted as the true representatives of the interests of the population of AOF.[20] Their language was uncompromising:

> We are afraid that, everywhere in Africa, in a few months' time perhaps, when the government councils have been established, various mafias will continue with their usual degrading work . . . We fear that for them the revolution is over and that, having gained a taste for the succulence of the poisoned cake of Colonialism, they will oppose the working masses who are the true revolutionaries in this country.

Houphouët-Boigny was singled out by the students for his membership of a French government that supported the Algerian war effort and African leaders in general were attacked for nepotism, corruption and opportunism. They were portrayed as the main obstacles to the maintenance of the unity of the federation.[21]

The students' watchword was unity: if the unity of AOF was to be maintained, a united, interterritorial nationalist movement, committed to independence for AOF as a federation, represented the best chance of attaining this objective. As part of their campaign to build such a movement, they set out to discredit African political leaders not only by portraying them as unrepresentative of the real interests of Africans, but also by highlighting the divisions within and between AOF political movements, for which these leaders were held responsible. Broadly, the students argued that, whereas the RDA had at its inception expressed and represented the aspirations of Africans for emancipation and had promised to become an effective anti-colonial front against French rule, the actions of its leaders in 1950 had betrayed and split the movement. According to them, it was the youth and student movements that now represented the true spirit of anti-colonialism, as expressed by the RDA at Bamako in 1946, because 'the RDA in its present form is not anti-colonial'.[22]

This strategy was, however, causing the students a number of problems, which indicate that the unity of their movement was, in practice, more fragile than the above suggests. The choice of a revolutionary, anti-imperialist form of syndicalism posed problems because it made it more difficult for them to carry all students with them. The strategy of attacking the political leaders of AOF was to some extent counter-productive because, insofar as the students claimed to be attached to the ideal of unity, such attacks rendered it much easier for their opponents to brand them as divisive and 'extremists'. Extremism in turn led to factionalism: 'This extremism was often associated with an aggressive intolerance of everything that was not in keeping with the general thrust of its demands, even if this meant terrorizing the ordinary student'.[23] It also facilitated the political containment of the students, who were portrayed by Houphouët-Boigny as immature: 'Our authority over the parents and the population in general is sufficient to ensure that recalcitrant students will be brought back into line if necessary'.[24] Another difficulty was that students from Côte d'Ivoire tended to be less radical than their colleagues from other territories, partly because a high proportion of them were on Ivoirian government grants and depended on Houphouët-Boigny's support for their renewal.[25]

In sum, the student movement genuinely strove for unity, but the discourse of unity was more the product of an act of faith and an expression of hope than it was based on political realities: the louder and more frequent the calls for unity became, the more problematic it was to maintain that unity in practice, as if there was a need to paper over the divisions, both potential and actual, within the movement by a discourse of unity. Furthermore, the students always had to battle against the popularly held view that they were a privileged group who enjoyed opportunities and career prospects way beyond the dreams of the vast majority of Africans. It was therefore relatively easy for African political leaders to continue to portray the students' views as those of an unrepresentative minority, whereas they represented the interests of all Africans. The response of the RDA leader, Doudou Guèye, in an interview in which he was asked about African students, exemplifies this:

> The RDA wants to be the movement for all Africans, which means that it does not want to sacrifice the interests of any part of the population for the benefit of any other part. Its present position is dictated by the need to represent the millions of peasant farmers who toil and suffer within a slave economy and under a colonial regime.[26]

As was the case with civil servants, and for similar reasons, students did not automatically enjoy widespread support among the population at large. The colonial authorities worried about the links the students were forging with the trade union and youth movements in French West Africa: 'This separatist action is no longer confined to France'.[27] They need not have done. When they were campaigning for equal rights or on specifically educational issues, the students were broadly supported, but when they ventured into the wider political sphere and demanded immediate independence for the federation, as they did in the 1958 referendum campaign, they were not followed. Their motives, and their judgment, were questioned.

The Youth Movement

The reaction of the youth movement to the Loi-cadre mirrored that of the students. The same themes recurred constantly: opposition to the Loi-cadre and to what was seen as the deliberate 'balkanization' of Africa; the denunciation of African political leaders; support for the Algerian liberation struggle; the aspiration for unity and the demand for immediate independence. The language was also remarkably similar, as the following resolution adopted by the Rassemblement de la Jeunesse Démocratique Africaine (RJDA), illustrates:

> At a time when the whole colonial system of imperialism is in crisis . . . a historic task falls to the African democratic movements, an urgent rallying call has emerged: independence . . .

> In this situation, the RJDA . . . deems it necessary to dispel once and for all
> the misconception that the political leaders insist on perpetuating . . .
> The RJDA, conscious of . . . its vanguard role, reaffirms clearly and unequi-
> vocally its commitment to the idea of national independence.[28]

By the time of their Abidjan congress in October 1957, the youth
organizations of AOF had come together to form the Conseil de la
Jeunesse d'Afrique (CJA) and were united behind an unequivocal
demand for independence: 'The Congress declares that the only way of
setting the oppressed peoples of Africa completely free is through the
struggle for national independence'.[29] It was no doubt because of its
espousal of such radical positions that Houphouët-Boigny refused
permission for a youth festival to be held in Abidjan in September 1957.

As with the trade union and student movements, the watchword of the
youth movement was unity. However, as in the case of the trade unions,
it faced difficulties in attempting to create a unified interterritorial
organization. The question of the degree of autonomy to be left to the
territory-based associations that made up the interterritorial organization
arose, notably over the issue of international affiliations, and the problem
was only resolved once the right of each territorial youth council to
affiliate to the international youth organization of its choice was recognized. The politicization of the movement, which was inevitable if it was
to play an effective role within the nationalist movement, also created
problems, as it did for the trade union movement. While it was pursuing
objectives about which there was a general consensus, such as the
expansion of schools, or the defence of members' interests, as for
example when it took up the case of the French authorities' refusal to
issue passports to delegates elected to attend congresses organized in the
Eastern bloc by the WFDY, or the transformation of *centres culturels* into
maisons des jeunes, political divisions remained largely latent. However,
once it started to adopt political positions in opposition to those adopted
by the main political parties and leaders of AOF, it was not automatically
followed. Moreover under the Loi-cadre, as the territories established
themselves as the relevant political units in AOF, it became increasingly
difficult for the youth councils to maintain interterritorial solidarity.

At the youth festival which opened in Bamako on 6 September 1958,
the CJA called for immediate independence and in the referendum later
that month it joined the students and the trade union movement in calling
for a 'no' vote.[30] The youth wings of the different parties also mostly
campaigned against their party leaderships' decision to call for a 'yes'
vote, thus further deepening the rift between them and their party leaders.

The exception to this was Soudan, where the youth movement accepted the US-RDA leadership's decision to support a 'yes' vote. Here, the overriding priority of Soudan's political leaders was to maintain African unity and the 'yes' vote was presented as a purely tactical manoeuvre in preparation for the goal of African independence. Elsewhere, the crushing defeat of the 'no' vote further marginalized the youth movement and left party leaders in an even stronger position to pursue their chosen line of negotiation and cooperation with France. By setting them on a collision course with the party leaders, it also paved the way for the co-opting and silencing of the AOF youth movement by the new African governments once independence was achieved.

The Quest for Unity II: Political Parties

The history of AOF's political parties during this period is immensely complicated: it is a story of mergers and attempted mergers, followed by new splits and renewed attempts by the parties to combine forces in a united movement for African liberation. There is not the space to tell this story here and it is in any case a story that has been told in detail elsewhere.[31] Instead, the focus in this section will be on explaining two developments: firstly, why did efforts to forge a united, federation-wide political movement for African emancipation ultimately fail, despite virtually everyone's stated belief in the need for unity? Secondly, how did AOF's political leaders and their parties manage to avoid the danger, which appeared very real in 1956, of being outflanked on the left by a radical nationalist movement that was increasingly unequivocally committed to African independence? In explaining these developments, it will be shown how ideology and astute political tactics, combined with the opportunities afforded by the Loi-cadre, enabled AOF's main political leaders to win support for their chosen strategy of working with France and, when independence became inevitable, of negotiating independence in cooperation with France. The exception to this was, of course, Sekou Touré, who led Guinea to independence in 1958.

In the years prior to the Loi-cadre, trade unions and, increasingly, the youth movement, were more active on the ground in French West Africa than the political parties. The action of political leaders was focused on the *métropole* and political parties tended only to come alive at election times.[32] With the intensification of activity in the political arena from 1956 onwards, the parties became more active. Within AOF, the 1956 legislative elections were followed by the introduction of the Loi-cadre, municipal elections in November, elections to the new territorial assemblies in the following March and the installation of the government councils. Barely had they established themselves than the Fourth Republic fell and a constitutional referendum was announced, following which the jockeying for political position escalated as leaders and parties sought to position themselves in the run-up to independence. The period 1956–60 was thus one of almost uninterrupted political campaigning, during which the focus for political action switched from the *métropole* to Africa.

The Mirage of Unity

In the struggle for African emancipation, the watchword was unity. Everyone professed to believe in it and to be working for it. The problem was that everyone also wanted unity on their own terms – in other words, they wanted people to unite behind them. Moreover, if one probes the rhetoric of unity just a little, it soon becomes clear that the different political leaders and groups who used the term were actually talking about very different conceptions of unity. The debate was an important one, because part of the key to political success lay in winning broad support for one's own conception of unity against that of one's rivals.

The intensification of political activity, against the background of territorialization under the Loi-cadre, served to sharpen rather than diminish political tensions, not only between but also within territories. In five of the territories, one party was in virtually unchallenged control. The PDCI dominated Côte d'Ivoire, as did the Bloc Populaire Sénégalais (BPS), formed out of a merger in 1956 between Senghor's BDS and a number of smaller parties, in Senegal. Against this background of political strength in their own territories, neither Houphouët-Boigny nor Senghor wanted to give ground in the struggle to play a leading role within the federation. The fact that Houphouët-Boigny was at the time a minister in France and that his arch-rival, Senghor, was in opposition added a further dimension to their rivalry. The PDG enjoyed a hegemonic position in Guinea, having won the 1956 assembly elections in the territory; it then pursued a policy of intimidation of its political opponents.[33] In Soudan, the US-RDA occupied an increasingly dominant position over its socialist rivals in the much-weakened Parti Progressiste Soudanais.[34] In Mauritania, the Union Progressiste Mauritanien dominated the political scene, although one of the leading opposition figures, Horma Ould Babana, had left the territory for Cairo after his defeat in the 1956 elections, from where he announced the formation of a Mouvement

Nationaliste Mauritanien. In the other territories, the situation had evolved in a different direction. Politically, Haute-Volta was split between the Parti Démocratique Unifié-RDA (PDU-RDA) and Nazi Boni's Mouvement Populaire d'Evolution Africaine (MPEA), and Niger between the Hamani Diori's Parti Progressiste Nigérien-RDA (PPN-RDA) and Bakary Djibo's more radical Sawaba movement.[35] In Dahomey, the situation was even more complicated. There was a north-south split between Hubert Maga's Mouvement Démocratique Dahoméen (MDD) and Sourou Migan Apithy's Parti Républicain du Dahomey (PRD). The territory's third main party, the Union Démocratique Dahoméenne (UDD), at first hesitated to join either, then announced its affiliation to the RDA in 1956, then split when three of its leaders, notably Emile Zinsou, rejected the affiliation. This, in summary, was the situation at the beginning of 1957, when AOF's main political parties, with the exception of the RDA, decided to swim against the territorialization tide and make an attempt at unification.

The project did not get off to an auspicious start because two separate attempts at unification were launched at different meetings in different towns of AOF on the same dates. The first took place in Dakar from 11–13 January 1957 in Dakar and brought together the BPS, Upper Volta's MPEA, Dahomey's MDD and a small Nigerien party, the Union Nigérienne des Indépendants et Sympathisants. A number of other parties, including the RDA, sent observers. The new grouping, which took the name Convention Africaine, confirmed the merger of the parties represented at Dakar, while expressing support for territorial autonomy within the framework of the existing federation. It demanded a ceasefire in Algeria but also expressed its 'undying friendship' for the people of France. Its stated objective was the unification of all the political parties of French Black Africa and it looked forward to the coming RDA Congress as marking another important step on the road to African unity.[36]

The second meeting, which sought to bring together the socialist parties of Black Africa into a single movement, to be called the Mouvement Socialiste Africain (MSA), took place from 11–13 January in Conakry. It elected Lamine Guèye as its president. Its policy declaration favoured a continuing partnership between France and its overseas territories and affirmed the Party's opposition to the creation of one-party states: in a minority position in those territories in which it was represented and seeing the trend towards single parties throughout AOF, it was clearly worried about its political future.

The RDA, which was at this time the only genuinely interterritorial political grouping, remained on the sidelines. It viewed these attempts at unification with some scepticism, pointing out that their stated objectives, of the Convention for a single unified movement and of the MSA against the creation of a single party, were mutually exclusive. The situation was further complicated by the creation in Senegal on 10 September 1957 of the Marxist Parti Africain de l'Indépendance, which was the first political party in AOF to be unequivocally committed to independence.

The territorial assembly elections of 31 March gave 243 seats to the RDA, including all sixty in Côte d'Ivoire, fifty-six out of sixty in Guinea, sixty-four out of seventy in Soudan and thirty-seven out of seventy in Haute-Volta. Convention Africaine parties had a total of ninety-six seats: they controlled Senegal and were represented in three other Assemblies. Finally, the Socialists had just sixty-two seats: they controlled Niger, thanks to some help from local colonial officials, and were represented in three other territories.[37]

The RDA was therefore in a position of unrivalled strength when its Third Interterritorial Congress opened on 25 September 1957 in Bamako. Convention Africaine and the MSA sent observers, as did the UGTAN, the CATC, the FEANF, the UGEAO and several metropolitan political parties, including the UDSR which was represented by François Mitterrand. The Vice-President of the Senegalese Government Council, Mamadou Dia, appealed to delegates on behalf of Convention Africaine to support the merger of African political parties into a single, unified movement, but Houphouët-Boigny, knowing that his party was in a position to call the shots, replied that his preference was for unity of action or, alternatively, for other parties to join the RDA. A majority of the delegates disagreed with him and the end of the Congress had to be put back two days, to allow time for a compromise to be reached so that a party split could be avoided. In the end, a somewhat woolly resolution was adopted, affirming the right of peoples to political independence, but at the same time emphasizing the importance of interdependence and the need to create a democratic Franco-African Community based on the principle of equality.[38]

On the key question of unification, the RDA stuck to its guns: it would not accept it unless the other parties agreed to adopt the name of the RDA. This was unacceptable to the other parties, so that in the end the Convention Africaine and the MSA came together in March 1958 to form the Parti du Regroupement Africain (PRA) without the RDA. Its inaugural congress opened in Cotonou on 25 July. The key political issue that divided them was the question of the creation of a primary federation with a federal executive. Basically, the RDA was against while the PRA was in favour, although the situation was, in practice, rather more complicated because the RDA was actually divided on the issue: whereas Houphouët-Boigny was opposed, other territorial sections of the Party, such as Modibo Keita's US-RDA in Soudan, were in favour, as were many of the Party's activists. They did, however, agree to form a Front Commun d'Action Africaine to press for AOF and AEF to become democratic federations composed of territories that enjoyed full internal autonomy while remaining closely linked to France.

By the time the PRA held its inaugural congress, the political situation in France had again changed. The Fourth Republic had collapsed, and De Gaulle had announced his intention to hold a constitutional referendum, with the residents of France's overseas territories being consulted on the nature of future links with the *métropole*. Senghor, as President of the PRA, favoured a free association with France, but with the right to political independence being recognized by France. However, delegates on the floor of the Congress drafted an alternative resolution demanding immediate independence, which was passed unanimously. When, shortly afterwards, the referendum campaign started, the PRA was unable to agree whether to campaign for a 'yes' or a 'no' vote and decided to leave the final decision to its territorial sections. Backpedalling from the commitment to immediate independence made at Cotonou, Senghor and Dia called for a 'yes' vote in Senegal, but not everyone in the Party accepted this and some of the Senegalese section of the Party, including the former student activist Abdoulaye Ly and the trade union leader Latyr Camara, broke away to form the PRA-Senegal and campaign for a 'no' vote. Meanwhile, the PRA's General Secretary, Bakary Djibo, called for a 'no' vote in Niger. He was defeated and subsequently forced to resign. The RDA, in contrast, decided to recommend all its sections to campaign for a 'yes' vote, although this did not prevent Sekou Touré from deciding to do the opposite and winning a resounding majority for a 'no' vote in Guinea.

The referendum campaign widened the gap between the two groupings. By the end of the campaign, they disagreed not only on the issue of the primary federation, but also on the duration of the new Community. Whereas Houphouët-Boigny envisaged a long-term future for the Community, the PRA viewed it as a more flexible arrangement that could allow the associate territories to evolve along different paths, albeit in partnership with France. Houphouët-Boigny rejected this and suspected the PRA leadership of seeing the Community simply as a staging post on the road to political independence. Not everyone in the RDA shared Houphouët-Boigny's views. Some Party sections, such as the US-RDA in Soudan, and many Party activists wanted to keep the territories of ex-AOF together and supported the idea of a primary federation and a federal executive. The RDA split over this issue and federalists in the PRA and RDA decided to come together to form a new party, the Parti de la Fédération Africaine (PFA). Its inaugural congress took place from 1–3 July 1959 in Dakar. Its watchword was 'unity'. The party's stated objective was African unity within the context of a federal republic, on the road to the creation of which the Mali Federation was seen as the first step, followed by independence: 'national independence in the context of the interdependence of nations', as it was put.[39] Its territorial sections were the Union Progressiste Sénégalaise (UPS), the Union Soudanaise (US-RDA), the Parti Progressiste Dahoméen (PPD) and two parties that were banned shortly afterwards, Sawaba (Niger) and Nazi Boni's Parti National Voltaïque (PNV).[40]

The RDA held a special conference two months later in Treichville (Côte d'Ivoire) to reaffirm its commitment to the Community and its opposition to a primary federation and to what it dubbed the supporters of 'African unity and Pan-Africanism'. The Guinea and Soudan sections having left since the previous conference, it brought together delegations from each of the Conseil de l'Entente countries – Côte d'Ivoire, Niger, Haute-Volta and Dahomey – from the former AOF, as well as several delegations from the territories of AEF. However, the scene was now set for the Mali Federation and the four Conseil de l'Entente countries to take their independence as separate states from France. The dream of federal unity was dead and even the Mali Federation only lasted a few months before it split into its two constituent states.

Throughout this time, the trade union, youth and student movements were pressing party leaderships to unite in a common movement for African independence. There were, however, many obstacles on the road to unity, and their efforts were ultimately doomed to failure.

First of all, and most importantly, they were attempting to swim against the territorialization tide. Although the devolution of power under the Loi-cadre was selective and partial, the powers that were devolved were nonetheless considerable. Territorialization gave Africans a taste of real power and offered opportunities for political patronage. In contrast, the federal Government-General was stripped of most of its powers and prerogatives. Thus, from 1957, whereas the territory had some political substance, the federation became increasingly politically irrelevant.

Secondly, Africans identified with their political leaders as leaders of their territories. Indeed, as founders of the first mass political parties in their territories, leaders such as Houphouët-Boigny, Senghor and Touré symbolized the nation for many party members and sympathizers, and indeed for the wider electorate. In contrast, the ideas of federal unity and Pan-Africanism, which were promoted by radical nationalist leaders, seemed abstract and remote and found little echo with the wider electorate.

Thirdly, as powers were transferred to Africans and independence approached, political leaders who stood to benefit did not have any reason to give up the prestige and influence that the transfer of power conferred on them as leaders of their territories, in order to share power within some kind of federal government in which their authority would be diluted. Moreover, in the case of the richer territories within the federation, such as Côte d'Ivoire, the sharing of power would be likely to involve some transfer of resources from the richer territories to the poorer ones.

Fourthly, even if the 'balkanization' of Africa was not the explicit aim of the French government in adopting the Loi-cadre – voices within the French governing élite were, even at a relatively late stage, speaking up in favour of keeping the federations of AOF and AEF together – once the Loi-cadre was in place, it was in the French government's interest to do everything in its power to make it work. This meant supporting Africa's political leaders who sought to implement it and whose chosen strategy was to work in cooperation with France. The government also had other weapons in its armoury. Although it could do nothing to prevent Guinea going its own way, its successful operation in Niger to defeat Djibo Bakary in the referendum campaign was evidence of its continuing power to influence political developments in French West Africa. Moreover, in Houphouët-Boigny, who remained a French government minister until 1959 and was the most vociferous opponent of federation among Black Africa's main political leaders, the government had an able African advocate of the 'territorialist' approach to the transfer of power.

Finally, the ability of African political leaders to appropriate the language of unity and portray their political opponents as obstacles to the realization of African national unity were of crucial importance to their success. In opposition to the nationalist movement's advocacy of federal unity and a rather nebulous Pan-Africanism, African political leaders promoted a different sort of unity. They appealed to Africans to come together in a common struggle for the economic, social and cultural development of Africa. Only once this had been realized, they argued, could African emancipation be achieved and Africa genuinely become independent and free.[41] By espousing the language of unity in the cause of national development, they were able to portray those in the wider nationalist movement as the true divisionists who, by their refusal to break the link with the Communist Party in 1950 and their subsequent maintenance of links with international communism through the trade union and youth movements, were responsible for dividing Africans against themselves. Thus, alienated from their own people and beholden to 'foreign' ideas, radical nationalists were portrayed by African political leaders as unrepresentative of the true interests of the majority of Africans.

Moderate African nationalist leaders were helped in this by a con-tradiction at the heart of the radical nationalists' position. Thanks to their French education, those at the political and ideological forefront of the nationalist movement – students, civil servants, UGTAN leaders – were among the minority of Africans who were the most 'assimilated' to French culture. Wearing their trade union hats, they demanded assim-ilation, on a professional level, with the *métropole*: this meant continuing to campaign for equal rights and benefits with their metropolitan counter-parts. Yet on a political level, they simultaneously demanded African self-determination. They belonged to a minority group within African society that was already perceived by many Africans as economically and socially privileged, so it was not difficult for African political leaders to portray this position as motivated by self-interest and divisive of African unity. Moreover, as independence approached, African leaders appealed to all Africans to unite together in the common struggle for African development and national construction. They used the language of unity to encourage others to join them in this project and to justify the creation of a single party to carry it forward. As the RDA leader, Ouezzin Coulibaly, stated to the inaugural congress of the Convention Africaine, which he attended as an observer: 'No under-developed country which has reached political maturity has done so without granting primacy either to a single party or to a party which had such a large majority that it controlled all the sectors of social life'.[42] Those who concentrated on the issue of immediate independence, it was implied, were not working in the national interest but threatening the stability and future prosperity of the nascent African states by fomenting divisions between Africans.

This strategy could not succeed without popular support. With the gradual expansion in the number of eligible voters at each election, the political importance of the rural population increased. This suited political leaders such as Houphouët-Boigny, whose main support base was the Ivoirian peasant farmers, and Senghor, who, since he left the Socialist Party, had been carefully cultivating the rural Senegalese vote, notably through his contacts with Muslim religious leaders.[43] Leaders of the poorer territories, fearful of the economic consequences of an abrupt break with France, similarly relied on the rural vote to support them in their call for a 'yes' vote in the 1958 constitutional referendum and in their strategy of continuing to work in cooperation with France. In Niger, where Bakary Djibo's call for a 'no' vote in the constitutional referendum was defeated, Hamani Diori's local section of the RDA, supported by the traditional chiefs, quickly replaced Djibo's Sawaba as the dominant party. In each case, their strategy of appealing over the heads of radical nationalists to the wider public for support was greatly facilitated by the introduction of universal suffrage, the effect of which was to drown the votes of the urban élite in the votes of the rural masses. The exception to this was Soudan, where this was not necessary because the US-RDA had retained the support of the rural masses with its campaign slogan of African unity first, then independence.[44] In general, the language of African development and modernization, accompanied by the prospect of continued economic support from France, resonated more loudly with the population at large than the call for immediate independence.[45] At the same time, in supporting the Loi-cadre, political leaders in the territories furthest from Senegal exploited the demand for African autonomy by laying stress on the need for greater independence vis-à-vis the federal capital, Dakar. This also helped to defuse some of the force of the demand for independence from France.

The Defeat of the Nationalist Movement

The nationalist movement continued to grow in strength in the period up to the installation of the government councils in 1957. The government was constantly under pressure from the movement's use of 'assimilationist' language to press its demands for equal rights and equal benefits with the *métropole*, which it could not simply reject but which it did not have the resources to satisfy. This led many of the French-educated élite to give up on the promise of integration into a 'one and indivisible' Greater France. They began to lose faith with France and looked, instead, towards new political horizons, to secession from France and political independence. The government, which was kept informed of the movement's activities by regular, and increasingly worried, Security Service reports, clearly took seriously the threat that it represented. However, less than three years later, this threat was defused and the movement politically marginalized, so that France was able to hand over power, apart from in Guinea, to so-called 'interlocuteurs valables', African political leaders who were friendly towards France and wanted to cooperate with it after independence.[46]

Part of the explanation for this success lies in the emerging convergence of interest between France's governing élites and African political leaders for the transfer of power to Africans. For the French colonial establishment, it was a way of extricating France from an increasingly unsustainable colonial situation. For Africans, on the other hand, it was a question of power. They wanted to cut free from French political parties and trade unions and create their own autonomous organizations, and they wanted greater freedom to govern their own affairs. Moreover, with the nationalist movement wanting to maintain the federations of AOF and AEF and advocating independence in unity, French political leaders and those African leaders who wanted direct links with France on a territorial basis had a shared interest in rejecting federalism.

The far-reaching significance of this change of heart from the French perspective cannot be over-emphasized. The whole thrust of French policy after the Second World War had been to create a French Union in which the overseas territories were indissolubly linked to the *métropole*. Within the Union, France sought to remake imperialism by creating a modern Africa in its own image. The project simply was not viable and the Loi-cadre represented a belated recognition of this. However, this was not the end of the story because France had, within the French Union, created a unique system that allowed colonial representatives to be elected to the National Assembly in Paris. In this way, it had forged a small élite of African political leaders who, because they were elected, were widely accepted by Africans as their legitimate leaders, but who also felt a deep sense of loyalty towards a France that treated them as equals and enabled them to rise to the very peak of the French political establishment. Using the prestige that this position conferred upon them, they appealed over the heads of the nationalist movement, in every territory apart from Guinea and Soudan, for support for their chosen policy of cooperation with France. Thus, although the 'assimilationist' dream of creating a modern Africa within the colonial system was dead, French political objectives were met as the manner of the transfer of power enabled France to maintain a sphere of influence in Africa after independence.

The defeat of the nationalist movement was comprehensive and its plans for African unity a failure. There were a number of reasons for this: institutional and structural factors, combined with the astute political manoeuvring of Houphouët-Boigny and the assistance of the colonial administration at key moments, all of these played a role in the movement's political marginalization. African political leaders were also able to hold out to their electorates the prospect of continuing French aid to promote the cause of African development, if friendly relations with France were maintained. Moreover, the nationalist movement's ideology of African unity and Pan-Africanism had little resonance beyond the French-educated élite that promoted it. The language of unity was, in any case, successfully appropriated by African political leaders, who were able to exploit the ambiguities of the nationalist movement's position to portray its actions as those of an unrepresentative and privileged minority. In portraying themselves as national leaders, they were able to play on the complex layering of multiple African identities, mobilizing their electorates as Ivoirians or Senegalese or Soudanese when it suited them, while at other times appealing to their 'African-ness' – their 'African personality' – when they wanted to emphasize their role as uniters and leaders of the African nation.

Yet this should not lead us to deny any significance to the contribution of the nationalist movement in the struggle for decolonization. The constant attacks on the colonial regime by the trade unions, by students and by the youth movement put the French government on the defensive. At the same time, French West African political parties and their leaders were forced to respond to the increasingly radical demands being articulated by the nationalist movement, in order to avoid losing the political initiative to it. This pressure from below played a crucial role in providing momentum for the decolonization process and in ensuring that independence came as quickly as it did. The unity and strength of the nationalist movement were dissipated by the Loi-cadre, and many of its former leaders were coopted into roles within the new African political establishments that were put in place from 1957 onwards. As a result, the nationalist movement played a key role in a victory – political independence – from which it was, ultimately, largely excluded.

Notes

1. Cf. G. W. Johnson, 'The Triumph of Nationalism in French West Africa: or, the Change from Assimilation to Nationalism as a Secular Faith for West African Élites', p. 2, paper given at the conference 'Décolonisations Comparées', Aix-en-Provence, 30 September–3 October 1993.
2. F. Cooper, *Decolonization and African Society* (Cambridge University Press, 1996), p. 415.

3. 'Confidential' security services report, dated 17 September 1957, in AAOF 17G612/152.
4. AAOF 17G620/152.
5. 'Confidential' letter dated 9 December 1957, Governor-General to Minister, in ANSOM Aff. Pol. 2200/3.
6. General resolution adopted by UGTAN's executive committee at its meeting in Bamako on 8–10 March 1958, political report, March 1958, in AAOF 17G633/152. Cf. also security services' report for June 1957, p. 1, in 17G630/152.
7. Cf. radio broadcast by Doudou Guèye, leading figure in the RDA and member of the Grand Conseil: 'We are asking the trade union organizations not to get so excited and not to make the workers think that they are putting their interests before those of the community as a whole', *Paris-Dakar*, 4 February 1958, p. 2; cf. also veiled warning issued by Mamadou Dia before the 1957 Territorial Assembly elections, 'Un régime d'austérité acceptée par tous', *Afrique Nouvelle*, 26 February 1957, p. 1; and report of a meeting between the Senegalese Government Council and trade unions at which Dia was reported as saying: 'The nature of the present situation is that the particular struggle of workers to resolve secondary contradictions risks compromising the general struggle being undertaken by the Government Council, the Trade Unions and the whole Senegalese People to resolve the fundamental contradiction which is a product of the regime of semi-autonomy', Political report, April 1958, in AAOF 17G633/165.
8. 'Monthly review of political events', April and September 1957, in ANSOM Aff. Pol., 2232/2.
9. 'Les syndicalistes peuvent-ils aussi être des Ministres?' *Afrique Nouvelle*, 6 August 1957, p. 1 and M. Dicko, 'Préservons l'autonomie syndicale', ibid, 17 September 1957, p. 1.
10. D. Soumah, 'L'unité syndicale étoufferait la voix du syndicalisme libre', *Afrique Nouvelle*, 14 March 1958, pp. 1, 8.
11. These tensions emerge clearly in the Dahomey Security Services' reports for 1957, in AAOF 17G588/152.
12. Report from Governor of Dahomey to Minister for Overseas France, 30 January 1958, pp. 6–13, in ANSOM Aff. Pol. 2189/12.
13. Political report, March 1958, in AAOF 17G633/152.
14. G. Chaffard, *Les Carnets secrets de la décolonisation française* (Calmann-Lévy, 1967), vol. 2, p. 205.
15. Interview with Amadou Ndene Ndaw, 31 March 1990.
16. 'The trade union movement is not and cannot be a separate entity from the "African" entity in its struggle for emancipation. It must . . .

undergo a reconversion with a view to making a more effective contribution to the organised campaign for complete decoloniz-ation', resolution adopted at the PDG's Third Congress, Conakry, 23–26 January 1958, FHB 1D–002. Prior to this, Sekou Touré had indicated, in speeches he made shortly after being appointed Vice-President of Guinea's Government Council, that his conception of unity would not allow space for dissenting voices: 'The country's development requires a rigorous discipline and a perfect order . . . We shall punish without weakness all those who attempt deliberately to sabotage our work', *La Liberté* (the PDG's weekly paper), 21 May 1957, p. 1; cf. also F. Cooper, *Decolonization*, pp. 423–4.

17. N. Khaly, 'Réflexions sur la situation politique de l'Afrique Noire', *L'Etudiant d'Afrique Noire*, 5 (new series), June-September 1956, p. 34. Cf. also editorial in ibid, 17, December 1957, p. 3, which complained at the way in which students were denounced as 'unreal-istic dreamers, too young and irresponsible'.

18. Cf. Ly Tidiane Baïdy, 'L'esprit de la loi-cadre', *Dakar-Etudiant*, 7, December 1956, pp. 7–8 and addressing a meeting in Kaolack, 'Le rôle des jeunes et des étudiants dans les mouvements de libér-ation nationale', reported in a 'confidential' security services' note dated 17 September 1957, AAOF 17G612/152; cf. also J. Pliya. 'L'étudiant d'Afrique noire face à ses responsabilités', *Tam-Tam*, 8, February–March 1957, p. 42; 'Loi-cadre: une manoeuvre colonial-iste', *L'Etudiant d'Afrique Noire*, 28, January–February 1960, p. 9.

19. 'Le RDA est-il encore anti-colonialiste?', *L'Etudiant d'Afrique Noire*, 13, June 1957, pp. 7–8.

20. Security Services' Bulletin, 'restricted circulation', Ministry for Overseas France, 26 July 1957, in ANSOM Aff. Pol. 2232/3.

21. 'Discours du Président de l'UGEAO au Congrès du BPS', in *L'Etudiant d'Afrique Noire*, 13, June 1957, p. 6; and special issue of *L'Etudiant d'Afrique Noire*, 5 (new series), June–September 1956, on Algeria, which included a joint declaration by the AGED and the FEANF condemning the use of *tirailleurs sénégalais* (French West African troops) in Algeria (pp. 8–9), an open letter to both Houphouët-Boigny and Senghor attacking their position on Algeria (p. 8) and 'Contre l'opportunisme en Afrique Noire', ibid, pp. 3–4. 'Colonialism' has a capital 'c' in the original text.

22. 'Le RDA est-il encore anticolonialiste?', p. 8.

23. C. Diané, *La FEANF et les grandes heures du mouvement syndical étudiant noir* (Chaka, 1990), p. 153.

24. Quoted in J. Capelle, *L'Education en Afrique noire* (Karthala/ACCT, 1990), p. 264.

25. One ex-FEANF member has even claimed that the Ivoirian students' association in France was wooed by Ivoirian political leaders, who used agents to infiltrate it, and that this acted as an extra disincentive to radical political activity among Ivoirian students, see C. Diané, *La FEANF* (Chaka, 1990), p. 55.

26. *Afrique Nouvelle*, 19 March 1957, p. 6.

27. Security Services' report on the FEANF's Eighth Annual Conference, December 1957, in AAOF 17G604/152.

28. 'Résolution sur l'orientation politique du RJDA', *L'Etudiant d'Afrique Noire*, 15, November 1957, p. 20.

29. Security service report dated 22 October 1957, p. 27, in AAOF 17G604/152.

30. H. d'Almeida-Topor and O. Goerg, *Le Mouvement associatif des jeunes en Afrique noire francophone au XXe siècle* (L'Harmattan, 1989), pp. 56, 108.

31. See for example, R. S. Morgenthau, *Political Parties in French-Speaking West Africa* (Clarendon Press, 1964); A. Blanchet, *L'Itinéraire des partis africains depuis Bamako* (Plon, 1958); A. Ly, *Les Regroupements politiques au Sénégal, 1956–70* (Codesria/Karthala, 1992); J. S. Coleman and C. G. Rosberg Jr., eds, *Political Parties and National Integration in Tropical Africa* (University of California Press, 1964).

32. Cf. Mamadou Dia: 'political groupings are often no more than electoral committees whose main role is to nominate a leader, and whose leaders are fetishists, more interested in shoring up their authority and increasing their prestige than in the political education of the masses', *Afrique Nouvelle*, 26 February 1957, p. 1.

33. The most serious incidents were in Conakry from 29 September to 3 October 1956, which left eight dead and nearly 300 injured.

34. A. C. Danioko, *Contribution à l'étude des partis politiques au Mali de 1945 à 1960* (Thèse de 3e Cycle, University of Paris-VII, 1984), pp. 372–5.

35. R. Higgott, 'Dependence and Decolonisation in a Land-Locked State: Niger', *African Review of Political Economy*, January-April 1980, pp. 47–8.

36. See party's own report on its inaugural meeting.

37. G. Chaffard, *Les Carnets*, vol. 2, p. 268.

38. 'Résolution politique votée au 3e Congrès Interterriorial du RDA', in A. Blanchet, *L'Itinéraire des Partis Africains*, pp. 187–9; see also J.-R. de Benoist, *L'Afrique Occidentale Française de 1944 à 1960* (Nouvelles Editions Africaines, 1982), pp. 352–4.

39. Quoted in J.-R. de Benoist, *L'Afrique*, pp. 453–4.
40. The UPS was created out of the BPS, the Socialists and the local, Senegalese section of the RDA; the PPD out of Dahomey's main political parties, with the exception of the local section of the RDA; Sawaba was Bakary Djibo's party that had fought and lost the campaign for a 'no' vote in Niger, and the PNV was created out of the former MPEA.
41. Cf. Doudou Guèye in an interview in Abidjan on 11 April 1979 with I. B. Kaké for Radio-France International: 'It was not through ignorance that we did not talk about independence. We chose the term emancipation because this was a process which led to independence by strengthening the man you wanted to make independent. This was therefore the basis for its action', in 'L'itinéraire intellectuel et politique d'un militant du RDA: Doudou Guèye', Service de Coopération, Paris, 1986, p. 14.
42. Quoted in A. Blanchet, *L'Itinéraire*, p. 58.
43. According to a report prepared by the AOF Bureau d'Etudes for 15–21 September 1957, the Mouride khalifa warned Senghor and Dia on 12 September of the dangers of calling for a 'no' vote, AAOF 17G633/152.
44. A. C. Danioko, *Contribution à l'étude des partis politiques*, p. 261.
45. Cf. 'Résolution économique votée au 3e Congrès Interterritorial du RDA', in ibid, pp. 190–2; interview with Pierre Kipré, Minister of Education of Côte d'Ivoire, 18 December 1997.
46. Mali, as Soudan was called after independence, was also an exception, insofar as the regime adopted increasingly anti-French positions after the split with Senegal and the collapse of the Mali Federation.

–8–

Conclusion: Decolonization and the French Colonial Legacy

One major difficulty of writing the history of decolonization is that 'the story lends itself to be read backwards'.[1] We know the *dénouement*: the end of colonial rule and the accession of the previously colonized territories to political independence. This can lead to a tendency to write linear history, to see decolonization as a process, the inevitable outcome of which was the coming to a close of the colonial era. It encourages us to view what precedes in the context of, and as a preparation for, this known outcome.

This reading of the history of decolonization takes different forms. From the point of view of the colonial power, it can lead to an emphasis being placed on policy making, which is implicitly, if not explicitly, conceived as a rational process in which the colonial power adopts policies that prepare the way for decolonization and eventual independence. According to this view, Black Africa was France's 'successful decolonization': there was no war of decolonization; the transition from colonial rule was not marked by large scale violence or bloodshed; it was a largely smooth process, and the transfer of power was managed in such a way as to enable France to maintain its presence and a sphere of influence in Black Africa after political independence. It is a view that has been carefully orchestrated by the French political establishment but finds expression in a variety of different forms. The Gaullist variant attaches central importance to the role played by De Gaulle at the Brazzaville Conference and in the immediate aftermath of the Second World War, downplays the role of Fourth Republic political parties and politicians, whose unstable parliamentary coalitions and governmental instability are held responsible for a series of disasters in French colonial policy, and then highlights the speed with which De Gaulle moved to reform France's imperial relationship with Africa following his return to power in 1958. The view that Black Africa was France's 'successful decolonization', in which the enlightened actions of a small number of

French politicians and officials played a determining role, is not, however, exclusively Gaullist and has been widely promoted by French
political leaders from across the political spectrum. In 1994, for example,
at his last Franco-African summit in Biarritz, François Mitterrand made
a valedictory speech in which he drew attention to the way in which
'France and its African partners organised a peaceful decolonisation' and
then went on to explain: 'if we have been able to overcome the obstacles,
it is because we have never lacked the will so to do'.[2] It is a view that has
hitherto also, implicitly if not explicitly, underpinned the approach of
many historians of French decolonization. By concentrating on events in
Indochina and Algeria and dedicating only a limited amount of space to
Black Africa, they have tended to lend credence to the view that the
decolonization process in Black Africa was essentially unproblematic and
produced a largely smooth transition from colonialism to cooperation.

 In parallel with, and not entirely in opposition to, this 'top-down'
reading of the decolonization process, is the nationalist reading. From this
perspective, the key event is still the culmination of the process – the
achievement of political independence – and, as in the previous reading,
there is a tendency to interpret what precedes in the light of, and as a
preparation for, this known outcome. The key difference is that, whereas
in the previous case the successful decolonization is attributed to the
process of preparation undertaken by the colonial power, in the nationalist
reading it is seen as the product of the anti-colonial struggle. Of course,
there is not just one nationalist reading of the anti-colonial struggle, but
all share a tendency to linearity to the extent that they view the different
manifestations of resistance to the colonial power, whether by political
parties, trade unions or peasant uprisings, as an integral and necessary
part of the movement for national liberation.[3] In practice, however, there
is a need to maintain the tension between the *political* and *socio-economic*
dimensions of the nationalist struggle. The political struggle for decolonization is a struggle for autonomy and subsequently independence.
The socio-economic struggle is a struggle against the colonial regime
for equal pay and benefits with Europeans. The two will periodically
converge and feed off each other, but the links between them cannot be
taken for granted. Indeed, as this study has shown, the relations between
the political parties, trade unions and other social movements, such as the
student movement, were often far from straightforward.[4] The decisions
by the new African governments to eliminate autonomous trade unions
once political independence was achieved, something the colonial power
had not dared to do, is a clear indication of the underlying tension
between the political and the socio-economic arms of the nationalist
struggle.

Conclusion

There is a particular, and at first sight paradoxical, twist to both the 'French' and the 'nationalist' reading of the decolonization process in French West Africa, in that both have attributed a key role to African political leaders such as Senghor and Houphouët-Boigny while marginalizing and downplaying the role of the wider nationalist movement in the struggle for national liberation. Both of these readings are, in their own way, compelling because each appears to provide elements of an explanation for France's 'successful decolonization' in Black Africa. Indeed, they have become part of a prevailing orthodoxy – the 'smooth transfer of power to Africa's 'natural' leaders – that has proved remarkably durable. This can be attributed to the fact that, despite their opposed starting-points – French policy and African agency – the two explanations are, ultimately, complementary. From their different standpoints, that of French policy-makers or African nationalists, each appears to explain a success story: for France, it was a successfully managed transition from colonialism to cooperation; for African political leaders it was the achievement of political independence by negotiation and without the need for bloodshed. This was not all that was at stake, however. From the French point of view, it has helped to legitimize and justify the maintenance of a French presence in sub-Saharan Africa after political decolonization, while from the point of view of African leaders, it has served to legitimize their takeover of the functions of government in the eyes of their own people. Outmanoeuvring their opponents in the nationalist movement, they have been able to portray themselves as true African nationalists, representing the interests of the whole African nation. 'History', as Alistair Cook once remarked, 'is written by the winners'.[5] The result has been that prominence has been given to the role of those who won power at independence and the relative neglect of the role of the broader nationalist movement in the decolonization process.

This study has shown that, within this prevailing orthodoxy, key questions remain unanswered and many voices remain unheard. However, in seeking to challenge this orthodoxy, the intention here has not been to replace it with a new orthodoxy but to open up a debate by suggesting that alternative histories are possible and necessary. A central argument here has been that activists in the wider nationalist *movement* played a key role in building pressure on both the French government and African political leaders for independence. Riven by divisions over strategy and ideological contradictions, this nationalist movement nonetheless played an important role in the decolonization struggle. In analysing the obstacles it faced as it sought to unite around a common project for African unity and independence, trade unions, students and youth organizations, as well as African parties and their leaders, have all found a voice here. But what of religious groups? Should we agree with Jean-Louis Triaud when he suggests that the 'Muslim factor' be discounted as 'rather marginal in the rise of, and in preparing the way for, independence'.[6] Yet we have seen that Muslim student associations in Dakar played a significant role in constructing a sense of cultural identity among students. What of the apparent absence of 'ethnic' tensions within nationalism? Was this the dog that did not bark in the night? Mention has been made of their growing importance in Dahomean politics towards the end of the colonial period, but more research remains to be done on the significance of ethnic loyalties and associations within the wider nationalist movement. What about Christian groups? What of women's role in the nationalist movement? Their voices remain largely unheard here. In this respect, this study has raised as many questions as it has provided answers. Clearly, more research is needed into the contribution of groups such as these to the anti-colonial struggle.

In revisiting the question of French decolonization in West Africa, three main themes have emerged. The first of these concerns French policy. We have seen how the Popular Front initiated a colonial reform project which sought to liberalize and humanize French colonialism while binding the colonies more closely to France. Decolonization, in the sense of preparing the colonies for self-government, was nowhere on the agenda. The Popular Front fell and its reform project remained largely still born, but the Popular Front was significant for revealing the extent to which the mainstream French left was now implicated in, and attached to, empire. As for the Popular Front's project to modernize French colonialism, it was to be revived and refined in the immediate aftermath of the Second World War. French experience during the war and the crucial role played by France's Black African colonies in the war effort convinced its post-war governing élites of the need to maintain the empire if France was to regain its status as a world power after the war. These élites, of both left and right, were therefore totally unprepared for decolonization. Indeed, in contrast to Britain, which had granted independence to its white dominions and where Labour governments in the 1930s were already talking of preparing colonies for self-government, albeit in some distant, unspecified future, there was nothing in France's colonial tradition that could serve as a precedent for such an approach to decolonization. The political imperative was, rather, to reform the colonial relationship in order to integrate the colonies more fully with France. This was the overriding objective that underpinned the creation of the French Union. Underlying this project was the idea that decolonization and the emancipation of colonial peoples would take place through integration with the *métropole* within a 'one and indivisible' Greater France, rather than through self-government and eventual secession from France. The definition of decolonization normally accepted in English today, which is associated with the transfer of power to local elected leaders and the granting of political independence, would not have been recognized by post-war French governing élites and did not form part of the French colonial agenda at this time. On the contrary, 'decolonization' (the term itself did not come into use until the early 1950s) was about reforming imperialism and creating a modern Africa *within the French colonial system*. Only once it was recognized that the cost of such a policy of assimilation on the French taxpayer was too high and that its political consequences were unacceptable to French politicians and metropolitan public opinion, did the mindset of policy makers begin to change and new solutions begin to be sought.

The key issue here is the question of treating decolonization as a process somehow willed or controlled, as the term implies, by the colonial power. Firstly, colonial projects are shot through with fundamental contradictions between universalist claims and particularist assertions about the nature of the colonized society. The project to maintain France's Black African colonies as part of the French empire by remaking them as modernized, 'Frenchified' overseas territories of the French Union was no exception to this. On the one hand, it made the 'universalist' claim that Africans, once they had been acculturated and assimilated to French ways through the creation of a modern economy and the provision of a French education, should be treated in the same way as, and the equal of, French people. On the other hand, it sought to maintain a range of distinctions against the colonized population in order to justify the maintenance of France's colonial presence, albeit in a reformed, 'modernized' form. Secondly, even if France's post-war governing élites shared the objective of maintaining Black Africa as part of the French empire, there were tensions within these élites, notably although not exclusively between the metropolitan and the local colonial state, over which policies should be pursued in order to achieve this objective. There was also the question of the long-running, and growing, divorce between the modernizing élites of French capitalism and colonial empire.[7] Thirdly, the metropolitan political situation made it virtually impossible for Fourth Republic governments to control the decolonization process in practice. The French Union was a rigid structure owing to the fact that, under the provisions of the Fourth Republic Constitution, substantial political reform was made subject to constitutional revision. This rendered incremental change to the institutions of the Union very difficult to achieve. Moreover, shifting political coalitions meant that it would, in any case, have been difficult for any government to construct a parliamentary majority for such a change. In addition, the multiplicity of political actors who became involved in colonial policy after the war meant that policy making was far from being either monolithic or homogeneous.

By throwing light on some of the political manoeuvrings that lay behind what has been seen as the largely 'successful' decolonization of French West Africa, this study has shown how the process of dissolution of the French colonial Empire in Africa was a product of the combination of these contradictions and of metropolitan indecision. Policy making was characterized by periods of policy inertia, leading to gathering political crises that were followed by belated concessions and political compromises at key moments. The most important of these was the Loi-cadre. By 1956, France had lost Indochina, it was implicated in an increasingly bloody war in Algeria, and it was under growing pressure from the nationalist movement in Black Africa. It was only the timely introduction of the Loi-cadre, via a procedure that was strictly unconstitutional, that enabled France subsequently to regain control of the colonial agenda in French West Africa at the eleventh hour. By devolving certain powers to elected assemblies at territorial level, which were dominated by African political leaders loyal to France, while maintaining French control over key areas of policy such as foreign affairs, defence, the currency, communications and the media, the Loi-cadre finally succeeded in breaking the colonial logjam and opened the way to the maintenance of the French presence in Black Africa after independence.

It is worth underlining the significance of this finding, because it indicates that, for all its policy inertia and political fumbling in the colonial field, it was actually under the Fourth Republic that this breakthrough was made and not, as proponents of the 'Gaullist' view have suggested, on the General's return to power in 1958. Indeed, in opposition to the traditional Gaullist view, it could be argued that the Loi-cadre created the new political structures that made it possible for France to maintain good relations with its former colonies in French West Africa after independence and that it was De Gaulle's intervention in Conakry in August 1958 that actually prevented Guinea from remaining in the French fold. It was also the Loi-cadre that enabled France to give an element of reality to the language of partnership between France and the overseas territories, on which the French Union was theoretically based but that actually accorded only very restricted powers to the local elected assemblies. The devolution of power to Africans under the Loi-cadre belatedly enabled France to develop a new discourse of development to replace that of the 'civilizing mission'. This new discourse on decolonization, in which the 'civilizing mission', freed from its colonial association, was able to find new expression, and gain increased acceptance, in the shared language of cooperation and partnership for the promotion of African development, was of crucial importance in allowing France to buy time to detach the messianism of the 'civilizing mission' from France's 'colonial vocation' and establish a new discourse of partnership and 'cooperation' with Black Africa.[8] Such a partnership was in the interest of France, which wished to maintain a sphere of influence in Black Africa after independence, and of the political leaders of newly independent Africa, who needed to consolidate their authority in a difficult economic and political environment. The new discourse of cooperation and equal partnership between sovereign nations thus served to legitimate, to both French and African opinion, the maintenance of close links between France and Black Africa in the post-colonial period. This discourse was then used, like the discourse of the civilizing mission before it, to justify a particularistic set of economic and political rewards to its African colonies, which were soon to become its client states.

The second theme running through this study has been the nature and political role of the nationalist movement in French West Africa. As in other colonial situations, nationalism initially was synonymous with anti-colonialism and the nationalist movement emerged as an expression of political opposition to colonial rule. The grievances that fuelled this anti-colonial nationalism were as diverse as the varied experiences of Africans of colonialism – forced labour, poor wages, the *indigénat*, the lack of education, its poor quality, conscription, and all the forms of discrimination that are the daily reality of colonialism – but the cement that held it together was anti-colonialism. However, the point has been made here that colonial rule was not a straightforward, dichotomous 'us' and 'them' situation, but a constant process of negotiation in which the colonizer and the colonized became implicated and in which they were mutually shaped by each other. Moreover, a range of means existed by which the colonized became implicated in the colonial project. They included working for the colonial administration in a variety of occupations, ranging from canton chief or law enforcement through to interpreter or medical assistant. But the colonized also became implicated in other, more-or-less subtle, ways, for example through receiving a French education, or being conscripted into the army, or becoming part of non-indigenous, 'European' organizations such as trade unions and political parties, or in a few cases being elected to parliament. Thus, nationalist feeling was shaped by the particular nature of colonial rule to which French West Africans were subject. It was the product of specific interactions between the colonizer and the colonized at local, territorial, federal and metropolitan level; for example, the colonial experiences of those educated in France and those educated in AOF, or the experiences of those conscripted into the standing army in AOF and those shipped to Europe to fight in the war were very different, and shaped attitudes to the colonial power in different ways. As a result, nationalist feeling was shot through with tensions and ambiguities, which made the creation of a unified nationalist movement problematic: different experiences of colonialism produced different sources of nationalist feeling, which could only be gelled into a single unified movement with difficulty, and even when some sort of unity was achieved, it did not endure. The multiple and shifting agendas of both the colonial power and the different groups within the nationalist movement, and the ongoing processes of negotiation between them, were sufficient to ensure that this was the case.

As the nationalist movement developed and opposition to colonial rule crystallized into the demand for self-determination and then independence, the nationalist movement was confronted with a new problem: what was the nature of the future African nation for which it was fighting? The first point to make is that the African nation they posited did not exist as such. The struggle for this imagined nation was thus a profoundly ambivalent one, 'at once both a product of colonial modernity and an attempt to steer it in a different direction'.[9] It was an élite project, put forward by members of the French-educated African élite, who were imbued with elements of the culture and value system of the colonial power and used its republican values – liberty and equality – both to legitimize their opposition to the ideology of colonialism and to contest the practice of colonial rule.[10] As such, it was not, indeed could not be, purely African; it was necessarily an amalgam, part-African, part-French. This was as true of the nationalist project of 'moderate' nationalist leaders, such as Houphouët-Boigny and Apithy who wanted decolonization through cooperation with France, as it was of the radical nationalists whose goal was 'immediate independence in unity'.

The competing nationalist models put forward by moderate and radical nationalists shared certain characteristics, in that they did not contest the colonial state *per se*. Rather, they sought to take it over, 'Africanize' it and redirect it towards the promotion of African-controlled, rather than European-controlled, development projects.[11] As independence approached, political success depended on winning over the majority of the population to 'your' vision for the future African nation.

If the Franco-African partnership promised by moderate nationalists won out over the radicals' vision of a pan-African future, this was largely because it promised more immediate benefits to the mass of Africans, through economic development in partnership with France, than did the vaguer, more distant, pan-Africanist dream of independence in unity. This does not mean that the latter was entirely without purchase over the mass of the population. However, in those territories where radical nationalists were in control, there were specific local reasons for their success. The particular political circumstances of Sekou Touré's rise to prominence, the undoubted economic wealth of Guinea, which appeared to hold out the promise of an indigenous industrialization, and his personal charisma, were factors in his successful construction of a coalition of forces in favour of immediate independence. In Modibo Keita's Soudan, on the other hand, the watchword was African unity as a prelude to independence. It was only once independence was achieved and this unity irreparably broken that Mali, as it now was, sought to break free from the Franco-African partnership.

There was, then, no consensus between these different groups over the nature of the future African nation that was supposed to be their common goal. Moreover, African identities under colonialism were constructed in different ways. This is especially pertinent in the case of French West Africa, where nationalists faced the additional problem that the geographical entity for which self-determination was being fought was far from self-evident. As a result, there was no firmly held, shared belief in a future single French West African nation. Even those in the nationalist movement who professed such a belief on a *political* level simultaneously felt *culturally* Senegalese or Guinean or Malian: the individual territorial units of the federation, it seems, worked more powerfully on the imagination than the federal model. Furthermore, after the devolution of powers to African-led government councils in each of the territories in 1957, they found themselves in a situation in which they were increasingly forced to express their political aspirations and identity at the territorial, rather than federal, level.

This leads us to the book's third main theme: the nature of French decolonization in West Africa and, related to this, the issue of the legacy of French colonialism. This has been the subject of an abundant literature, much of which has focused on the various mechanisms that have continued to bind France to its former colonies in Black Africa since independence.[12] As Jean-François Médard put it: 'Without Africa, France found itself naked, if we can put it that way, limited to the Hexagon and reduced to the status of a medium-sized country whose only ambition was to survive as best it could'.[13] The crucial importance of Black Africa to France after the Second World War has been underlined here. France's post-war governing élites of both left and right saw the re-establishment of French Great Power status after the debacle of the Second World War as a, if not the, key foreign policy priority. Unable to maintain its Great Power status by proxy, as Britain sought to do after the war, by hanging onto America's coat-tails, the maintenance of a French sphere of influence in Black Africa was integral to this ambition. Indeed, together with European construction and the establishment of France as one of the world's recognized nuclear powers, Black Africa has been one of the three lynchpins of French foreign policy throughout the post-war period. From the French point of view, therefore, the French colonial legacy in West Africa, as in the rest of former French Africa, has been globally positive, because the outcome has been to enable France to maintain its presence and interests in the region.

This study has thrown light on the origins of some of the structures and patterns of the continuing French presence in West Africa in the post-colonial period. The French Union played a key role in preparing the ground for the maintenance of the French presence in Black Africa after independence. However, once it was belatedly acknowledged that the post-war project of creating a modern Africa within the colonial system was not viable, a new project for partnership with Black Africa was devised, which was effectively a modernized version of the old French colonial project of association. Its aim was to protect French strategic interests by maintaining France's presence in the region, but without incurring the costs of direct colonial rule. The Loi-cadre lay the foundation for this new project and in this respect prefigured French African policy in the post-colonial period. Two years later, the Constitution of the Fifth Republic, which installed the French President as the President not only of France but also of the new French Community, lay the basis for presidential primacy over French African policy after independence. Then, in the run-up to independence, the Ministry for Overseas France was renamed the Ministry of Cooperation and became, effectively, the Ministry for Francophone Black Africa; the FIDES was replaced by the Fonds d'Aide et de Coopération; and the University of Dakar was created as France's eighteenth university in 1957, thus laying one of the foundation stones for what was to become a key element of 'Francophonie' under the Fifth Republic: the promotion of the French language through the provision of French higher education. Many of the multiple instruments of French African policy in the post-colonial period were thus put in place before 1960. Moreover, it was during this period that the close links between France's governing élites and African political leaders were forged, firstly in the National Assembly under the Fourth Republic, then subsequently in the web of personal relationships maintained by French political leaders and officials under the Fifth Republic. De Gaulle, in particular, enjoyed close personal relations with a number of African political leaders, but other key political actors also had close links with African political leaders that were an essential component of the maintenance of close ties between French and African governing élites after 1960. They included François Mitterrand, Pierre Messmer, Gaston Defferre, Jacques Foccart and Fernand Wibaux.

It was thus during the last years of colonial rule that the framework for French African policy in the post-colonial period was established. It laid the foundation for the signature of a series of defence, military, technical and cultural assistance accords that, together with the maintenance of the Franc zone, were to keep sub-Saharan Africa firmly in the French sphere of influence after independence. It also brought a multiplicity of political actors into the policy-making process, which opened the door to the incoherences and inconsistencies that have been a characteristic of French African policy, and established the *modus operandi* of this policy, which often operated 'invisibly', that is, without going through the normal political channels and without being subject to the kind of scrutiny to which policy-making is usually subject in a democracy. Indeed, the Loi-cadre, which was unconstitutional and therefore of dubious legality, set a significant precedent in this respect.

If we now turn to the legacy of French colonialism in West Africa from an African perspective, the balance sheet is a mixed, and in many ways an ambivalent, one. The colonial state that African nationalists sought to control was not modelled on Western 'universal', democratic and liberal values, but was a particularistic creation of European imperialism. It was a coercive state that was, 'by its very nature purely administrative and authoritarian [and which] for this reason found itself directly contradicting the principles on which the Republic was founded'.[14] There was thus no tradition of democratic rules or accountability to be observed; the overriding imperative in the exercise of power was administrative efficiency in the name of a certain conception of modernity. It is not therefore surprising that, once nationalist leaders took power, they progressed rapidly to the establishment of authoritarian, one-party states.[15] This was true whether the leaders of the newly independent states were moderate nationalists, as in Côte d'Ivoire, Senegal or Dahomey, or radical nationalists, as in Guinea or Soudan. In each case, opposition movements were routinely co-opted, suppressed or eliminated; opposition leaders were imprisoned and others lost their lives. Many of those affected had been at the forefront of the nationalist movement, but now excluded from power, they became the main victims of efforts by the governments of the newly independent African states to eliminate any form of organized opposition: opposition political parties, autonomous trade unions and youth organizations, even a free press, disappeared in much of former French West Africa after 1960. Ironically therefore, much of the space that had existed under colonial rule after the Second World War for the expression of opposition voices was closed off in the post-colonial period. This policy was justified by African political leaders by reference to the need to unite the newly independent country behind a project for national development. The language was one of 'unity for development'. However, it is not at all clear that this strategy has brought long-term benefits to the countries concerned. Economic development has not taken off and, even in the richest country of ex-AOF, Côte d'Ivoire, the economic benefits to the population of the development strategy that has been pursued have been extremely unevenly spread. Moreover, corruption, which has taken various forms, from misappropriation of funds to lack of transparency in the allocation of and accounting for public expenditure, has been rife and has further undermined the development process.

What is the explanation for this? If we view decolonization not as a simple dichotomous relationship in which the colonizer and the colonized confront each other, but as a complex web of relationships in which a range of political actors are caught up, it is clear that the political choices of the various actors in the decolonization process were not entirely free. The parameters within which these choices were made were determined by the play of uncontrollables, which included the international situation, together with a particular combination of political and economic circumstances and a particular set of ideological and cultural attitudes. Moreover, it is important to note that the political, economic and logistical strength of each of these actors was not equal, because some were clearly more powerful than others. Within this web, the choices of African political leaders in the immediate post-independence period were very much about the art of the possible. In a situation in which their hold on power was often fragile, thanks to the difficult economic and political circumstances in which power was transferred to them, African political leaders had few options. They needed a dependable source of political, economic, and indeed military, support in order to consolidate their position. Unavailable internally, this was what France offered, in return for which African leaders provided certain political services to France. While this relationship was in many ways a dependent one, it was not one of straightforward dependency and can best be described using a different frame of reference: 'It is the model of international clientelism, rather than dependency, which provides the best framework for analysing the particular nature of the links between France and its African sphere of influence (*"pré-carré"*)'.[16] This complicity between France's governing élites and African leaders has been one of the most enduring political aspects of the French colonial legacy in Black Africa. By enabling France, through the creation of a network of client states, to continue to punch above its weight, not only in the region but also in the wider international arena, it has played a central role in the maintenenace of France's status as a world power.

Notes

1. F. Cooper, *Decolonization and African Society* (Cambridge University Press, 1996), p. 6.
2. Quoted in *Jeune Afrique Economie*, December 1994, p. 29.
3. Fred Cooper, in his study of trade unions in French and British Africa during the decolonization period, has underlined the dangers of such a reductionist approach, *Decolonization*, esp. pp. 6–8 and 241–8.
4. According to Amadou Ndene Ndaw, under colonialism, the trade unions were supported when they were pursuing economic demands, but when it came to political demands, people generally preferred to give their support to the main political parties and their leaders, interview, Dakar, 19 December 1994.
5. Alistair Cook, quoting from Justice Holmes, in his 'Letter from America', BBC Radio 4, 9 May 1999.
6. J.-L. Triaud, 'L'islam sous le régime colonial', in C. Coquery-Vidrovitch, ed., *L'Afrique occidentale au temps des Français* (La Découverte, 1992), p. 150.
7. See J. Marseille, *Empire colonial et capitalisme français. Histoire d'un divorce* (Albin Michel, 1984).
8. This was symbolized most strikingly in the renaming of France's former Colonial Ministry, which had been re-christened the Ministry for Overseas France in 1946 and which was renamed the Ministry of Cooperation shortly before independence.
9. G. Prakash, *Another Reason: Science and the Imagination of Modern India* (Princeton University Press, 1999), p. 179.

10. As Herman Lebovics has pointed out, we need to be wary of concepts of identity when theorizing the struggles of oppressed peoples, and he has warned of the danger of focusing too narrowly on their otherness to understand their resistance to colonial rule, in *True France* (Cornell University Press, 1992), p. 101.
11. Gyan Prakash makes a similar point about the contrasting nationalist stances of Nehru and Gandhi during decolonization: 'Both formulated powerful critiques of colonial modernity while seeking to seize control of its territory and institutions and establish over it the authority of the nation', *Another Reason*, p. 225.
12. See for example W. H. Morris-Jones and G. Fischer, eds, *Decolonisation and After: the British and French Experience* (Frank Cass, 1980); J. Adda and M.-C. Smouts, *La France face au sud. Le miroir brisé* (Karthala, 1989).
13. J.-F. Médard, 'Les avatars du messianisme français', in *L'Afrique Politique 1999: Entre transition et conflits* (Karthala, 1999), p. 25.
14. Ibid, p. 21.
15. Indeed Lamine Guèye had warned, at the MSA's inaugural congress in 1956, that, as an ideology, it opened the door to fascism, see A. Blanchet, *L'Itinéraire des partis africains depuis Bamako* (Plon, 1958), p. 59.
16. J.-F. Médard, 'Les avatars', p. 27.

Chronology

1936

April–May — Popular Front comes to power. Marius Moutet becomes Colonial Minister.

27 September–5 October — Moutet tours French West Africa.

1937

11 March — Authorization of trade unions for French-educated Africans.

13 July — Creation of region of Haute Côte d'Ivoire (out of the *cercles* of former Haute-Volta).

1940

23–25 September — Dakar bombardment by FFL/British force, codenamed Operation Menace: 175 dead, 350 injured.

1941

14 August — Atlantic Charter.

25 December — General Catroux proclaims independence of Syria and Lebanon.

1943

3 June — Formation of CFLN in Algiers.

1 July — Pierre Cournarie becomes Governor-General of AOF.

26 August — André Latrille becomes Governor of Côte d'Ivoire.

1944

30 January–8 February — Brazzaville Conference.

2 June — CFLN becomes Provisional Government.

9 November — Paul Giaccobi becomes Minister for the Colonies.

1 December — Tiaroye massacre: thirty-five killed, thirty-five wounded.

1945

24 March	Government declaration on future of Indochina.
June	End of French mandate in Syria and Lebanon.
18 June	San Francisco Charter (UN).
14 August	Latrille replaced by Mauduit as Governor of Côte d'Ivoire while Latrille on leave.
September	Etats Généraux de la Colonisation Française, Douala.
21 October	Elections to First Constituent Assembly.
21 November	Jacques Soustelle becomes Minister for the Colonies.

1946

19 January	Ministry of Colonies is renamed Ministry for Overseas France.
29 January	Marius Moutet becomes Minister for Overseas France.
16 February	Governor Mauduit leaves Côte d'Ivoire, to be replaced by Latrille.
12–14 March	Réunion, Guadeloupe, Guyane and Martinique become Départements d'Outre-Mer.
29 March	Latrille returns from leave to Côte d'Ivoire.
11 April	The Houphouët-Boigny Law abolishing forced labour in France's overseas territories is promulgated (it had been adopted by the Constituent Assembly on 5 April).
30 April	Law passed creating the Fonds d'Investissement pour le Développement Economique et Social (FIDES).
3 May	René Barthes becomes acting Governor-General of AOF.
5 May	Constitutional referendum - constitution rejected.
7 May	Law proclaiming all residents of France's overseas territories citizens – First Lamine Guèye Law.
2 June	Elections to Second Constituent Assembly.

August	Etats Généraux de la Colonisation Française, Paris.
17 October	Constitutional referendum.
19–21 October	Inaugural congress of the Rassemblement Démocratique Africain (RDA), Bamako.
10 November	First National Assembly elections.
19 December	Beginning of Indochina War in Tonkin.

1947

20 February	Durand replaces Latrille as Governor of Côte d'Ivoire.
29 March	Beginning of Madagascar uprising.
4 September	Adoption of law reconstituting Haute-Volta as a territory.
20 September	Algeria statute voted.
3 November	First Grand Conseil elections.
22 November	Paul Coste-Floret becomes Minister for Overseas France.

1948

27 January	Paul Béchard becomes Governor-General.
27 September	Senghor resigns from the SFIO.
4 December	End of Madagascar uprising.

1949

January	RDA Congress, Treichville.
6 February	Political meeting at Treichville meeting, following which a number of PDCI activists (including the writer Bernard Dadié) are arrested and imprisoned.
23 March	Decree creating the FERDES (Fonds d'Equipement Rural et de Développement Economique et Social: fund for small-scale rural development projects) is adopted.
15–17 April	Founding Congress of BDS.
19 July	France-Laos agreement – Laos becomes an 'independent associated state'.
27 October	Jean Letourneau becomes Minister for Overseas France.
8 November	Cambodia becomes an 'independent associated state'.

1950

29–30 January	Disturbances at Dimbokro (Côte d'Ivoire).
8 March	Doudou Guèye condemned to three months' prison.
8 May	RDA decides to disaffiliate from the PCF.
30 June	Second Lamine Guèye Law.
11 July	François Mitterrand becomes Minister for Overseas France.

1951

24 May	Paul Chauvet becomes temporary Governor-General.
17 June	Second National Assembly elections.
8 August	Louis Jacquinot becomes Minister for Overseas France.
21 September	Bernard Cornut-Gentille becomes High Commissioner (Governor-General) of AOF.

1952

7 February	Pierre Pflimlin becomes Minister for Overseas France.
February	Disturbances in Tunisia.
30 March	Territorial Assembly elections.
30 April	Grand Conseil elections.
23 November	Adoption of new Labour Code.

1953

6 January	Louis Jacquinot becomes Minister for Overseas France.

1954

13 Mar-7 May	Dien Bieu Phu battle, culminating in the defeat of France.
17 June	Robert Buron becomes Minister for Overseas France.
21 July	Geneva accords – peace in Indochina.
1 November	Beginning of Algerian revolution.

1955

23 February	Pierre-Henri Teitgen becomes Minister for Overseas France.

16 April	Law creating the Government Council in Togo and granting it internal autonomy.
18–24 April	Bandung conference.
3 June	Tunisia gains internal autonomy.

1956

1 January	Gaston Defferre becomes Minister for Overseas France.
2 January	Third National Assembly elections.
2 March	Independence of Morocco.
20 March	Independence of Tunisia.
23 June	Loi-cadre voted by National Assembly.
5 July	Gaston Cusin becomes High Commissioner of AOF.
8 July	By-election in Soudan to replace Mamadou Konaté (died 11 May 1956).
July	France announces plebiscite in Togo for the creation of an autonomous Republic within the French Union.
1 September	Proclamation of the autonomous Republic of Togo within the French Union.
25 October	Plebiscite in Togo – 70 per cent vote 'yes'.

1957

31 March	Territorial Assembly elections.
1 May →	Establishment of new Government Councils in each territory.
15 May	Grand Conseil elections.
12 June	Gérard Jaquet becomes Minister for Overseas France.
25 September	RDA Congress opens, Bamako.

1958

1 June	De Gaulle returns to power; Bernard Cornut-Gentille becomes Minister for Overseas France (until 16 January 1959).
15 July	Pierre Messmer becomes High Commissioner of AOF.
28 September	Constitutional referendum. Victory of 'yes' vote except in Guinea.
2 October	Independence of Guinea.

| 14 October–8 December | The Franco-African Community is established. |

1959

| 14–17 January | Federal Constituent Assembly meets in Dakar to create the Mali Federation with delegations from Dahomey, Haute-Volta, Senegal and Soudan. |
| 4 April | First federal government of Mali (Senegal, Soudan only). President: Modibo Keita; Vice-President: Mamadou Dia. |

1960

27 April	Independence of Togo.
20 June	Independence of Mali.
1 August	Independence of Dahomey.
3 August	Independence of Niger.
5 August	Independence of Haute-Volta.
7 August	Independence of Côte d'Ivoire.
19 August	Break-up of Mali Federation.
11 September	Independence of Senegal.
22 September	Former Soudan becomes the Mali Republic.
28 November	Independence of Mauritania.

Bibliography

Primary Sources

Archival sources

(Abbreviations used in the endnotes are in brackets.)

Archives of the Government-General of AOF, Dakar (AAOF):
4E: Conseil général of Senegal;
Series 15E-21E: Territorial assemblies;
Series 22E: Grand Conseil;
Series 2G: Periodic reports by governers, administrators et heads of
    services (the two figures after the '2G' refer to the year of the report
    and the figures after the '/' are the number of the report, for example
    2G46/57 is report no. 57 for the year 1946);
Series 13G: Senegal;
Series 17G: Political affairs, generalities;
Series 21G: Police and security;
Series K: Labour;
Series O: Education;
Series 'FIDES'.

Archives of Senegal (colonial period), Dakar (AS):
Series D: Government of Senegal.

Archives Nationales, Paris (AN):
The French National Archives have an incomplete collection on microfilm
    of certain series of documents from the Archives du Gouvernement-
    Général de l'AOF. The private papers of some former colonial admin-
    istrators, notably Henri Laurentie (AN 72 AJ), are also conserved
    there.

Archives Nationales, Section Outre-Mer (ANSOM) and Library (CAOM),
    Aix-en-Provence:
Series AP: Affaires Politiques.

Ministry of Education Archives (Paris/Fontainebleau) (MinEd):
F17bis series.

Public Record Office, London (PRO):
FO series;
CO series.

Bibliothèque Nationale, Département des Périodiques, Versailles:
Newspaper collection.

Centre de Recherche et de Documentation Africaine, Paris and Fondation
 Houphouët-Boigny, Yamoussoukro (FHB):
Documents covering the history of the RDA 1946–60; Party newspapers.

Institut Fondamental d'Afrique Noire, Dakar:
Library, newspaper and periodical collection.

Private archives:
J.-R. de Benoist, Dakar;
J. Eyraud, Pontcharra;
A. Ndene Ndaw, Dakar;
J. Suret-Canale, Ste Foy la Grande.

Official publications:
Annuaire de l'Union Française Outre-Mer
AOF, Conseil de Gouvernement
Bulletin du Grand Conseil de l'AOF
Journal Officiel de l'Afrique Occidentale Française (JOAOF)
*Journal Officiel de la République Française. Débats parlementaires
 (JODP)*
Journal Officiel de la République Française. Lois et Décrets (JOLD)
Outre-Mer. Revue générale de colonisation.

Official party reports on party congresses and meetings:
RDA Inaugural Congress, Bamako, 19–21 October 1946.
Second Interterritorial Congress of the RDA, Treichville, 2–6 January
 1949.
Indépendants d'Outre-Mer Congress, Bobo-Dioulasso, 12–15 December
 1953.
RDA Coordinating Committee, Conakry, 8–11 July 1955.
Convention Africaine, Dakar, 11–13 January 1957.

MSA Inaugural Congress, Conakry, 11–13 January 1957.
Third Interterritorial Congress of the RDA, Bamako, 25–29 September 1957.
PRA Inaugural Congress, Cotonou, 25–27 July 1958.

Interviews:
Thierno Bâ, Dakar, 3 April 1990, 6 April 1990;
Joseph-Roger de Benoist, Dakar, 8 April 1990, 11 April 1992;
Paul Désalmand, Paris, 8 February 1990, 8 September 1990;
Joseph Eyraud, Pontcharra, 10 September 1990;
Abdoulaye Fofana, 31 March 1990;
Abdoulaye Gueye, Dakar, 10 April 1990;
Boubacar Ly, Dakar, 26 March 1990;
Amadou Ndene Ndaw, Dakar, 31 March 1990, 4 April 1990, 6 April 1992, 13 April 1992; 19 December 1994;
Souleymane Ndiaye, Dakar, 27 March 1990;
Assane Seck, Dakar, 21 March 1990;
Jean Suret-Canale, Paris, 30 November 1991;
Iba Der Thiam, Dakar, 19 March 1990;
Pierre Kipré, Abidjan, 18 December 1997;
Mme Dagri Diabaté, Abidjan, 18 December 1997;
Thierno Ibrahima Barry, Abidjan, 20 December 1997;
Monsieur Konaré, Department of History, Bamako University, 8 June 1999;
Assouan Usher, Abidjan, 17 June 1999;
Joachim Bonny, Abidjan, 18 June 1999.

Secondary Sources

Abdul-Raheem, T., ed, *Pan Africanism*. London: Pluto Press, 1996.
Actes du Colloque International sur l'Histoire du RDA, Yamoussoukro, 18–25 October 1986, 2 vols. Abidjan: CEDA, 1987.
Adda, J. and Smouts, M.-C. *La France face au sud. Le miroir brisé*. Paris: Karthala, 1989.
Africanus, *L'Afrique noire devant l'indépendance*. Paris: Plon, 1958.
L'Afrique Politique 1999: Entre transition et conflits. Paris: Karthala, 1999.
Ageron, C.-R., *France coloniale ou parti colonial?* Paris: Presses Universitaires de France, 1978.
Ageron, C.-R., *La Décolonisation française*. Paris: A Colin, 1991.

Ageron, C.-R., ed., *Les Chemins de la décolonisation française*. Paris: Eds. du CNRS, 1986.

Ageron C.-R., 'Novation et immobilisme de la politique française vis-à-vis de l'outre-mer dans les premières années de la IVe République', unpublished paper delivered at the Fondation Nationale des Sciences Politiques, 1981.

Ajayi, A. D. E. and Crowder, M., eds, *History of West Africa*, vol. 2, 2nd ed. Harlow: Longman, 1987.

Akpo-Vaché, C., *L'AOF et la seconde guerre mondiale*. Paris: Karthala, 1996.

Alduy, P., *L'Union Française. Mission de la France*. Paris: Fasquelle, 1948.

Almeida-Topor, H. de and Goerg, O., *Le Mouvement associatif des jeunes en Afrique noire francophone au XXe siècle*. Paris: L'Harmattan, 1989.

Anderson, B., *Imagined Communities*. London: Verso/New Left Books, 1983.

Andrew, C. M., *France Overseas*. London: Thames & Hudson, 1981.

Ansprenger, F., *The Dissolution of the Colonial Empires*. London: Routledge, 1989.

Auchnie, A, 'The Commandement Indigène in Senegal, 1919–47', PhD thesis, University of London, 1983.

Bakary, D., *Silence! On décolonise . . .* Paris: L'Harmattan, 1992.

Bathily, A., Diouf, M. and Mbodj, M., 'Le mouvement étudiant sénégalais, des origines à 1989', in *Mouvements sociaux, mutations sociales et lutte pour la démocratie en Afrique*. Dakar: unpublished manuscript, undated [1991].

Baulin, J., *La Politique intérieure de Houphouët-Boigny*. Paris: Eds. Eurafor-Press, 1982.

Baulin, J., *La Politique africaine de Houphouët-Boigny*. Paris: Eds. Eurafor-Press, 1980.

Benoist, J.-R. de, *La Balkanisation de l'Afrique Occidentale Française*. Dakar: Nouvelles Editions Africaines, 1979.

Benoist, J.-R. de, *L'Afrique Occidentale Française de 1944 à 1960*. Dakar: Nouvelles Editions Africaines, 1982.

Benot, Y., *Les Députés africains au Palais Bourbon de 1914 à 1958*. Paris: Chaka, 1989.

Berg, E. J., 'The Economic Basis of Political Choice in French West Africa', *American Political Science Review*, 54, 2, June 1960, pp. 391–405.

Betts, R. F., *Assimilation and Association in French Colonial Theory*. New York: Columbia University Press, 1961.

Betts, R. F., *France and Decolonisation 1900–1960*. Basingstoke: Macmillan, 1991.

Betts, R. F., *Decolonization*. Basingstoke: Palgrave: 1998.

Biarnès, P., *Les Français en Afrique Noire de Richelieu à Mitterrand*. Paris: A Colin, 1987.

Blanchet, A., *L'Itinéraire des partis africains depuis Bamako*. Paris: Plon, 1958.

Bouche, D., 'L'école rurale en Afrique Occidentale Française', in *Etudes africaines offertes à Henri Brunschwig*. Paris: Publications de l'Ecole des Hautes Etudes en Sciences Sociales, 1982, pp. 271–96.

Bourcart, R., *Le Grand Conseil de l'Afrique Occidentale Française*. Paris: Société des Journaux et Publications du Centre, 1955.

Bragança, A. de and Wallerstein, I., *The African Liberation Reader: Documents of the national liberation movements*, 3 vols. London: Zed Press, 1982.

Capelle, J., *L'Education en Afrique noire à la veille des indépendances*. Paris: Kathala/ACCT, 1990.

Cartier, R., 'En France Noire avec Raymond Cartier', *Paris-Match*, 11 August, pp. 38–41, 18 August, pp. 34–7, and 1 September 1956, pp. 39–41.

Castle G., ed., *Postcolonial Discourses. An Anthology*. Oxford: Blackwell, 2001.

Cerny, P., *The Politics of Grandeur: ideological aspects of De Gaulle's foreign policy*. Cambridge University Press, 1980.

Chafer T, 'African Perspectives: the Liberation of France and its Impact in French West Africa', in Kedward, H. R. and Wood, N., eds, *The Liberation of France: Image and Event*. Oxford: Berg, 1995.

Chafer, T., 'French African Policy in Historical Perspective' *Journal of Contemporary African Studies*, 19, 2, July 2001, pp. 165–82.

Chafer, T., 'Students and Nationalism: the Role of Students in the Nationalist Movement in Afrique Occidentale Française', in Becker, C., Mbaye, S. and Thioub, I., eds, *AOF; réalités et héritages. Sociétés ouest-africaines et ordre colonial, 1895–1960*, vol. 1. Dakar: Direction des Archives du Sénégal, 1997, pp. 388–407.

Chafer T. and Sackur, A., eds, *Promoting the Colonial Idea: Propaganda and visions of empire in France*. Basingstoke: Palgrave, 2002.

Chafer T. and Sackur, A., eds, *French Colonial Empire and the Popular Front*. Basingstoke: Macmillan, 1999.

Chaffard, G., *Les Carnets secrets de la décolonisation*, 2 vols. Paris: Calmann-Levy, 1965 and 1967.

Chipman, J., *French Power in Africa*. Oxford: Blackwell, 1989.

Clauzel, J., *Administrateur de la France d'outre-mer*, Avignon: J. Laffitte/ A. Barthélemy, 1989.

Clayton, A., *France, Soldiers and Africa*. London: Brassey's, 1988.

Cohen W B, *Rulers of Empire: The French colonial service in Africa*. Stanford: Hoover Institution Press, 1971.

Coleman, J. S. and Rosberg, C. G., eds, *Political Parties and National Integration in Tropical Africa*. Berkeley: University of California Press, 1964.

Colombani, O., *Mémoires coloniales*. Paris: La Découverte, 1991.

Cooper, F. *Decolonization and African Society. The Labor Question in French and British Africa*. Cambridge University Press, 1996.

Cooper F, 'Le mouvement ouvrier et le nationalisme. La grève générale de 1946 et la grève des cheminots de 1947–48', *Historiens-Géographes du Sénégal*, 6, 1991, pp. 32–42.

Coquery-Vidrovitch, C., *Afrique Noire. Permanences et Ruptures*. Paris: Payot, 1985.

Coquery-Vidrovitch, C., 'French black Africa', in Roberts, A. D., ed., *The Cambridge History of Africa*, vol. 7. Cambridge University Press, 1986, pp. 329–92.

Coquery-Vidrovitch, C., 'Nationalité et Citoyenneté en Afrique Occidentale Française: Originaires et Citoyens dans le Sénégal Colonial', *Journal of African History*, 42, 2001, pp. 285–305.

Coulibaly, O., *Combat pour l'Afrique, 1946–58. La lutte du RDA pour une Afrique nouvelle*. Abidjan: Nouvelles Editions Africaines, 1988.

Crowder, M., *West Africa under Colonial Rule*. London: Hutchinson, 1968.

Crowder, M., 'Independence as a goal in French West African politics, 1944–60', in Lewis, W. H. ed., *French-Speaking Africa: the Search for Identity*. New York: Walker & Co, 1965, pp. 15–41.

Cruise O'Brien, D., 'The limits of political choice in French West Africa, 1956–60', *Civilisations*, 15, 2, 1965, pp. 206–26.

Cruise O'Brien, R., *White Society in Black Africa: The French in Senegal*. London: Faber & Faber, 1972.

Dalloz, J., *Textes sur la décolonisation*. Paris: Presses Universitaires de France, 1989.

Danioko, A. C., 'Contribution à l'étude des partis politiques au Mali de 1945 à 1960'. Thèse de 3e cycle, University of Paris VII, 1984.

Darwin, J., 'Diplomacy and Decolonization', *Journal of Imperial and Commonwealth History*, XXVIII, 3, 2000, pp. 5–24.

Davidson, B., *Modern Africa. A Social and Political History*. 3rd ed. London: Longman, 1994.

De Gaulle, C., *Discours et messages*. Paris: Plon, 1970.

Delanoue, P., 'La CGT et les syndicats de l'Afrique noire de colonisation française, de la Deuxième Guerre Mondiale aux indépendances', *Mouvement social*, 122, 1983, pp. 103–16.

Delavignette, R., *Freedom and Authority in French West Africa*. Oxford University Press, 1950.

Delavignette, R., *Service africain*. Paris: Gallimard, 1946 (originally published in an earlier version as *Les vrais chefs de l'empire*).

Delval, J., 'Le RDA au Soudan français', *L'Afrique et l'Asie*, 4, 1951, pp. 54–67.

Dewitte, P., 'La CGT et les syndicats d'Afrique occidentale française', *Mouvement social*, 117, 1981, pp. 3–32.

Dewitte, P., *Les Mouvements nègres en France, 1919–1939*. Paris: L'Harmattan, 1985.

Dewitte, P., 'Réponse à Paul Delanoue', *Mouvement social*, 122, 1983, pp. 117–21.

Dia, M., *Mémoires d'un militant du tiers-monde*. Paris: Publisud, 1985.

Diané, C., *La FEANF et les grandes heures du mouvement syndical étudiant noir*. Paris: Chaka, 1990.

Dicko, A., *Journal d'une défaite autour du référendum du 28 septembre 1958 en Afrique noire*. Limoges: Imprimerie Rivet, 1959.

Dieng, A. A., *La Fédération des Etudiants d'Afrique Noire en France (FEANF), 1950–55*. Dakar: typescript, Cheikh Anta Diop University, undated, (c. 1986).

Diop, C. A., *Nations nègres et culture*, 2 vols. Paris: Présence Africaine, 1979.

Dore-Audibert, A., *Une Décolonisation pacifique*, Paris, Karthala, 1999.

Echenberg, M., '"Morts pour la France": the African soldier in France during the Second World War', *Journal of African History*, 26, 1985, pp. 363–80.

Echenberg, M., 'Tragedy at Tiaroye: the Senegalese soldiers' uprising of 1944', in Gutkind, P. C. W., Cohen, R. and Copans, J., eds, *African Labour History*, vol. 2. London: Sage, 1978, pp. 109–28.

Fedorowich, K. and Thomas, M., eds, *International Diplomacy and Colonial Retreat*. London: Frank Cass, 2001.

Filipovich, J., 'Destined to fail: forced settlement at the Office du Niger, 1926–45', *Journal of African History*, 42, 2001, pp. 239–60.

Fischer, G., 'Syndicats et décolonisation', *Présence africaine*, 34–5, October 1960–January 1961, pp. 17–60.

Foltz, W., *From French West Africa to the Mali Federation*. New Haven: Yale University Press, 1965.

Fuglestad, F., *A History of Niger* 1850–1960. Cambridge University Press, 1984.

Gann, L. H. and Duignan, P., eds, *Colonialism in Africa 1870–1960. 2. The History and Politics of Colonialism, 1914–60.* Cambridge University Press, 1970.

Gardinier, D., 'The Second World War in French West Africa and Togo: recent research and writing', in P. P. Boucher, ed., *Proceedings of the Tenth Meeting of the French Colonial Historical Society, April 12–14, 1984.* Lanham: University Press of America, 1984.

Gbagbo, L., *Réflexions sur la conférence de Brazzaville.* Yaoundé: Editions Clé, 1978.

Gérard, C., *Les Pionniers de l'indépendance.* Paris: Inter-Continents, 1975.

Gerteiny, G., *Mauritania.* London: Pall Mall Press, 1967.

Gide, A., *Voyage au Congo.* Paris: Gallimard, 1927.

Gifford, P. and Louis, W. R., *Decolonization and African Independence. The Transfers of Power, 1960–80.* New Haven: Yale University Press, 1988.

Gifford, P. and Louis, W. R., eds, *The Transfer of Power in Africa. Decolonization 1940–60*, New Haven: Yale University Press, 1982.

Gifford, P. and Louis, W. R., *France and Britain in Africa: Imperial Rivalry and Colonial Rule*, New Haven: Yale University Press, 1971.

Ginio, R., 'Marshal Pétain spoke to schoolchildren: Vichy propaganda in French West Africa, 1940–1943', *International Journal of African Historical Studies*, 33, 2, 2000, pp. 291–312.

Glélé, M.-A., *Naissance d'un état noir.* Paris: Librairie Générale de Droit et de Jurisprudence, 1969.

Grimal, H., *La Décolonisation de 1919 à nos jours.* Brussels: Editions Complexe, 1985.

Guèye, D., *Sur les sentiers du temple. Ma rencontre avec Félix Houphouët-Boigny.* Ventabren: Les Rouyat, 1975.

Guèye, L., *Itinéraire africain.* Paris: Présence Africaine, 1966.

Guèye, L., *Etapes et perspectives de l'Union Française.* Paris: Editions de l'Union Française, 1955.

Guitard, O., *Bandoeng et le réveil des peuples colonisés.* Paris: Presses Universitaires de France, 1961.

Hargreaves, J. D., 'Approaches to Decolonization', in Rimmer, D. and Kirk-Greene, A., eds, *The British Intellectual Engagement with Africa.* Basingstoke: Macmillan, 2000, pp. 90–111.

Hargreaves, J. D., *Decolonisation in Africa*, 2nd ed. Harlow: Longman, 1996.

Hargreaves, J. D., *West Africa: The Former French States*. New Jersey: Prentice-Hall, 1967.

Higgott, R., 'Structural Dependency and Decolonisation in a West African Land-Locked State: Niger', *Review of African Political Economy*, 17, January–April 1980, pp. 43–59.

Hodgkin, T., *Nationalism in Colonial Africa*. London: F. Muller, 1956.

Houphouët-Boigny, F., *Anthologie des discours 1946–1978*, 4 vols. Abidjan: CEDA, 1978.

Hymans, J. L., *Léopold Sédar Senghor. An Intellectual Biography*. Edinburgh: Edinburgh University Press, 1971.

Institut Charles de Gaulle/Institut d'Histoire du Temps Présent, *Brazzaville. Janvier-Février 1944. Aux sources de la décolonisation*. Paris: Plon, 1988.

Johnson, G. W., *The Emergence of Black Politics in Senegal*. Stanford: Stanford University Press, 1971.

Kahler, M., *Decolonization in Britain and France*. Princeton University Press, 1984.

Kake, I. B., *Sekou Touré: le héros et le tyran*. Paris: Jeune Afrique Livres, 1987.

Kennedy, D., 'Imperial History and Post-Colonial Theory', *Journal of Imperial and Commonwealth History*, 24, 3, 1996, pp. 345–63.

Kipré, P., *Le Congrès de Bamako ou la naissance du RDA*. Paris: Chaka, 1989.

Kobelé-Keita, S., *Ahmed Sekou Touré, l'homme du 28 septembre*. Conakry: INRDG, Bibliothèque Nationale, 1977.

Kohn, H. and Sokolsky, W., eds, *African Nationalism in the Twentieth Century*. Princeton: Van Nostrand, 1965.

La Conférence africaine française. Brazzaville: 30 janvier–8 février 1944. Paris: Ministère des Colonies, 1945.

Langley, J. A., *Pan-Africanism and Nationalism in West Africa 1900–45*. Oxford: Clarendon Press, 1973.

Lawler, N., 'Reform and repression under the Free French: economic and political transformation in the Côte d'Ivoire, 1942–45', *Africa*, 60, 1, 1990, pp. 88–110.

Lebovics, H., *True France*. Ithaca: Cornell University Press, 1992.

Lemaire S., Blanchard P. and Bancel N., '1931! Tous à l'Expo', *Le Monde Diplomatique*, January 2001, p. 10.

Lewis, M. D., 'One hundred million Frenchmen: the 'assimilation' theory in French colonial policy', *Comparative Studies in Society and History*, IV, 1962, pp. 129–53.

Lisette, G., *Le Combat du Rassemblement Démocratique Africain pour la décolonisation pacifique de l'Afrique noire*. Paris/Dakar: Présence Africaine, 1983.

Loucou, J. N., 'La vie politique en Côte d'Ivoire de 1932 à 1952', Thèse de 3e cycle, 2 vols., University of Provence, 1976.

Luchaire, F., *Les Institutions politiques et administratives des territoires d'outre-mer après la loi-cadre*. Paris: Librairie Générale de Droit et de Jurisprudence, 1958.

Lukes, S., *Power*. Basingstoke: Macmillan, 1974.

Ly, A., *Les Masses africaines et l'actuelle condition humaine*. Paris: Présence Africaine, 1956.

Ly, A., *Les Regroupements politiques au Sénégal (1956–70)*. Dakar: CODESRIA/Karthala, 1992.

Manifeste du GAREP. Paris: J. Marx et Cie., 1951.

McNamara, F. T., *France in Black Africa*. Washington DC: National Defense University, 1989.

Maddox, G. and Welliver, T., *Colonialism and Nationalism in Africa*. New York: Garland, 1993.

Manchuelle, F., 'Assimilés ou patriotes africains? Naissance du nationalisme culturel en Afrique française (1853–1931)', *Cahier d'Etudes Africaines*, 138–9, XXXV, 2–3, 1995, pp. 333–68.

Manning, P., *Slavery, Colonialism and Economic Growth in Dahomey, 1640–1960*. Cambridge University Press, 1982.

Marseille, J., *Empire colonial et capitalisme français. Histoire d'un divorce*. Paris: Albin Michel, 1984.

Marshall, D. B., *The French Colonial Myth and Constitution-Making in the Fourth Republic*. New Haven: Yale University Press, 1973.

Martens, G., 'Industrial Relations and Trade Unionism in French-Speaking West Africa', in Damachi, U. G., Seibel, H. D. and Trachtmann, L., eds, *Industrial Relations in Africa*. New York: St Martin's Press, 1979, pp. 16–72.

Martens, G., 'Le syndicalisme en Afrique Occidentale Française de 1946 à 1960', *Syndicalisme et Développement*, special issue, March 1982. (Originally published in *Le Mois en Afrique*, 178-9, October–November 1980, pp. 74–97; 180–1, December 1980-January 1981, pp. 53–92; 182–3, February–March 1981, pp. 52–83.

Mazrui, A. A. and Tidy, M., *Nationalism and New States in Africa*. Nairobi: East Africa Educational Publishers, 1984.

Mbaye, S., *Histoire des Institutions Coloniales Françaises en Afrique de l'Ouest (1816-1960)*. Dakar: Imprimerie Saint-Paul, 1991.

Mbembe, A., *De la postcolonie*. Paris: Karthala, 2000.

Médard, J.-F., 'Les avatars du messianisme français', in *L'Afrique politique 1999: entre transition et conflits*. Paris: Karthala, 1999, pp. 17–34.

Messmer, P., *Après tant de batailles*. Paris: Albin Michel, 1992.

Messmer, P., *Les Blancs s'en vont: récits de décolonisation*. Paris: Albin Michel, 1998.

Milcent, E., 'Les syndicats de Côte d'Ivoire reprochent au RDA son alliance avec le grand patronat européen', *Le Monde*, 27 November 1956, p. 12.

Morgenthau, R. S., *Political Parties in French-Speaking West Africa*. Oxford: Clarendon Press, 1964.

Morris-Jones, W. H. and Fischer, G., eds, *Decolonisation and After: the British and French Experience*. London: Frank Cass, 1980.

Mortimer E, *France and the Africans, 1940–60. A Political History*. London: Faber & Faber, 1969.

Ndaw, A. N., 'Réflexions sur la jeunesse: mieux comprendre la jeunesse', lecture given at Dakar Chamber of Commerce, 1 February 1989 (typescript), A. Ndene Ndaw personal archives.

Ndaw, A. N., 'Jeunesse. Messages d'hier. Défis d'aujourd'hui', Dakar, unpublished manuscript, 1990.

Nkrumah, K., *Towards Colonial Freedom*. London: Heinemann, 1962.

Nwaubani, E., *The United States and Decolonization in West Africa, 1950–60*. Rochester: University of Rochester Press, 2001.

Person, Y., 'Colonisation et décolonisation en Côte d'Ivoire', *Le Mois en Afrique*, August–September 1981, pp. 15–30.

Peyrefitte, A., *C'était de Gaulle*. 3 vols. Paris: Eds de Fallois/Fayard, 1997.

Prakash, G., *Another Reason: Science and the Imagination of Modern India*. Princeton University Press, 1999.

La République du Sénégal. Paris: Notes et Etudes Documentaires, 22 February 1961.

Richard-Molard, J., *Afrique Occidentale Française*. Paris: Berger-Levrault, 1956

Rioux P, *La France et la Quatrième République. 1. L'ardeur et la nécessité 1944–52*. Paris: Seuil, 1980.

Rivière, C., *Guinea: the Mobilisation of a People*. Oxford: Ithaca, 1977.

Ronen, D., *Between Tradition and Modernity*. Ithaca: Cornell Univeristy Press, 1975.

Said, E. W., *Culture and Imperialism*. London: Vintage Books, 1994.

Sartre, J.-P., 'Le colonialisme est un système', *Les Temps Modernes*, 123, March–April 1956, reproduced in *Situations V. Colonialisme et néo-colonialisme*. Paris: Gallimard, pp. 25–48.

Searing, J., 'Accommodation and Resistance: Chiefs, Muslim Leaders, and Politicians in Colonial Senegal, 1890–1934', 2 vols, PhD thesis, Princeton University, 1985.

Secrétariat d'Etat chargé des Affaires Culturelles de la Côte d'Ivoire, *Le Président Houphouët-Boigny et la nation ivoirienne*. Dakar: Nouvelles Editions Africaines, 1975.

Semidei, M., 'De l'Empire à la décolonisation à travers les manuels scolaires français', *Revue Française de Science Politique*, XVI, 1966, pp. 56–86.

Senghor, L. S., 'Nous ne voulons plus être des SUJETS ni subir un régime d'occupation', *Gavroche*, 8 August 1946, p. 7.

Senghor, L. S., 'Le problème culturel en AOF', *Paris-Dakar*, 6–8 September 1937.

Senghor, L. S., *Liberté I. Négritude et humanisme*. Paris: Seuil, 1964.

Senghor, L. S., *Liberté 2. Nation et voie africaine du socialisme*. Paris: Seuil, 1971.

Senghor, L. S., *Liberté 3: Négritude et civilisation de l'universel*. Paris: Seuil, 1977.

Shennan, A., *Rethinking France. Plans for Renewal*. Oxford: Clarendon Press, 1989.

Siriex, P.-H., *Félix Houphouët-Boigny: l'homme de la paix*. Paris: Seghers, 1975.

Siriex, P.-H., *Une Nouvelle Afrique. AOF 1957*. Paris: Plon, 1957.

Spiegler, J. S., 'Aspects of Nationalist Thought among French-Speaking West Africans, 1921–39', PhD thesis, Nuffield College, Oxford, 1968.

Springhall, J., *Decolonization since 1945*. Basingstoke: Palgrave, 2001.

Suret-Canale, J., *Afrique noire occidentale et centrale. 2. L'Ere coloniale 1900–45*. Paris: Editions Sociales, 1964.

Suret-Canale J, *Afrique noire occidentale et centrale. 3. De la colonisation aux indépendances 1945–60*. Paris: Editions Sociales, 1977.

Suret-Canale, J., *Les Groupes d'Etudes Communistes (GEC) en Afrique Noire*. Paris: L'Harmattan, 1994.

Thobie, J., Meynier, G., Coquery-Vidrovitch, C. and Ageron, C.-R., *Histoire de la France coloniale. 1. Des origines à nos jours*. Paris: A. Colin, 1991.

Thomas, M., *The French Empire at War, 1940–45*. Manchester: Manchester University Press, 1998.

Topouzis, D., 'Popular Front, War and Fourth Republic Politics in Senegal: from Galandou Diouf to L S Senghor, 1936–52', PhD thesis, University of London, 1989.

Traoré, S., *La Fédération des Etudiants d'Afrique Noire en France (FEANF)*. Paris: L'Harmattan, 1985.

Vaillant, J. G., *Black, French and African. A Life of Léopold Sédar Senghor*. Cambridge MA: Harvard University Press, 1990.

Viard, R., *La Fin de l'empire colonial français*. Paris: Maisonneuve et Larose, 1963.

Wallerstein, I., *The Road to Independence. Ghana and the Ivory Coast*. Paris: Mouton & Co, 1964.

Wallerstein, I., *Africa. The Politics of Independence*. New York: Vintage Books, 1961.

Wasserman, G., *Politics of Decolonization: Kenya Europeans and the Land Issue, 1960–1965*. Cambridge University Press, 1976.

White, O., *Children of the French Empire. Miscegenation and Colonial Society in French West Africa, 1895–1960*. Oxford: Clarendon Press, 1999.

Yacono X, *Les Etapes de la déclonisation française*. Paris: Presses Universitaires de France, 1985.

Zan, Semi-Bi, *Ouezzin Coulibaly, le Lion du RDA*. Abidjan: Presses Universitaires de Côte d'Ivoire, 1995.

Zolberg, A. R., *One-Party Government in the Ivory Coast*. Princeton University Press, 1969.

Zuccarelli, F., *Un parti politique africain, l'Union Progressiste Sénégalaise*. Paris: Librairie Générale de Droit et de Jurisprudence, 1970.

Index

Index

Index

Index